Green Bonds and Sustainable Finance

This book introduces green bonds and their significance in portfolio management and sustainable finance. It emphasizes the significance of green bonds in terms of two primary factors: environmental sustainability and investor return.

The book establishes the definitions, features, and typology of green bonds, and explains the characteristics that separate it from traditional ones. It delves into the benefits and challenges of investing in these financial instruments, and outlines the process by which green bonds are certified, focusing on the widely accepted Climate Bonds Standard. It also covers transparency, reporting, and monitoring measurements of green bonds. In its second section, the book focuses on investor and policy perspectives. The authors discuss asset allocation strategies for investors as well as various methods for integrating ESG issues into investment portfolio design. New estimating methodologies and case studies of successful green bond investments are also provided.

Pitched at graduate students and researchers in finance, accounting, as well as related fields of energy and environmental economics, this book will also interest practitioners and investors looking to understand this emerging area in finance.

Muhammad Saeed Meo is a Senior Lecturer at Sunway Business School (AACSB), Sunway University. He is a leading researcher in financial economics, applied finance, sustainable finance, and energy finance.

Marcin W. Staniewski is a researcher and academic at the University of Economics and Human Sciences in Warsaw, Poland. He is currently the Development Director of the Faculty of Management and Finance and has published research on topics such as human resources, retirement and pensioner problems, and business process management.

Routledge International Studies in Money and Banking

For more information about this series, please visit: www.routledge.com/Routledge-International-Studies-in-Money-and-Banking/book-series/SE0403

Green Bonds and Sustainable Finance

The Evolution of Portfolio Management in Conventional Markets

Edited by
**Muhammad Saeed Meo and
Marcin W. Staniewski**

Routledge
Taylor & Francis Group

LONDON AND NEW YORK

First published 2025
by Routledge
4 Park Square, Milton Park, Abingdon, Oxon OX14 4RN

and by Routledge
605 Third Avenue, New York, NY 10158

Routledge is an imprint of the Taylor & Francis Group, an informa business

British Library Cataloguing-in-Publication Data
A catalogue record for this book is available from the British Library

ISBN: 9781032686837 (hbk)
ISBN: 9781032686820 (pbk)
ISBN: 9781032686844 (ebk)

DOI: 10.4324/9781032686844

Typeset in Galliard
by codeMantra

Contents

Contributors

Saad Babatunde Akanbi is presently affiliated with the University of Ilorin, Nigeria. He possesses extensive research and teaching expertise spanning several decades, focusing on economics and financial matters.

Sajid Ali is presently employed in the School of Economics, Bahauddin Zakariya University, located in Multan, Pakistan. His research interests encompass sustainable finance, energy finance, applied energy finance, and applied economics.

Alade Ayodeji, ADEMOKOYA is presently employed in the Department of Accounting & Finance at Kwara State University in Nigeria. He possesses extensive teaching and research experience spanning several decades.

Eşref Savaş BAŞCI is a specialist in finance and experienced in both teaching and research in this field. He currently works at the Hitit University, Turkey.

Calvin Cheong Wing Hoh is presently employed as an Associate Professor at Sunway Business School, Sunway University, Malaysia. He holds the position of department chair and oversees doctoral students.

Ferhat Çıtak is currently affiliated with Hitit University, Turkey. He is a very known young economist in the country and a very dedicated researcher. He published on economics and financial issues.

Md. Mahmudul Haque is presently associated with the Labuan Faculty of International Finance at the University Malaysia Sabah. He is a very experienced researcher and a highly skilled instructor. He is mostly interested in studying financial markets.

Tella Oluwatoba Ibrahim is presently affiliated with the University of Ilorin, Nigeria. He possesses extensive research and teaching expertise spanning several decades, focusing on economics and financial matters.

Laeeq Razzak Janjua works in the financial sector as a compliance officer in the TMF group and as an academic researcher and teaching assistant at WSB University, Poland.

Ebere Ume Kalu, Senior Lecturer with the University of Nigeria, Nsukka, holds a PhD with Distinction in Banking and Finance and is an Edx/International Monetary Fund and African Heritage Institution graduate of a short course in Econometric and Forecasting.

Uzma Kashif, Assistant Professor at Superior University, recognized by the Pakistani Higher Education Commission, specializes in Finance, Islamic Banking, Green Finance and Venture Financing.

Bezon Kumar, Assistant Professor at Rabindra University, has been teaching economics for over six years. He also taught at Varendra University after completing Master's in Economics from the University of Rajshahi.

Lianne Lee Mei Quin is presently employed at Sunway Business School, located inside Sunway University, Malaysia. Her research interest lies in financial markets and economic issues.

Muhammad Saeed Meo is a Senior Lecturer at Sunway Business School (AACSB), Sunway University. He is a leading researcher in financial economics, applied finance, sustainable finance, and energy finance.

Raima Nazar is presently associated with the Department of Economics at the Women University Multan, Pakistan. She has extensive expertise in teaching and doing research, spanning 15 years.

Rosemary Ifeoma Nwokike obtained her BSc degree in 1998 from the University of Nigeria Nsukka. In 2005, she obtained her LLB, and she was called to the Nigerian Bar in 2006.

Chinwe Ada Olelewe is a Lecturer in the Department of Banking and Finance, University of Nigeria, Nsukka. A first-class honours graduate from the University of Nigeria, Nsukka (UNN), she also holds a PhD in banking and finance from the same University. She is a chartered accountant and a positive model in the educational and financial space where she has published in referred journals in her area of specialty.

Agatha Okeke is a distinguished administrator at the University of Nigeria Enugu Campus. She is presently the Unit Head, Examinations Unit, Registry Department, University of Nigeria, Enugu Campus.

Nouman Maqbool Rao is presently pursuing a PhD at Superior University in Lahore, Pakistan. Additionally, he is actively engaged in research and works with the Higher Education Commission of Pakistan.

Priyanka Sahu is an Assistant Professor in the Economics Department of Humanities and Social Sciences, Ghani Khan Choudhary Institute of Engineering and Technology, West Bengal. Her research interests include inflation, poverty, and sustainable development.

Orhan Şanli is a research assistant at Adnan Menderes Üniversitesi-Aydin, Turkey. He has published more than 15 research papers in different international journals. His research interests include international trade, energy economics, inflation, and economic integration.

Atman Shah serves as an Assistant Professor in the Department of Economics, St. Xavier's College (Autonomous) Ahmedabad. He completed his postgraduation at the Mumbai School of Economics and obtained his PhD from VNSGU in Surat.

Manjeet Kaur Harnek Singh is employed at Sunway Business School, Sunway University, Malaysia. She is now pursuing a PhD in Economics, with a research focus on financial and economic concerns.

Afia Mubasshira Tiasha is currently working as a Senior Research Associate at the South Asian Network on Economic Modeling (SANEM). She has completed both her Master of Social Sciences (MSS) and Bachelor of Social Sciences (BSS) in Economics from the Department of Economics, Jagannath University, Dhaka.

Afrida Jinnurain Urbee is currently serving as a Lecturer of Economics in the Department of Economics at Noakhali Science and Technology University (NSTU). Prior to joining NSTU, Urbee worked as an Adjunct Lecturer in the Department of Economics of Barishal Government Women's College.

Ayesha Zahid is presently employed as the Director of Academics at Superior University, Lahore, Pakistan. She focuses on developing unique ideas for entrepreneurship and promoting sustainability.

1 Green Bonds Unveiled

Investor Preferences and the Rise of Sustainable Finance

Ebere Ume Kalu, Agatha Okeke, Rosemary Ifeoma Nwokike and Chinwe Ada Olelewe

Introduction

At the heels of the expiration of the Millennium Development Goals (MDGs) in 2015 (a program criticized for its beam on specifically developing economies) came the transformative 2030 Agenda for Sustainable Development tagged Sustainable Development Goals (SDGs). The universality of SDGs and its focus on sustainable development of the planet and people accounted for its wide acceptability (United Nations (2000) 55/2. United Nations Millennium Declaration. Online, http://www.un.org/millennium/declaration/ares552e.pdf). Huge finance, which should be sustainable, is required to achieve such global goals hence the carving out of a niche to integrate private companies, supranational institutions, and public entities, and this gave birth to the Green/Climate Bond. This type of bond, which is a departure from the traditional corporate and public bonds, is connected to financing for safe environment, biodiversity conservation, safe living, healthy climate, and other things in that similitude.

This chapter presents first definitional issues on green bonds; second, classifications and characteristics of green bonds; also, the regulation, certification, and verification processes for green bonds are presented. Greens around sustainable finance are presented and the interface between green bonds and sustainable finance is also discussed. This chapter makes a case for the increased adoption of green bonds for the imperatives of sustainable finance and financing in not just developed financial systems but also in emerging and developing financial markets.

Definition of Green Bonds

"Green" or "Climate" bond is a relatively new financial instrument. Green bonds are debt instruments. They are fixed-income securities, taxable, and tax-exempt, issued with the aim of raising funds for climate-related or environmentally sustainable projects or activities (World Bank, 2016). Unlike the traditional/conventional or regular bonds, green bonds address the major challenge of climate change by using its proceeds to finance or re-finance green projects. In simple

DOI: 10.4324/9781032686844-1

terms, green bond operates like a traditional bond. It is a type of investment that represents a loan between a lender and a borrower. Here, the lender is called the "investor" while the borrower, usually a government or corporation/institution, is called the "issuer." The proceeds of the debt instrument are used in any project the issuer deems fit and is adjudged to be suitable for a green bond exposure (in the case of green bond, proceeds are invested specifically on climate or environment-related projects) (Adeojo, 2022).

Green bonds are structured under the issuer's medium term notes programs. This protects the investors from being exposed to the risk of the bonds' underlying projects hence its full backing by the issuer's entire balance sheet (World Bank, Dec 2016). Green bonds were initially issued mainly by multilateral banks because of their enormous financial involvement but are gradually slipping into the issuance purview of private and public concerns. Sovereign governments are major investors for the sole purpose of investing the funds in climate or environmentally related projects such as promoting sustainable agriculture, ensuring availability and sustainable management of water and sanitation, ensuring access to affordable, reliable, sustainable and modern energy, combating climate change and its impacts in line with the agreements made by the UNFCCC forum, it is majorly for funding biodiversity conservation (www.iclei.org/publications).

Evidently, proceeds are recorded and managed with dependability; they are only assigned to Green Projects. Following the bond's issuance, reporting ensures transparency. Green bonds make it possible to raise money and make investments for both new and ongoing environmentally beneficial projects.

Origin and Concept of Green Bonds

Green bond is a brainchild of the World Bank aimed at sustainably financing investments in climate change and environmentally friendly projects. The World Bank is focused on transitioning to low-carbon and climate-resilient development and growth (UN Publication, 2017; Rezai, 2021). Such an effort is capital intensive and cannot be achieved only with public sponsorship. There is a need to incorporate private funding. Therefore, the World Bank initiated effective policies and introduced novel strategies for more financing to achieve these goals. Introducing other varieties of bonds into the capital market will hopefully generate more and robust interest in bond business. The World Bank achieved this through the introduction of green bonds which, in all respects, function like any other bond except that it is tied to the use of its proceeds for handling climate and environmentally focused projects. Green bonds, aside facilitating the diversification of investments from the regular bond, help to create awareness for the issuer's activities (World Bank).

Core Characteristics of Green Bonds

Presently, green bonds lack legal definition, and as such, they are exposed to regulations and guidelines as defined by the issuing body. A good case in point is the guidelines and regulations on green bonds prepared by Asia and China. However, for the purpose of standardizing the nascent market, a team comprising bond issuers, investors, and underwriters has articulated a number of general principles and certification programs which are non-prescriptive but intended to enhance the growth of green bond market in order to avert obstacles to entry by emerging economies. The Green Bond Principles and the Climate Bond Standards currently in use are coordinated by the International Capital Market Association (ICMA) (www.ifc.org). These guidelines were initially released in 2014 but a reviewed copy was published in June 2016. The ICMA put forward four principles which include:

i Use of proceeds which recognizes several broad categories of potential eligible green projects.
ii Process for Project Evaluation and Selection addressing the decision-making process to determine projects to be funded and transparent selection eligibility.
iii Management of proceeds taking care of funds handling through the appointment of proceeds managers in the form of specific sub-portfolio allocation, use of auditors or other third parties, and
iv Reporting with attention on frequency of reports on use of proceeds, project descriptions, and expected environmental impact (www.ifc.org).

Still in the spirit of standardization, a not-for-profit organization called Climate Bond Standard (CBS) came up with the initiative to provide sector-specific eligibility criteria for asset classes and projects, with the goal of allowing investors to screen a bond to assess its environmental impact (www.ifc.org).

Overall, the issuer's activities, in collaboration with investors and third-party opinions, ascribe the features attributed to green bond. It is peculiar to green bond that the issuer determines projects that could be considered as "green," designs and implements choice of eligibility index, develops internal process to be employed to ensure that proceeds from green bond are applied as earmarked. The bond is "green" when the issuer defines expected project outcomes and metrics in order to measure the impact of selected projects, and reports to investors (ex-ante and, as available, ex-post). Finally, in green bond deals, the issuer establishes internal and/or external procedures to ensure compliance with its stated transparent process.

Historical Evolution of Green Bonds

As mentioned above, the green bond initiative was established to quell the alarm on biodiversity loss and climate change raised by scientists and economist in pursuance to eco-friendly planet.

The World Bank has it that the first green bond was issued by European Investment Bank in 2007 to the tune of €600 million. The purpose of which was to focus attention on renewable energy and energy efficiency. This was followed, in 2008, by the issue of green bond of approximately US$440 million by the International Bank for Reconstruction and Development (IBRD). This was in response to specific demand from Scandinavian pension funds seeking to support climate-focused projects. Closest to this was in 2010 when the International Finance Corporation (IFC), a member of World Bank Group, issued their first green bond. Then in October 2013, the African Development Bank (AFDB) issued their first green bond amounting to US$500 million. This was geared toward supporting the financing of climate change solutions as part of a broader strategy to support inclusive and sustainable growth in Africa. Thereafter, other financial institutions joined in the race, among which are the Asian Development Bank (ADB), the European Bank for Reconstruction and Development (EBRD), the Nordic Investment Bank (NIB). Apart from the first issue by IBRD, by June 2015, it has issued about US$8.5 billion worth of green bonds in over 70 climate-related projects around the developing countries. The European Union issued the largest number of green bonds worth US$11.8 billion before June 2022. This landmark record was followed by Bank of China with green bond issue of about US$8.13 billion. Globally, the green bond market is estimated to have exceeded US$430 billion by 2022 (World Bank; Bisultanova, 2023). Evidently, awareness for sustainable investments is growing among issuers and investors alike.

Nigeria as the leading green bond market in the African continent issued her first sovereign green bond in 2017 worth NGN10.69 billion and in 2019 issued a second one to the tune of NGN15 billion. With that issue, Nigeria delivered its Nationally Determined Contributions (NDCs) to the Paris Climate Agreement. The proceeds were channeled toward energy and land use projects (Adeojo, 2022). In the work done at Kadyrov Chechen State University Russia, Bisultanova succinctly summarized the evolution of green bond in Table 1.1.

Eligibility Criteria for Green Bonds

A Process – Green-themed (self-labeled) bond identification A green bond issuer is required to identify the bond with a statement stating that it is meant to have a positive environmental impact. Though alternative designations like climate-awareness, climate, environmental, carbon, sustainability, and environment, social, and governance (ESG) are all acceptable, the term "green" is the most widely used. For a label to be valid, the issuer must use the label or description in a document that is made public. The bond may be mentioned by the label, for instance, in a press statement from the issuer or a virtual statement on the website, the bond prospectus, or any supporting documentation for the bond offering.

B Adequacy of the bond configurations – Asset-linked and asset-backed bond structures are the two categories of qualifying bond structures. Bonds that are asset-linked or use profits have designated funds from the bond sale for projects that qualify. Certain asset-linked bond issuers may decide to ring-fence proceeds by utilizing different accounts or vehicles. While

Table 1.1 Historical Stages in the Development of Green Bonds

Year	Event
2007	Berlin Declaration – organizations from the green banking sector have begun discussing the concept of green bonds.
2008	Verdict on climate bonds – The Climate Bonds Initiative has begun work on creating a standard for green bonds.
2010	First green bond – The World Bank has issued its first green bond for $174million.
2013	Companies are getting in on the act – Major companies such as EDF and Toyota have started to issue green bonds.
2014	First perfect green government bond – Poland has issued the first perfect green government bond.
2015	Creation of the Green Commission – The Green Bond Commission is set up to standardize green bonds.
2016	Market growth – The green bond market has reached $81billion.
2017	Green bonds around the world – Organizations and governments around the world have started to issue green bonds.
2018	First green bond – Apple has issued its first billion-dollar green bond to finance sustainable projects.
2020	Record year – In 2020, the green bond market reached $269 billion.

Source: Aza Bisultanova.

ring-fencing is not a condition for inclusion, at least some of the proceeds must go toward qualifying green projects. Bonds are separated into Project Bonds and Securitized Bonds for asset-backed arrangements.

- Securitized bonds are eligible if proceeds support green projects or assets.
- Project bonds are eligible if they are backed by a green project and the proceeds from the bond sale are used exclusively to finance the same green project. Thus, assets that are collateralized must not be labeled as "green."

C **Openness on the use of proceeds from green bonds** – Issuers agree to finance qualifying green projects or assets with the entire proceeds from the bond sale, minus the bond arrangement fees. The bond will not be allowed to be included if more than 5% of the proceeds are utilized for projects that are not considered green or for "general corporate purposes." The bond would not be qualified if the proceeds were to be distributed among several projects such as an ESG Bond with separate social initiatives and green projects.

D **Using green credentials for screening** – Based on the green credentials of the revenues used, each bond is examined. These could be designated proceeds for senior unsecured bonds that are asset-linked, projects that support a project bond, or assets that support an Asset-Backed Securities (ABS). In accordance with the Green Bond Principles, the issuer is required to specify at the time of issuance the kinds of green assets or projects that qualify for funding.

Allocation and Utilization of Green Bonds Proceeds

The Green Bond issuer ought to put in place and ensure the following:

i An approach for ascertaining the projects' compatibility with the eligible Green Projects categories.
ii Associated qualifying standards and the goals of environmental sustainability.
iii The Green Bond Principles (GBP) must promote openness to the fullest and advise that an external review be added to an issuer's project evaluation and selection process.
iv Green Bond investors have the option to evaluate an issuer's overall profile quality and environmental sustainability performance, in addition to the information the issuer discloses about its criteria, procedure, and external evaluation.
v The issuer must track the net proceeds of Green Bonds appropriately, either by crediting them to a sub-account, moving them to a sub-portfolio, or in some other way, and establishing a formal internal process that is connected to the issuer's lending and investment operations for Green Projects.
vi The balance of the monitored profits should be periodically modified to meet allocations to qualifying Green Projects made during the period that the Green Bonds are outstanding. Investors should be informed by the issuer of the types of temporary placements for the remaining unallocated cash.
vii The GBP advocacy for a high degree of transparency and advises that an issuer hire an auditor or other outside entity to help with the administration of proceeds.

Types of Green Bonds

Four types of green bonds could be identified following the World Bank:

Use-of-proceeds bonds,
Use-of-proceeds revenue bonds,
Project bonds-proceeds and,
Securitized bonds.

Use-of-proceeds Green Bonds

The concept of flat pricing, in which the bond price is the same as that of regular bonds, has given rise to the green "use of proceeds" bond market. Proceeds bonds are used to finance initiatives that have specific environmental and/or social benefits, as their name implies. The foundation of a Green Bond is the use of the bond proceeds for Green Projects, which must be suitably detailed in the security's legal documentation. Every approved Green Project category should have measurable environmental benefits that the issuer will evaluate and, if practical, quantify. It is advised that issuers offer an estimate of the share of financing vs. refinancing and, where applicable, further specify which investments or project portfolios may be refinanced if all or a portion of the funds are or may be used for refinancing.

A "green use of proceeds revenue bond" is a type of non-recourse financial obligation where the proceeds of the bond are used for either connected or unrelated green initiatives, and the credit exposure of the bond is based on the pledged cash flows of revenue streams, fees, taxes, etc.

The purpose of these bonds is to provide funding for both new and ongoing initiatives that have a positive environmental impact. Impactful green bonds, in our opinion, ought to be issued in accordance with the ICMA's GBP, a voluntary set of standards that encourage more open, consistent reporting on the environmental goals and anticipated impact of bonds. Since ICMA offers standards for all types of green, social, or sustainability-linked bonds, it is actually applicable for these kinds of bonds.

Asset – Linked and Revenue Linked Green Bonds

- "Use of Proceeds" Bonds: These bonds are intended to fund environmentally friendly projects, but in the event of a liquidation, the lenders may seize other assets of the issuer. The issuer's other bonds and these instruments have the same credit rating.
- "Use of Proceeds" Revenue Bonds or ABS: These securities can be used to finance or refinance environmentally friendly projects, but the debt is secured by the issuer's revenue streams, which include taxes and fees. When issuing green bonds, state and local governments may choose to use this kind of arrangement.

Climate Bonds, Sustainability Bonds and Transition Bonds

Sustainability Bonds

Sustainability bonds are issued with the intention of using the money raised to either refinance or finance a mix of social and environmental projects. Companies, governments, and municipalities may issue these bonds for assets and projects, and they should adhere to the ICMA Sustainability Bond Guidelines, which are in line with the SBP and GBP. They may be secured by security on a particular asset, unsecured, or guaranteed by the government's or company's creditworthiness.

Project categories that fall within the green and social bonds categories are a couple of examples of those that qualify for sustainability bonds.

Sustainability-linked Bonds

Connections to sustainability Bonds are structurally tied to the issuer's accomplishment of climate or more general SDG targets. One example of this is a covenant that links the coupon of a bond. These bonds are known as key performance indicator (KPI)-linked or SDG-linked Bonds. In this instance, advancement—or lack thereof—against the SDGs or particular KPIs subsequently causes the instrument's coupon to fluctuate. These bonds have the potential to be extremely effective in motivating businesses to take corporate sustainability pledges, especially when it comes to joining the Paris Agreement or the UN SDGs. ICMA. Sustainability-linked bonds support an issuer's overall operations and have stated sustainability targets that are connected to the bond's financing terms, rather than funding specific projects.

The bond is known as a sustainability bond when there is a deliberate combination of social and environmental advantages; the ICMA offers a distinct set of rules for this type of bond, called the Sustainability Bond rules.

Transition Bonds

A novel type of bonds known as transition bonds is issued with the intention of using the profits to finance a company's shift to a lower carbon footprint or environmental effect. Only qualifying transition initiatives, either new or already underway, may be financed using the money raised (Riordan, 2017). As a condition of issuing these bonds, the issuer must pledge to switch to more environmentally friendly business methods. The issuer of transition bonds must use the funds for activities relevant to climate transition, but neither the project nor the issuer must be categorized as "green." One way to finance efforts to collect and store carbon would be for a coal-mining company to issue a transition bond. Transition bond proponents contend that it is preferable for businesses looking to go "greener" to finance their assets with bonds rather than risk being shut out of the green bond market and having no other way to pay for transition projects. New types of bonds are frequently issued in industries that would not typically be eligible for green bonds. Transition bonds can be thought of as a cross between sustainability-linked bonds and green bonds.

Green bonds typically offer a direct funding source for environmentally favorable projects that have already been identified, including solar power plants or environmentally acceptable waste disposal facilities.

Importance of Transition Bonds

Transition bonds can provide financing for sustainable projects to businesses that would not be able to issue green bonds. Furthermore, because there is a limited supply of green bonds, they may not be able to meet the growing demand for sustainable investment possibilities. Transition bonds provide a means of bridging this investment gap.

Climate Bonds

Bonds with fixed income associated with climate change solutions are called climate bonds. They are released to generate funds for projects connected to adaptation or mitigation in response to climate change. These could be energy efficiency or clean energy initiatives aimed at reducing greenhouse gas emissions, or they could be climate change adaptation projects like constructing flood barriers in the Nile Delta or assisting the Great Barrier Reef in adjusting to warming waters.

Climate bonds may be issued by governments, multinational banks, or businesses, much like regular bonds. In addition to a fixed or variable rate of return, the issuing entity promises to repay the bond over a specific period. The majority of Climate Bonds are use-of-proceeds bonds, in which the issuer guarantees investors that all funds obtained will only be used to certain climate-related assets or initiatives, including supporting programs for climate mitigation or renewable energy plants. Investors should be aware that they are funding efforts to combat climate change.

Certification and Verification Processes

Asset managers and their principals must be able to recognize the bonds that genuinely improve the environment or the climate in order for green bond investments to take off. Asset managers might possess the means to independently make a well-informed decision. Global efforts to improve environmental information accessibility include the financial stability (UNEP, 2016). However, external certification may be more economical and enables asset managers to verify to beneficiaries that they are, in fact, investing in green bonds upon request.

The "voluntary process guidelines" known as the ICMA Green Bond Principles set forth broad standards that the majority of certification programs adhere to. Under the auspices of the ICMA, they were assembled by significant private financial institutions (ICMA, 2015). The principles offer prospective issuers direction on the essential elements of issuing green bonds, which include: (i) allocating proceeds to ecologically sustainable projects; (ii) establishing a procedure for project eligibility; (iii) handling proceeds in an open, verifiable, and transparent manner; and (iv) submitting an annual report on the use of proceeds. Many countries have created their own national taxonomies that define what qualifies as a green bond.

Certification of Climate Bonds

As was previously mentioned, the CBI keeps track of all green bonds that have been issued since 2009. Although the bonds in its database have green labels, CBI does not express a judgment on the accuracy of the label just because it is included in the database.

In addition, the CBI offers guidelines and a certification process. The CBI's Climate Bonds Standard defines industry-specific qualifying standards to assess an asset's low carbon value and appropriateness for issuing a green bond, even if the Green Bond Principles are somewhat broad. After an authorized external verification that the bond satisfies environmental criteria and that the issuer has the necessary controls and procedures in place, assets that meet the CBI standard can subsequently be eligible for Climate Bond Certification.

Concept of Sustainable Finance

The key focus of Sustainable finance is the integration of ESG principles into business and managerial decisions, economic and developmental planning, and policies, as well as investment strategies. Documented evidence abounds as to how sustainability consideration exerts multidimensional impact on financial stability (IMF, 2022). Beyond actualizing traditional financial objectives, sustainable finance among other things focuses on containing risks such as:

1 **Environmental risk exposures** – risks, uncertainties, and losses that come from climate and other environment-related variations.
2 **Governance failures** – risks, uncertainties, and failures that come from governance at social, corporate, or public levels.
3 **Social risks** – risks, uncertainties, and instabilities that come from such social factors as inequality, poverty, unemployment, and social exclusions.

Prominently used financial instruments in sustainable finance include green bonds, green loans, and sustainability-linked loans which are designed to finance reduction in emission intensity and other climate and environment-related challenges.

Growth Trajectory in Sustainable Finance

In an era where global challenges like climate change, social inequality, and environmental degradation loom large, the financial world has undergone a remarkable shift toward sustainability. This transition to sustainable finance represents a profound evolution in investment strategies and capital allocation, fueling a trajectory of growth that is reshaping the global financial landscape. Financing is considered sustainable when investment decisions take into consideration the ESG factors of an economic activity or project (Goel, Guatam, & Natalucci, 2022). The roots of sustainable finance could be traced back to the concept of socially responsible investing (SRI) and ethical investing, which emerged in the 1960s and 1970s, driven by concerns about the societal and environmental impact of corporations. However, the evolution of sustainable finance has seen a paradigm shift from merely excluding certain industries to actively integrating ESG factors into investment decisions (Niyazbekova et al., 2021). Environmental factors include mitigation of the climate crises or use of sustainable resources. Social factors consider human and animal rights, as well as consumer protection and diverse hiring practices while governance factors refer to the management, safe labor practices, employee relations, and compensation practices of both government and corporate organizations. The momentum behind sustainable finance has gained unprecedented traction in recent years. Investors, from institutional giants to individual stakeholders, are increasingly recognizing the importance of aligning their financial goals with broader societal and environmental objectives. This surge in interest has led to a proliferation of sustainable investment products, including green bonds, ESG-focused funds, and impact investing vehicles. Key drivers of growth in sustainable finance include:

Regulatory Initiatives: Governments and regulatory bodies worldwide are enacting policies and regulations that motivate sustainable investment. These measures include disclosure requirements, tax incentives, and the integration of ESG considerations into financial frameworks.

Changing Investor Preferences: Millennials and younger generations, in particular, are vocal about their desire to invest in companies that prioritize sustainability and social responsibility. This shift in preferences is exerting a substantial influence on investment trends and decision-making.

Corporate Accountability: Companies are under increasing pressure to demonstrate their commitment to sustainability. Investors are demanding greater transparency regarding corporate ESG practices, prompting companies to adopt more sustainable business models to attract capital.

While the growth trajectory of sustainable finance appears promising, challenges persist. Concerns regarding standardization of ESG metrics, greenwashing, and the need for comprehensive data remain issues yet to be fully attended to. Ironically, these challenges appear to present opportunities for innovation, collaboration, and the development of robust frameworks to address these issues. Looking ahead, the trajectory of sustainable finance seems unstoppable. The global shift toward a more sustainable future is driving the integration of ESG factors into investment decisions, reshaping capital markets, and influencing corporate behaviors (Dodds, 2015). As sustainable finance continues to evolve, stakeholders across the financial ecosystem will play a pivotal role in shaping its future trajectory.

The Significance of Green Bonds in Sustainable Finance

Green bonds have gained immense grip in recent years as a financial tool to address pressing environmental concerns while mobilizing capital for sustainable projects. Their importance in sustainable finance is evident in their capacity to attract a wide range of investors and finance initiatives aimed at mitigating climate change and promoting environmental sustainability (FGN, 2017). Green bonds hold significant importance in the realm of finance and sustainability for several reasons:

Funding Environmental Projects: Green bonds are specifically designed to finance or re-finance projects that have positive environmental impacts, such as renewable energy initiatives, sustainable water management, clean transportation, and energy efficiency projects. They provide a crucial avenue for raising capital dedicated exclusively to these environmentally friendly endeavors.

Promoting Sustainable Finance: By earmarking proceeds for environmentally beneficial projects, green bonds play a pivotal role in advancing sustainable finance. They help mobilize capital toward initiatives that mitigate climate change and promote sustainable development, aligning financial investments with broader environmental objectives.

Attracting Diverse Investors: Green bonds attract a wide range of investors who prioritize both financial returns and positive environmental impact. This diversified investor-base includes institutional investors, socially conscious individuals, and entities seeking to align their portfolios with ESG criteria.

Market Growth and Trends: The market for green bonds has witnessed substantial growth, with increasing issuance volumes and a broadening range of issuers. This trend reflects growing demand from investors seeking opportunities to support environmentally responsible projects and signifies a shift toward more sustainable investment options.

Alignment with ESG Objectives: Green bonds facilitate responsible and sustainable investing by enabling investors to align their portfolios with ESG objectives. Investors can support projects that not only offer financial returns but also positively impact the environment and society.

Risk Mitigation and Reputation Enhancement: Issuers of green bonds may benefit from enhanced reputation and improved risk management. By demonstrating a commitment to sustainability, issuers can attract a broader investor-base concerned about sustainability factors, potentially reducing financing costs.

Challenges and Mitigation Strategies: Challenges such as standardization of frameworks and transparency persist in the green bond market. Efforts are ongoing to establish clearer guidelines and metrics for evaluation, aiming at enhancing credibility and trust in these financial instruments.

Addressing Environmental Challenges

The urgency of addressing environmental challenges has prompted the exploration of innovative financial instruments designed to fund sustainable initiatives. The escalating environmental challenges, including climate change, resource depletion, and biodiversity loss, necessitate proactive measures. Goel et al. (2022) posit that green bonds, as financial instruments dedicated to funding eco-friendly projects, hold promise in redirecting capital toward initiatives aimed at addressing these challenges. The benefits and impacts of addressing environmental challenges cannot be over-emphasized. First, green bonds facilitate investments that are aligned with ESG criteria, encouraging sustainable financial practices. Second, issuers of green bonds stand to benefit from improved risk management and enhanced reputation by demonstrating a commitment to sustainability. Environmental challenges could be strategically addressed by standardizing green bond frameworks and ensuring transparent reporting. Also, by developing a more liquid market and establishing pricing benchmarks (ADB, 2013). The future of green bonds in addressing environmental challenges appears promising. The ongoing regulatory support, efforts toward standardization, and heightened awareness about environmental concerns are expected to drive further growth and innovation in this space. Green bonds stand as a powerful financial instrument capable of steering capital toward environmentally beneficial projects, significantly contributing to global sustainability efforts.

Advancing Sustainability Goals in Finance

Advancing sustainability goals in finance represents a critical shift toward integrating ESG factors into financial decision-making. This shift acknowledges the importance of aligning economic growth with broader societal and environmental well-being (Kaminker, 2016). It involves several key aspects:

ESG Integration: Incorporating ESG criteria into investment decisions ensures that financial activities consider environmental impact, social responsibility, and corporate governance. This integration allows investors to support companies committed to sustainable practices and responsible business conduct.

Sustainable Investing Strategies: Finance is increasingly directed toward sustainable investing strategies, such as impact investing, SRI, and thematic investing. These strategies focus on generating positive social or environmental impacts alongside financial returns.

Green Finance Instruments: The development of financial tools like green bonds, sustainability-linked loans, and ESG-focused funds offers avenues to mobilize capital for projects addressing sustainability challenges. These instruments channel investments toward renewable energy, conservation, sustainable infrastructure, and other eco-friendly initiatives.

Corporate Accountability and Reporting: Companies are encouraged to adopt transparent reporting practices regarding their sustainability efforts. Enhanced disclosure and accountability mechanisms allow stakeholders to assess a company's environmental and social performance, fostering responsible corporate behavior.

Regulatory Support: Governments and regulatory bodies play a crucial role in advancing sustainability in finance by implementing policies that incentivize ESG integration, impose reporting requirements, or offer tax incentives for sustainable investments. This support encourages financial institutions and corporations to prioritize sustainability in their operations.

Risk Management and Long-Term Value Creation: Integrating sustainability into financial practices mitigates risks associated with environmental and social factors, ensuring long-term value creation. Companies that embrace sustainable practices are better positioned to navigate regulatory changes, market shifts, and changing consumer preferences.

Stakeholder Engagement: Collaboration among various stakeholders—such as investors, businesses, governments, and civil society—is essential for driving sustainable finance. Engaging stakeholders foster dialogue, knowledge sharing, and collective efforts toward achieving sustainability goals.

Conclusion and Policies

There has been increasing emphasis on sustainability on every front and in every facet of economic, social, and political life. Consideration for environmental safety, biodiversity conservation, social equality, and safe habitation have been at the forefront of most policies at supranational, national, and corporate levels. Sustainable finance is one of the evolving issues in finance and financial system stability discourses. One of the financial instruments that come into consideration in sustainable finance literature is green bond. Most countries, pursuant to the actualization of sustainability goals as enshrined in the United Nation's Sustainable Development Goals (SDG) have continued to make green bonds a part of their financial system. Evidently, like most financial innovations, the level of adoption has not been the same across different jurisdictions. While the developed economies have taken more to the issuance and use of green bonds, the pace has been slow in emerging financial markets and expectedly at its slowest pace in developing economic systems of Asia and Africa.

With the increasing level of significance of green bonds and their advancement as veritable tools for sustainable finance, their prospects continue to increase in financial systems with slow pace of adoption. Moreso, the increasing spate of financial globalization and the benchmarking of financial best practices across the international financial space will continue to enhance the acceptability and use of green bonds.

The regulatory architectures at national, subnational, and international levels are expected to continually adjust to the need for adequate regulation of the green bonds markets. This is to contain counterparty and other associated risks while engendering the confidence of issuers and investors alike, in the use of this sustainability focused financial instrument.

References

Adeojo, J. (2022). *Nigeria's Green Bond Programme: Aspirations, Realities and Solutions.* Heinrich Boll Stiftung.

African Development Bank (2013). *Green Bonds Framework: Portfolio Selection, Allocation of Proceeds and Monitoring.*

Bisultanova, A. (2023). "Green" Bond: Historical Aspects of Implementation. https://doi.org/10.1051/e3sconf/202345805013

Dodds, F. (2015). *Negotiating the Sustainable Development Goals: A Transformational Agenda for an Insecure World.* Routledge Environment & Sustainability Posts. Online. https://www.routledge.com/sustainability/posts/8516.

Environmental Theme Bonds: A Major New Asset Class Brewing, Excerpt from Sustainable Banking – Risk and Opportunity in Financing the Future, edited by Joti Mangat, published by Thomson Reuters, 2010.

Federal Government of Nigeria (FGN) (2017). Offer for Subscription of N10,690,000,000 Series I: 5 Year [13.48] Per cent Fixed Rate Bonds Due 2022: Pricing Supplement (Prospectus). https://dmo.gov.ng/fgn-bonds/green-bond/2292-green-bond-pricing-supplement.

Goel, R., Gautam, D., & Natalucci, F. (2022). *Sustainable Finance in Emerging Markets: Evolution, Challenges, and Policy Priorities.* IMF WORKING PAPERS Monetary and Capital Markets Department, WP/22/182.

ICMA. (2015). *Green Bond Principles.* Retrieved March 28, 2024, from https://www.icmagroup.org/assets/documents/Regulatory/Green-Bonds/GBP_2015_27-March.pdf

ICMA Group (2021). *The Green Bond Principles: Voluntary Process Guidelines for Issuing Green Bonds.* www.icmagroup.org.

IMF. (2022). *Shaping The Frontier of Sustainable Finance in Emerging Markets.* Retrieved March 28, 2024, from https://www.imf.org/en/News/Articles/2022/04/26/sp-042622-shaping-the-frontier-of-sustainable-finance-in-emerging-markets

International Capital Market Association 2015 Governance Framework for Green Bon

International Finance Corporation (World Bank Group) (2016). *Mobilizing Private Climate Finance – Green Bond and Beyond.* www.ifc.org.

Kaminker, C. (2016). Green Bonds – Ecosystem, Issuance Process & Case Studies. Deutsche Gesellschaft für Internationale Zusammenarbeit (GIZ) GmbH Implemented through develoPPP.de.

Niyazbekova, S., Moldashbayeva, L., Kerimkhulle, S., Dzholdoshev, N., Dzholdosheva, T., & Serikova, M. (2021). "Green" Bonds – A Tool for Financing "Green" Projects in Countries. EDP Sciences. http://creativecommons.org/licenses/by/4.0/.

Rezai, A. (2021). Yahoo! Finance. Global Green Bond Market Report 2022: Analysis by Energy, Building & Industry, Transport, Water, & Multi-Sector – Forecast to 2027. 7.

Riordan, R. (2017). Sustainable Finance Primer Series. Smith School of Business Journal.

UNEP. (2016). *Task Force on Climate-Related Financial Disclosures: Draft Recommendations Report out 14th December.* United Nations Environment Programme - Finance Initiative. Retrieved March 28, 2024, from https://www.unepfi.org/industries/banking/task-force-on-climate-related-financial-disclosures-draft-recommendations-report-out-14th-december/

United Nations (2000) 55/2. United Nations Millennium Declaration. Online. http://www.un.org/millennium/declaration/ares552e.pdf.

Velloso, H., Bustillo, I., & Játiva, T. (2017). The Rise of Green Bonds: Financing for Development in Latin America and the Caribbean. United Nations Publication. LC/WAS/TS.2017/6.

World Bank. (2016). *The world bank green bond.* Retrieved March 28, 2024, from https://thedocs.worldbank.org/en/doc/614431507751962913-0340022017/original/investorupdategreenbond2016.pdf

2 Environmental and Social Criteria in Green Bond Selection

Raima Nazar, Sajid Ali, Manjeet Kaur Harnek Singh and Ayesha Zahid

Introduction

Green bonds are specially developed securities meant to foster sustainability by financing projects with a clear vision of improving the environment (Zhao et al., 2022). They are called "green bonds" because they were created only to finance activities and projects aimed at saving the environment. This includes energy efficient projects, pollution control projects, sustainable agricultural practices, preservation of aquatic and terrestrial ecosystems, forestry and fisheries management, eco-friendly transportation solutions, clean water resources, and sustainable water management (Anh Tu et al., 2020; Sartzetakis, 2021).

It is important to note that the specific criteria for green bonds may vary by issuer and region. Various organizations, including the Climate Bonds Initiative, have developed standards and guidelines to help define what qualifies as a green bond, and they continue to evolve to align with sustainability goals and best practices (Anh Tu et al., 2020; Zhao et al., 2022). Environmental and social (E&S) criteria are important components in the selection and issuance of green bonds (Azhgaliyeva et al., 2020). When evaluating and selecting projects for green bond issuance, issuers and investors typically consider the following environmental and social criteria.

Environmental Criteria

Environmental criteria (Hu & Jin, 2023) for green bonds are stringent and encompass several key aspects. First, projects funded by green bonds must offer clear, measurable environmental benefits, including renewable energy, energy efficiency, and clean transportation (Mankata et al., 2022). These projects should also contribute to climate change mitigation and adaptation by reducing greenhouse gas emissions, improving carbon sequestration, and enhancing climate resilience. Resource efficiency, biodiversity conservation, and pollution prevention are crucial considerations, as green bonds promote the responsible use of natural resources, protect ecosystems and wildlife, and reduce pollution (Wu et al., 2021; Chang et al., 2022). Finally, green bonds may support sustainable land use practices, ensuring a comprehensive approach to environmental sustainability.

DOI: 10.4324/9781032686844-2

Measurement of Carbon Footprint

Measuring the carbon footprint of a project involves calculating and reporting the total amount of greenhouse gases (usually expressed in CO_2-equivalents) emitted as a result of the project's activities. This can include emissions from energy use, transportation, production processes, and other project-related sources. The measurement of the carbon footprint provides insights into the project's environmental impact and helps in setting reduction targets.

- **Alignment with Climate Goals (e.g., Paris Agreement)**
  This criterion ensures that the project aligns with international climate goals, such as the Paris Agreement's objective to limit global warming to well below 2°C and to pursue efforts to limit the temperature increase to 1.5C°. Projects must demonstrate their contribution to achieving these goals through emission reductions, sustainable practices, and climate resilience measures.
- **Projects Promoting Renewable Energy, Energy Efficiency, etc.**
  Projects promoting renewable energy typically involve developing and deploying clean and sustainable energy sources, such as wind, solar, hydro, geothermal, and bioenergy. Energy efficiency projects focus on reducing energy consumption and improving energy performance in various sectors, including buildings, transportation, and industry. Both types of projects aim to reduce the carbon footprint and environmental impact associated with energy production and consumption.
- **Natural Resource Conservation**
  Natural resource conservation encompasses projects that aim to protect and preserve essential resources, such as water, forests, and land. For instance, it may include the sustainable management of forests, responsible water use, and land use practices that prevent deforestation, overgrazing, and soil erosion. The goal is to ensure the long-term availability of these critical resources.
- **Protection of Biodiversity and Ecosystems**
  This criterion emphasizes the importance of protecting biodiversity and maintaining ecosystems. Projects in this category may involve habitat restoration, wildlife conservation, reforestation, and efforts to prevent habitat destruction. The goal is to safeguard the rich variety of plant and animal species and the stability of ecosystems.
- **Sustainable Use of Natural Resources**
  Sustainable use of natural resources refers to projects that promote responsible resource management. This includes practices that reduce waste, minimize resource depletion, and support circular economy principles, such as recycling and upcycling. The objective is to extend the lifespan of natural resources and reduce environmental harm.
- **Pollution Prevention and Control**
  Pollution prevention and control criteria require projects to adopt technologies and practices that minimize the release of harmful substances into the environment. This can involve pollution control measures, using cleaner

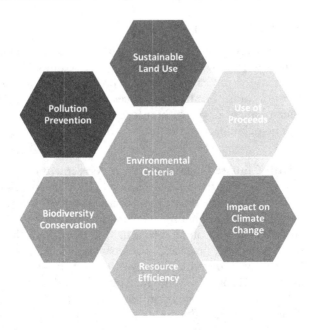

Figure 2.1 Environmental criteria for Green Bond issuance

Source: Authors own creation

production processes, and implementing pollution reduction strategies to protect air, water, and soil quality.

- **Reduction of Air, Water, and Soil Pollution**
  This criterion stresses the importance of projects that specifically aim to reduce pollution in air, water, and soil. Projects should have clear strategies and technologies in place to lower emissions of air pollutants, prevent the discharge of pollutants into water bodies, and avoid soil contamination from industrial activities.
- **Compliance with Environmental Regulations**
  Compliance with environmental regulations is a fundamental requirement for all projects. It ensures that projects adhere to relevant local, national, and international environmental laws and standards. This criterion emphasizes the necessity of legal and regulatory compliance to prevent environmental harm and protect ecosystems, human health, and communities (Figure 2.1).

Social Criteria

Green bonds extend their support to projects with a positive social impact, including affordable housing, healthcare facilities, education infrastructure, and clean water supply systems (Sartzetakis, 2021). These projects prioritize community engagement, local job creation, inclusivity, and equality. They involve the local community, adhere to labor and human rights standards, and prioritize health and safety for workers and the community (Chang et al., 2022).

- **Social Impact**: Green bonds may support projects that have a positive social impact, such as affordable housing, healthcare facilities, education infrastructure, and clean water supply systems.
- **Community Engagement**: Projects should involve the local community and respect the rights and needs of affected communities. Socially responsible projects often prioritize community consultation and benefit sharing.
- **Job Creation**: Green bond-financed projects may be evaluated based on their potential to create local jobs and improve the livelihoods of communities.
- **Inclusivity and Equality**: Projects should aim to reduce social inequalities and promote inclusivity, such as projects that benefit underserved or marginalized populations.
- **Labor and Human Rights**: Adherence to labor and human rights standards is crucial, ensuring that workers involved in green bond projects are treated fairly and with dignity.
- **Health and Safety**: Projects should prioritize the health and safety of workers and the surrounding community, especially in potentially hazardous industries.

It is important to note that the specific criteria for green bonds may vary by issuer and region. Various organizations, including the Climate Bonds Initiative, have developed standards and guidelines to help define what qualifies as a green bond, and they continue to evolve to align with sustainability goals and best practices. Investors and issuers use these criteria to ensure that the funds raised through green bonds are allocated to environmentally and socially responsible projects, making a positive impact on both the planet and society. Third-party verification and reporting are often used to provide transparency and accountability in the selection and use of green bond proceeds.

Significance of Incorporating E&S Criteria into the Selection and Issuance of Green Bonds

The significance of incorporating environmental and social criteria into green bonds lies in their ability to drive sustainable and responsible financing, tackle pressing global challenges, and contribute to the transition to a more environmentally and socially sustainable economy. They provide a structured and transparent way to link financial markets with sustainability objectives.

- Green bonds play a crucial role in financing projects that address pressing environmental and social challenges. By channeling capital into initiatives that promote sustainability, they contribute to mitigating climate change, protecting natural ecosystems, conserving resources, and addressing social issues like affordable housing and healthcare access.

- The criteria for green bonds help align investment and financing activities with international and national sustainability goals. For example, they support the objectives of the United Nations Sustainable Development Goals (SDGs) and the Paris Agreement on climate change.
- Green bonds attract investors who are specifically looking to put their money into projects that have a positive impact on the environment and society. This helps mobilize capital for projects that might not have been funded through traditional financing channels.
- The use of environmental and social criteria encourages responsible investment practices. Investors are increasingly concerned about the long-term risks associated with climate change and social issues, and green bonds offer a way to address these concerns.
- Issuers of green bonds benefit from a positive reputation and increased transparency. By adhering to stringent criteria, issuers can build trust with investors and demonstrate their commitment to sustainability.
- Bonds are a key tool for supporting sustainable development, as they help finance the transition to a low-carbon and socially inclusive economy. This is particularly important in the context of the global push for sustainable development.
- The growth of the green bond market has encouraged regulatory bodies to establish standards and guidelines, further promoting environmentally and socially responsible investment. It has also fostered innovation in financial products and services.
- Environmental and social criteria in green bonds require issuers to track and report on the use of proceeds, ensuring accountability for the intended positive impact. This transparency is essential for building and maintaining investor confidence.
- By funding projects with strong environmental and social credentials, green bonds can help mitigate long-term environmental and social risks. This, in turn, can reduce financial risks for investors and issuers alike.

Rationale of Incorporating E&S Factors in Green Bond Selection

The rationale for incorporating environmental and social factors into bond selection, encompassing green, sustainable, and social bonds, is substantiated by various economic, ethical, and risk management rationales (Zou et al., 2023). First and foremost, it serves to mitigate environmental and social risks by proactively addressing potential hazards linked to unsustainable practices, thereby safeguarding investors' portfolios. This approach promotes long-term sustainability, reducing the likelihood of stranded assets and sudden financial losses. Additionally, it aligns investments with stakeholders' values, accommodating ethical and values-based preferences (Park, 2021). Moreover, adhering to environmental, social, and governance (ESG) factors is essential for compliance with regulatory and reporting requirements, ensuring transparency and reliable information. Beyond risk management and regulatory compliance, it enhances reputation, attracts a broader investor base, taps into market opportunities, fosters resilience to change, strengthens community and stakeholder relations, and bolsters competitive advantage (Cicchiello et al., 2022). In sum, integrating E&S factors in bond selection yields benefits that span financial, ethical, and strategic dimensions.

Integration of E&S Criteria in Bond Selection

- **Screening and Exclusion Criteria**
  Screening criteria encompass a range of factors such as industry, geographic location, and financial performance (Billio et al., 2021). For example, an investor may screen out companies involved in weapons manufacturing, tobacco production, or fossil fuel extraction. Exclusion criteria are based on predefined E&S standards. These may include specific quantitative thresholds, such as maximum allowable carbon emissions, as well as qualitative factors like human rights violations or involvement in controversial activities.
- **Identifying and Excluding Controversial Industries**
  Controversial industries often include areas like arms production, tobacco, gambling, or companies with a history of severe environmental violations. Excluding bonds associated with these industries aligns the investment portfolio with ethical values and can help mitigate reputational risks for investors.
- **Ethical and Values-Based Considerations**
  Ethical and values-based considerations vary from investor to investor. They can encompass a wide range of principles, including religious beliefs, ethical convictions, and personal values. For example, an investor may exclude bonds linked to companies involved in animal testing due to their ethical beliefs.
- **Positive Selection Criteria**
  Positive selection criteria aim to identify projects and issuers that actively contribute to E&S goals. For example, a positive selection criterion may prioritize bonds from companies that have committed to a specific level of renewable energy generation or that allocate a portion of their profits to community development programs.
- **Identifying E&S Leaders and Positive Impact Issuers**
  Identifying E&S leaders involves evaluating an issuer's historical E&S performance, recognizing companies with exemplary records in sustainability, and giving preference to their bonds. Positive impact issuers are entities whose projects have shown a clear, measurable positive impact on environmental and social goals, making their bonds appealing to investors seeking meaningful E&S outcomes.
- **Evaluating Green and Social Projects**
  When evaluating green projects, investors assess the environmental benefits, such as carbon emissions reductions, energy efficiency improvements,

or the use of renewable energy sources. For social projects, the focus is on their societal impact, which could include improved healthcare access, poverty reduction, or educational advancements.

- **Quantitative E&S Metrics**
  Quantitative metrics can encompass various indicators, such as carbon emissions reductions in tons, energy efficiency improvements as a percentage, water use reductions in cubic meters, or the number of jobs created. These metrics provide a clear, measurable basis for evaluating projects.
- **Scoring Systems and Rankings for E&S Performance**
  Scoring systems assign scores or rankings based on predefined criteria and metrics. For example, a green bond may receive a higher score if it has a more significant impact on reducing carbon emissions, while a social bond may be ranked higher if it delivers measurable benefits to underserved communities.
- **Integration with Financial Analysis and Risk Assessment**
  Integrating E&S criteria with financial analysis involves evaluating the potential financial risks and returns associated with E&S factors. For instance, a company with a high carbon footprint may face future regulatory risks and increased operational costs.
- Risk assessments may also consider the reputational and legal risks associated with non-compliance with E&S regulations and standards.

Due Diligence and Research Process

The due diligence and research process serves as a foundation for making informed and responsible investment decisions, ensuring that E&S criteria are integrated into the selection of bonds and projects. It enhances transparency, risk management, and alignment with ethical and sustainable investment objectives.

- **Stakeholder Engagement**
  Stakeholder engagement is a proactive and ongoing process that involves identifying and interacting with a diverse set of stakeholders such as shareholders, bondholders, local communities, environmental groups, labor unions, and other organizations with an interest in the bond or project. Engagement methods may encompass meetings, surveys, public hearings, and direct communication to solicit feedback, share information, and address concerns. The goal is to create a transparent and inclusive dialogue with stakeholders.
- **Engaging with Issuers, NGOs, and Communities**
  When engaging with issuers, investors seek comprehensive information about the issuer's E&S commitments and practices. They may request data on emissions, sustainability initiatives, and adherence to ethical standards. Interaction with NGOs and communities often involves conducting impact assessments and gathering qualitative data on social and environmental

concerns. These groups may provide insights into potential E&S risks and opportunities, as well as help identify the most relevant E&S criteria.

- **Assessing Stakeholder Feedback and Concerns**
  Assessment includes analyzing the feedback and concerns collected from various stakeholders. The significance of each concern is evaluated in relation to its potential impact on the investment. For instance, a high level of community opposition to a project can carry significant reputational and regulatory risks. The concerns may be categorized as environmental, social, or governance-related and scored according to their materiality and relevance to investment decisions.

- **E&S Risk Assessment**
  E&S risk assessment is a comprehensive process that identifies, evaluates, and quantifies risks that could affect the bond or project. It encompasses a range of considerations, including regulatory compliance, resource scarcity, labor practices, and supply chain risks. Risk assessments may also consider factors such as climate change, political stability, and cultural considerations, as these can have profound E&S implications.

- **Identifying and Managing E&S Risks in Bond Portfolios**
  After evaluating individual E&S risks, the next step is to consider the composition of the bond portfolio as a whole. Investors must balance the bonds with varying E&S profiles to create a well-diversified portfolio. Strategies for managing E&S risks include setting thresholds for E&S performance, divesting from high-risk bonds or industries, and incorporating bonds that contribute to portfolio resilience in the face of potential E&S challenges.

- **Scenario Analysis and Stress Testing for E&S Events**
  Scenario analysis involves simulating potential E&S events and their impact on the bond portfolio (Sakurai & Kurosaki, 2020). These scenarios range from extreme weather events to social disruptions or sudden policy changes. Stress testing is a rigorous assessment of the portfolio's resilience under various E&S conditions. It helps investors identify vulnerabilities, assess potential losses, and develop strategies to mitigate these risks, including adjustments to asset allocation or risk hedging measures.

Reporting and Transparency

Reporting and transparency in E&S criteria are essential for promoting responsible and sustainable investment practices. They provide a clear framework for communicating an organization's or an investment portfolio's E&S performance, facilitate comparisons, and enable stakeholders to make informed decisions while fostering a culture of accountability and compliance with regulatory requirements.

- **Disclosure Standards**
  Disclosure standards refer to the set of guidelines, frameworks, and principles that dictate how issuers and investors report their E&S performance

(Quatrini, 2021). These standards provide a structured and consistent way to convey E&S information to stakeholders. They encompass internationally recognized reporting frameworks like the Global Reporting Initiative (GRI), the Sustainability Accounting Standards Board (SASB), and the Task Force on Climate-related Financial Disclosures (TCFD). These standards offer a common language for E&S reporting and are widely adopted by organizations globally.

- **Global Reporting Initiative (GRI), Sustainability Accounting Standards Board (SASB), etc.**
  GRI is a global standard for sustainability reporting that helps organizations measure and communicate their E&S performance. GRI provides a comprehensive framework for disclosing E&S data, promoting transparency, and enabling stakeholders to assess an organization's sustainability efforts (Diwan & Amarayil Sreeraman, 2023).

  SASB focuses on industry-specific standards for E&S disclosure. SASB's standards are designed to help organizations communicate financial material E&S information to investors (Diwan & Amarayil Sreeraman, 2023).

- **Communicating E&S Performance to Stakeholders**
  Effective communication of E&S performance is crucial for building trust and accountability with stakeholders. This involves regular and transparent reporting on E&S metrics, initiatives, and progress toward goals. Communication methods include sustainability reports, annual disclosures, websites, and direct engagement with stakeholders, such as shareholders, customers, employees, and local communities. Investors use this information to make informed decisions and assess the alignment of their investments with E&S goals.

- **Regulatory Compliance**
  Regulatory compliance refers to adherence to laws and regulations that require organizations to disclose E&S information. These regulations vary by jurisdiction and may include mandatory reporting on E&S issues, climate risk, and other sustainability-related matters.

- **Meeting Regulatory Requirements for E&S Reporting**
  Meeting regulatory requirements entails ensuring that organizations and investors provide E&S disclosures as mandated by local, national, or international regulations. Compliance may involve specific reporting formats, content, and deadlines. Organizations and investors must stay current with evolving regulatory requirements to avoid non-compliance and associated legal and reputational risks.

- **Implications of Non-Compliance**
  Non-compliance with E&S reporting requirements can have various repercussions, including legal and financial penalties, reputational damage, and the potential loss of investors or customers who prioritize E&S transparency and accountability (Mertens et al., 2023). Investors may also face consequences for non-compliance, including potential regulatory sanctions and loss of reputation. Non-compliance hinders the ability to attract responsible investors and can limit access to sustainable financing options.

Case Studies: Effective Integration of E&S Criteria

These case studies highlight the diverse ways in which organizations and institutions integrate E&S criteria into their operations, from sustainable bond issuance and supply chain management to ESG investing and shareholder engagement. They showcase the positive impact of such integration on both business performance and sustainability outcomes, demonstrating the value of E&S criteria in decision-making and reporting.

Bank of America is a notable example of a financial institution that has effectively integrated E&S criteria into its operations. They issued their first sustainable bond in 2013, raising $500 million to support renewable energy and energy efficiency projects. Bank of America's sustainable bond program incorporates green and social bond principles, adhering to established E&S standards. The proceeds from these bonds are allocated to projects that align with these principles, including renewable energy, affordable housing, and healthcare access.This case illustrates how a major financial institution has embraced E&S criteria in bond issuance, attracting responsible investors and supporting projects that contribute to a sustainable and inclusive economy.

Unilever, a global consumer goods company, has made significant strides in integrating E&S criteria into its supply chain and reporting practices. They have set ambitious sustainability goals, such as reducing their environmental footprint and enhancing social impact. Unilever's Sustainable Living Plan outlines specific targets, including sourcing 100% of agricultural raw materials sustainably and improving the livelihoods of millions of people. They regularly report progress against these targets in their annual sustainability report, demonstrating transparency and accountability.This case exemplifies how a multinational corporation can effectively incorporate E&S criteria into its business strategy, leading to positive social and environmental outcomes.

Nuveen, a subsidiary of TIAA, is a global asset manager known for its focus on ESG investing. They offer ESG-themed mutual funds and actively engage with companies to improve their E&S performance. Nuveen provides detailed ESG impact reports outlining the positive contributions of its ESG investments. These reports showcase the environmental benefits, social improvements, and governance enhancements achieved through their investment choices. This case demonstrates how asset managers can effectively integrate E&S criteria into investment decisions and provide transparent impact reporting to investors.

CalPERS, one of the largest public pension funds in the United States, is known for its active engagement with companies on E&S issues. They advocate for improved corporate governance, climate risk disclosure, and human rights practices. CalPERS engages in shareholder activism, filing resolutions at annual meetings to address E&S concerns and promote sustainable practices. Their efforts have influenced numerous companies to adopt E&S measures and enhance their transparency. This case illustrates how a major institutional investor can effectively use its shareholder influence to drive positive changes in corporate behavior regarding E&S criteria.

Real-world Examples of Successful Integration of E&S Criteria in Green Bond Selection

The real-world examples demonstrate the successful integration of E&S criteria in green bond selection, with organizations and institutions using such bonds to fund projects that benefit the environment and society. These investments not only align with ethical and sustainable goals but also attract responsible investors who seek both financial returns and positive E&S impacts.

In 2016, Apple issued a $1.5 billion green bond, the largest ever at the time, to finance renewable energy and energy efficiency projects. The bond was oversubscribed, highlighting investor demand for environmentally responsible investments. Apple's green bond funds initiatives like its massive solar farm in North Carolina and renewable energy projects across its operations. These projects not only reduce the company's carbon footprint but also create jobs and support local communities. Apple's commitment to green bonds underscores its dedication to sustainability and innovation.

Iberdrola, a Spanish multinational electric utility company, is a leader in green bond issuance. They have issued several green bonds to fund renewable energy projects, grid improvements, and other environmentally friendly initiatives. Iberdrola's green bonds have attracted significant investor interest and have allowed the company to finance a large portfolio of renewable energy projects. These bonds align with the company's commitment to clean energy and contribute to a reduction in greenhouse gas emissions.

Real-world Examples of Successful Integration of E&S Criteria in Green Bond Selection

BNP Paribas issued a €500 million green bond in 2017, demonstrating the financial industry's role in promoting sustainability. The bond's proceeds were allocated to renewable energy and energy efficiency projects. BNP Paribas actively supports the green bond market and encourages sustainable investment practices. They have demonstrated their commitment to E&S criteria through their issuance and promotion of green bonds.

In 2017, the City of Cape Town in South Africa issued a climate resilience bond to fund projects that enhance the city's ability to adapt to climate change. The bond aimed to finance initiatives like water conservation, improved infrastructure, and flood control measures. The City of Cape Town's bond demonstrated the application of E&S criteria at the municipal level The funds raised supported projects that contribute to environmental sustainability and community resilience in the face of climate challenges.

Performance Evaluation and Impact Assessment

Performance evaluation and impact assessment are critical processes for determining the effectiveness of investments, projects, or initiatives that incorporate Environmental and Social (E&S) criteria. These assessments help investors, organizations, and stakeholders gauge the outcomes and alignment with E&S goals.

- **Performance Evaluation**
  Performance evaluation focuses on assessing the overall effectiveness of investments or projects concerning their E&S objectives. It involves the following key elements:

  1 **Setting Clear Objectives**: The first step in performance evaluation is defining clear and measurable E&S objectives. These objectives should be specific, realistic, and time-bound, allowing for meaningful assessments.
  2 **Data Collection and Monitoring**: Ongoing data collection and monitoring are essential to track progress. Organizations should gather relevant E&S data, such as carbon emissions, resource usage, or social impact metrics, and regularly update this information.
  3 **Comparative Analysis**: To evaluate performance, organizations can compare current E&S outcomes with baseline data or industry benchmarks. This helps determine whether the investment or project is achieving its intended impact.
  4 **Regular Reporting**: Transparent and accessible reporting mechanisms are crucial for sharing performance data with stakeholders, such as investors, regulators, and the public. Reporting should include both quantitative metrics and qualitative narratives.
  5 **Feedback and Continuous Improvement**: Performance evaluation should be a continuous process that allows organizations to learn from their successes and failures. Feedback mechanisms, including stakeholder engagement, can inform adjustments and improvements to E&S strategies.

- **Impact Assessment**
  Impact assessment delves deeper into understanding the direct and indirect effects of investments or projects on the environment and society (Wang et al., 2023). It goes beyond measuring outputs to evaluating outcomes and potential long-term effects. Key elements of impact assessment include:

  1 **Defining Impact Metrics**: Impact assessment requires identifying specific metrics to measure the environmental and social effects of the investment or project. These metrics should align with the project's objectives and may include indicators like emissions reductions, water savings, job creation, or improved healthcare access.
  2 **Baseline Data Comparison**: To assess impact, organizations must establish baseline data to represent the situation before the investment or project begins. Comparing baseline data to current data provides insights into the extent of impact.

3 **Attribution and Contribution Analysis**: Impact assessments aim to determine whether the observed changes are attributable to the investment or project. Attribution analysis assesses the direct influence, while contribution analysis considers the broader impact.

4 **Long-Term and Indirect Effects**: Effective impact assessment accounts for both short-term and long-term effects. It also examines indirect effects, such as ecosystem services, economic ripple effects, or community empowerment, which may not be immediately apparent.

5 **Stakeholder Feedback**: Involving stakeholders in impact assessment is essential. Feedback from communities, employees, and other relevant parties can provide insights into how E&S outcomes are perceived and experienced on the ground.

6 **Impact Reporting**: Similar to performance evaluation, impact assessment involves reporting the assessment results to stakeholders. This reporting should focus on the actual changes in environmental and social well-being.

7 **Learning and Adaptation**: Impact assessments should contribute to organizational learning and adaptive management. If the assessment reveals areas where the project falls short, it can inform corrective actions and improvements.

Effective performance evaluation and impact assessment ensure that investments and projects incorporating E&S criteria achieve their intended goals. They provide transparency, accountability, and data-driven insights for continuous improvement, contributing to responsible and sustainable practices in various sectors, from finance to development.

Challenges and Considerations

Data Quality and Availability for E&S Metrics

- **Data Sources**: One of the challenges in E&S integration is sourcing reliable and comprehensive data for E&S metrics. Many organizations struggle to obtain accurate, up-to-date data due to varying standards and reporting practices across industries and regions.
- **Data Consistency**: Data consistency is crucial for effective comparisons and assessments. Inconsistent data formats, definitions, and measurement units make it challenging to create meaningful E&S benchmarks.
- **Quality Assurance**: Ensuring data quality is essential. Inaccurate or incomplete data can lead to misleading assessments and investment decisions. Organizations may need to invest in data verification and validation processes.

Balancing E&S Objectives with Financial Goals

- **Financial Performance**: Balancing E&S objectives with financial goals can be challenging. Investors and organizations may face pressures to prioritize short-term financial returns over long-term E&S gains.

- **Risk and Return Trade-offs**: Some E&S investments may carry higher upfront costs or lower short-term returns but can lead to substantial long-term benefits. Finding the right balance between E&S risks and financial returns is a complex task.
- **Investor Expectations**: Organizations must consider the expectations and preferences of their investors. Some investors prioritize E&S goals, while others focus on financial performance. Striking the right balance requires aligning with the interests of diverse stakeholders.

Addressing Trade-offs in E&S Criteria Selection

- **Conflicting Goals**: E&S criteria may sometimes conflict with one another. For example, a project aiming to reduce emissions might involve land use changes that impact biodiversity. Balancing these conflicting goals requires careful consideration.
- **Materiality**: Deciding which E&S criteria are most material to an investment or project can be challenging. What is material may vary between industries and over time. Organizations must prioritize the most relevant criteria while acknowledging the trade-offs.
- **Flexibility and Adaptability**: E&S criteria should be adaptable to changing circumstances and evolving priorities. Flexibility in criteria selection can help address trade-offs and respond to emerging E&S issues.

To effectively integrate E&S criteria into decision-making and investment processes, organizations and investors must address these challenges and consider the following:

Standardization: Encouraging the development and adoption of standardized E&S metrics and reporting practices can enhance data quality and consistency.

Scenario Analysis: Organizations can employ scenario analysis to assess the potential impact of different E&S criteria and trade-offs. This can help in making informed decisions that align with desired E&S outcomes.

Stakeholder Engagement: Engaging with a diverse range of stakeholders, including investors, regulators, NGOs, and local communities, can provide valuable input and perspectives on E&S goals and trade-offs.

Continuous Monitoring and Reporting: Regular monitoring and transparent reporting on E&S performance can help organizations demonstrate their commitment to E&S objectives and adjust strategies as needed.

Navigating these challenges and considerations is essential for achieving responsible and sustainable investment practices that prioritize both environmental and social goals alongside financial objectives.

Future Trends and Innovations

Emerging Technologies for E&S Data Analysis

- **Artificial Intelligence (AI) and Machine Learning**: AI and machine learning are expected to play a significant role in E&S data analysis. These technologies can process vast datasets, identify patterns, and provide real-time insights into environmental and social performance.
- **Satellite and Remote Sensing Technologies**: These technologies offer the ability to monitor environmental factors, such as deforestation, carbon emissions, and land use changes, with high precision. They can enhance the accuracy of E&S impact assessments.
- **Blockchain and Distributed Ledger Technology**: Blockchain can improve the transparency and traceability of E&S data, making it more resistant to manipulation and fraud. It has the potential to enhance the integrity of E&S reporting.

Evolving Regulatory Landscape for E&S Reporting

- **Mandatory E&S Reporting**: Many countries are moving toward mandatory E&S reporting for organizations. This trend will likely continue with stricter regulations on E&S disclosures to promote transparency and accountability.
- **Climate Risk Disclosure**: Climate-related financial disclosure requirements are expected to become more prevalent, driven by the need to assess and disclose climate risks. Organizations will be required to integrate climate risk into their financial reporting.
- **Standardization and Harmonization**: There is a growing movement toward global E&S reporting standards. Harmonized reporting frameworks aim to simplify the reporting process, making it easier for organizations to meet diverse regulatory requirements.

Shaping the Future of E&S Criteria in Green Bond Selection

- **Social Bonds and Sustainability-Linked Bonds**: The green bond market is evolving to include social bonds, focusing on social and community projects. Sustainability-linked bonds are also emerging, offering financial incentives for achieving specific E&S targets.
- **Thematic Bond Categories**: Green bonds are expanding to include thematic categories, such as water bonds, affordable housing bonds, and biodiversity bonds (Tirumala & Tiwari, 2023). These specific themes align with the SDGs and provide investors with more diverse options.
- **Impact Measurement and Reporting**: The future of green bond selection will likely emphasize more robust and standardized impact measurement and reporting. Investors will demand clear and quantifiable evidence of E&S impact to make informed investment decisions.

- **Inclusive Finance Bonds**: Bonds aimed at promoting financial inclusion and addressing economic disparities, particularly in underserved regions, are becoming increasingly relevant. These bonds support E&S criteria that foster economic empowerment and social equity.

As E&S criteria continue to gain prominence in investment decisions, these future trends and innovations will shape how organizations, investors, and regulators approach E&S reporting, data analysis, and green bond selection. Integrating advanced technologies, evolving regulations, and developing new E&S criteria will drive more responsible and sustainable investment practices.

Conclusion and Recommendations

In a nutshell, the incorporation of environmental and social (E&S) criteria into investment practices highlights several key takeaways: E&S integration is no longer optional but essential for investors and organizations committed to responsible and sustainable principles. Data quality and availability are pivotal, demanding standardization and transparency. Balancing E&S objectives with financial goals is challenging yet necessary, with long-term sustainability and financial returns in focus. The ever-evolving regulatory landscape necessitates vigilance and adaptability. Leveraging emerging technologies such as AI and blockchain reshapes E&S data analysis. Lastly, impact assessment goes beyond performance evaluation, offering a comprehensive understanding of the real-world effects of investments on the environment and society.

In conclusion, responsible and sustainable investment practices are imperative for addressing environmental challenges, promoting social equity, and driving positive societal change. Integrating E&S criteria into investment decisions not only aligns with ethical and sustainable principles but also contributes to long-term financial resilience. Encouraging responsible and sustainable investment practices involves collaboration among investors, organizations, regulators, and other stakeholders. By promoting transparency, setting clear E&S objectives, and embracing emerging technologies and innovations, we can ensure that the integration of E&S criteria becomes an integral part of investment practices, fostering a more responsible and sustainable financial landscape. This transition will not only benefit the environment and society but also contribute to the long-term success and resilience of investors and organizations.

Recommendations for Effective E&S Integration

To effectively integrate E&S criteria into investment practices, several essential steps must be taken. First, organizations and investors should prioritize investments in data quality by implementing data verification, validation, and management systems to ensure the reliability of E&S data. Staying well-informed about evolving E&S regulations and standards and adapting reporting and investment strategies accordingly is crucial for compliance and alignment with best practices. Maintaining transparent E&S reporting practices is essential to communicate performance and impact effectively to stakeholders. Regular stakeholder engagement is also paramount, providing insights into concerns, expectations, and preferences regarding E&S criteria. Emphasizing robust impact assessment is necessary to furnish clear evidence of E&S outcomes to stakeholders and investors. Lastly, education and training should be provided to personnel involved in E&S integration, ensuring they possess the knowledge and skills necessary for effective implementation, ultimately fostering responsible and sustainable investment practices.

References

Anh Tu, C., Sarker, T., & Rasoulinezhad, E. (2020). Factors influencing the green bond market expansion: Evidence from a multi-dimensional analysis. *Journal of Risk and Financial Management*, *13*(6), 126.

Azhgaliyeva, D., Kapoor, A., & Liu, Y. (2020). Green bonds for financing renewable energy and energy efficiency in South-East Asia: A review of policies. *Journal of Sustainable Finance & Investment*, *10*(2), 113–140.

Billio, M., Costola, M., Hristova, I., Latino, C., & Pelizzon, L. (2021). Inside the ESG ratings: (Dis) agreement and performance. *Corporate Social Responsibility and Environmental Management*, *28*(5), 1426–1445.

Chang, L., Taghizadeh-Hesary, F., Chen, H., & Mohsin, M. (2022). Do green bonds have environmental benefits? *Energy Economics*, *115*, 106356.

Cicchiello, A. F., Cotugno, M., Monferrà, S., & Perdichizzi, S. (2022). Which are the factors influencing green bonds issuance? Evidence from the European bonds market. *Finance Research Letters*, *50*, 103190.

Diwan, H., & Amarayil Sreeraman, B. (2023). From financial reporting to ESG reporting: A bibliometric analysis of the evolution in corporate sustainability disclosures. *Environment, Development and Sustainability*, 1–37.

Hu, Y., & Jin, Y. (2023). Unraveling the influence of green bonds on environmental sustainability and paving the way for sustainable energy projects in green finance. *Environmental Science and Pollution Research*, 1–16.

Mankata, L. M., Owusu-Manu, D. G., Hosseini, M. R., & Edwards, D. J. (2022). Analysis of success-dependent factors for green bond financing of infrastructure projects in Ghana. *Journal of Sustainable Finance & Investment*, *12*(3), 832–848.

Mertens, D., Klingenberger, L., Frère, E., Harder, D., & Zureck, A. (2023). Management of environmental and social risks within sustainable project finance: Solving tensions to enable sustainable development. *International Journal of Sustainable Development & Planning*, *18*(3).

Park, S. K. (2021). Legal strategy disrupted: Managing climate change and regulatory transformation. *American Business Law Journal*, *58*(4), 711–749.

Quatrini, S. (2021). Challenges and opportunities to scale up sustainable finance after the COVID-19 crisis: Lessons and promising innovations from science and practice. *Ecosystem Services*, *48*, 101240.

Sakurai, Y., & Kurosaki, T. (2020). A simulation analysis of systemic counterparty risk in over-the-counter derivatives markets. *Journal of Economic Interaction and Coordination*, *15*(1), 243–281.

Sartzetakis, E. S. (2021). Green bonds as an instrument to finance low carbon transition. *Economic Change and Restructuring*, 54(3), 755–779.

Tirumala, R. D., & Tiwari, P. (2023). Diverse applications: Thematic bonds catching up. In *Advances in Infrastructure Finance* (pp. 107–133). Singapore: Springer Nature Singapore.

Wang, J., Ulibarri, N., Scott, T. A., & Davis, S. J. (2023). Environmental justice, infrastructure provisioning, and environmental impact assessment: evidence from the California Environmental Quality Act. *Environmental Science & Policy*, 146, 66–75.

Wu, M., Liu, Y., Xu, Z., Yan, G., Ma, M., Zhou, S., & Qian, Y. (2021). Spatio-temporal dynamics of China's ecological civilization progress after implementing national conservation strategy. *Journal of Cleaner Production*, 285, 124886.

Zhao, L., Chau, K. Y., Tran, T. K., Sadiq, M., Xuyen, N. T. M., & Phan, T. T. H. (2022). Enhancing green economic recovery through green bonds financing and energy efficiency investments. *Economic Analysis and Policy*, 76, 488–501.

Zou, F., Huang, L., Asl, M. G., Delnavaz, M., & Tiwari, S. (2023). Natural resources and green economic recovery in responsible investments: Role of ESG in context of Islamic sustainable investments. *Resources Policy*, 86, 104195.

3 Integrating Sustainability in Portfolio Construction

Models and Approaches

Calvin Cheong Wing Hoh, Tella Oluwatoba Ibrahim, Saad Babatunde Akanbi and Lianne Lee Mei Quin

Introduction

The integration of Environmental, Social, and Governance (ESG) considerations into portfolio construction marks a transformative shift in the investment landscape, heralding a new era where financial performance and sustainable impact are inextricably linked. This groundbreaking approach not only redefines the ethos of investing but also presents complex challenges and opportunities for investors globally. As the world grapples with pressing environmental issues, social inequities, and governance dilemmas, the traditional paradigms of portfolio construction are being reevaluated and reshaped. This article explores the innovative models and approaches that are at the forefront of integrating ESG factors into investment portfolios, offering a comprehensive guide into this practice. Through a blend of theoretical insights and practical strategies, we explore how ESG considerations are reshaping asset allocation, risk management, and performance metrics. This marks a shift toward responsible investing that aligns financial objectives with the broader goals of sustainability and ethical stewardship.

Theories of Portfolio Investment

Before exploring the integration of ESG considerations in portfolio construction, it is essential to review the prevailing theories of portfolio investment. Given the substantial impact of portfolio investments on both private and public sector growth, a myriad of theories has been developed by scholars worldwide over the past two centuries. For clarity, these theories can be broadly categorized into two primary groups: traditional theories and sustainable theories of portfolio investment.

Traditional Theories of Portfolio Investments

Seminal portfolio investment models including classical, Keynesian, and modern theories, posits that investors' primary objective should be to maximize monetary returns capital gains by investing in profit-maximizing business

DOI: 10.4324/9781032686844-3

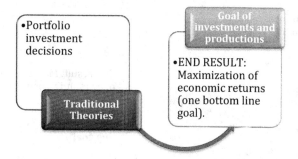

Figure 3.1 Traditional theories of portfolio investment construction

organizations (Ozili, 2021). These traditional theories consistently emphasize that profit-driven action is the fundamental goal of all business practices (Ozili, 2023). Furthermore, the magnitude of business profits serves as the principal metric for traditional investors, as evidenced in various studies (see, e.g., Ben, Yong, & Darren, 2019; Correia, 2019). These are typically used:

i   to measure the overall performance of business organizations.
ii to formulate investment decisions with regards to the companies' economic performance; and
iii in the selection of the companies' debt or equity issues.

Figure 3.1 illustrates a traditional portfolio construction model where the singular objective of profit predominantly drives investment and production decisions. This profit-centric ethos, as espoused by traditional investment theories, have prompted organizations and investors to evolve into highly profit-driven economic agents (Hummel & Szekely, 2021). However, this approach often overlooks the detrimental effects of business and investment practices on the ecosystem (refer to Charlin, Cifuentes, & Alfaro, 2022). Unfortunately, the traditional investment practices' singular focus on profit has resulted in environmental pollution and degradation, adversely impacting the health of humans, animals, and plants (Korpela et al., 2021). In light of the rise in global warming, drought, environmental pollution, pandemics, wildfires, and human conflicts, a global reassessment of our lifestyle is urgently needed to protect the survival of living beings within the ecosystem. The growing prevalence of negative externalities arising from profit-focused business and investment practices has catalyzed the rise of sustainable theories in business operations, consumption, and investment strategies (Pederson, Fitzgibbons, & Pomorski, 2023).

Sustainable Theory of Portfolio Investment

Proponents of sustainable portfolio investment theory advocate for responsible investment, production, and consumption within economies (Hill, 2020;

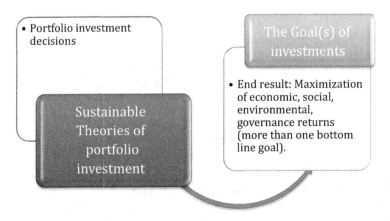

Figure 3.2 Sustainable (ESG) theories of portfolio investments

Ioannou & Serafeim, 2019). They argue that integrating sustainability or ESG practices into business operations and investment decisions can mitigate the ecological harm often associated with traditional investment and business models, which focuses primarily on profit (refer to Elkington, 1994). Advocates of sustainability argue that it is more advantageous for economic agents to concurrently pursue economic objectives (profit) while fulfilling environmental (planet), social (people), and governance responsibilities. This approach creates a mutually beneficial scenario for business organizations and other stakeholders in the industry (Kumar, 2023; Sandu, 2023).

Figure 3.2 illustrates that the sustainable portfolio investments theory necessitates the inclusion of ESG factors in investment or financing decisions (Luo, 2022; Ozili, 2021). Consequently, when incorporating ESG considerations into portfolio investments, investors aim not to incur losses but to generate profit, even if it means forging some potential gains to meet ESG objectives. Ozili (2023) has identified various theories pertinent to sustainable finance or ESG portfolio investment:

i **Priority Theory**: This theory posits that a country's or economic agents' prioritization of sustainable finance greatly impacts their investment in sustainable portfolio investment (Ozili, 2023; Parent & Deephouse, 2007). To gauge the extent of prioritization of sustainable investments by economic agents in a given country, it is essential to consider three-dimensional questions:

  a *Efforts and Commitments:* What is the level of joint efforts and commitments among economic agents toward achieving the proposed actions and predefined sustainability or ESG goals?

  b *Speed of General Consensus:* At what pace do economic agents reach a consensus for accomplishing their ESG goals, in line with their joint efforts and commitments?

   c *Actions Taken:* How swiftly or sluggishly are actions undertaken to achieve the predetermined ESG goals?

     In essence, Priority Theory suggests that a high (or low) preference for sustainable or ESG finance by economic agents will correspondingly lead to an increase (or decrease) in investments in sustainable portfolios over time (refer to Kuhn, 2020; Wilson, 2010).

ii **Peer Emulation Theory**: This theory contends that without a uniform standard or methodology for evaluating sustainability or ESG portfolio investments, economic agents tend to emulate the actions, policies, and strategies of their peers when constructing their sustainable portfolio investments and making investment decisions (Ditlev-Simonsen & Midt-tun, 2011). This suggests that the investment behavior of peers significantly influences an economic agent's portfolio investment decisions. It implies a state of interdependence among economic agents, where the degree of information sharing is vital in shaping portfolio investment strategies.

iii **Life-Span Theory**: This theory asserts that the anticipated life cycle of a sustainable finance product is a key determinant in the economic agents' portfolio investment decisions. It suggests that an economic agent's knowledge of a sustainable finance product's life cycle influenced their predictions about the product's expected lifespan. These predictions then guide their sustainable finance products' investment decisions (refer to Ozili, 2023). Consequently, economic agents are likely to boost their investments or financing in sustainable portfolios when they perceive these portfolios will be long-term or become permanent endeavors. Conversely, their support or commitment to sustainable investments tends to diminish or become short-term if they anticipate that the sustainable products will have a short lifespan or obsolete quickly.

iv **System Disruption Theory**: Proponents of this theory argue that the pursuit of sustainable finance goals has the potential to disrupt traditional/mainstream business financing. They assert that the cost-benefit analysis of transitioning from unsustainable to sustainable investment practices is crucial in guiding economic agents' decisions about construction and selection of portfolio investments (see Minoja, 2012; Ozili, 2023). Therefore, if economic agents believe that the costs associated with transitioning from unsustainable investments will outweigh the benefits, they are likely to be without support for such initiatives and decrease their investment in sustainable products. Conversely, economic agents are inclined to invest in sustainable portfolios when they expect to derive net positive benefits from these sustainable investment options.

v **Positive Signaling Theory**: This theory suggests that the pursuit for sustainability is motivated by the desire to boost reputations. Economic agents view sustainability as a powerful incentive to enhance their public image and gain support from external parties (Ngu & Amran, 2021). Consequently, they actively disclose information about their sustainable finance goals and achievements to attract positive feedback and support, thereby enhancing marketing and sales of their sustainable products (2021). For example, business organizations may emphasize their sustainability performance in annual reports to improve their public image which in turn can boost their sales.

vi **Resource Theory of Sustainable Finance**: This theory asserts that the extent of sustainable portfolio investment by an economic agent or country depends on their resources or overall wealth. It posits that countries with high debt, significant budget dependence, a weak financial sector, limited technical expertise, low technological advancement, widespread poverty, and substantial income disparity tend to have fewer economic agents investing in sustainable portfolios. Moreover, in these countries, the shift from unsustainable to sustainable practices is often sluggish due to institutional constraints (Wai-Khuen, Boon-Heng, & Siow-Hoon, 2023). The theory's key implication is that countries with a robust financial sector, advanced technical expertise, high technological development, effective environmental monitoring, sustainability awareness, and a large investor base, coupled with a lower income disparity, are likely to exhibit higher levels of sustainable portfolio investment.

Building a Model of ESG Portfolio Construction

Incorporating ESG considerations into portfolio construction involves embedding ESG factors into investment analysis and decision-making, aiming to bolster risk management and improve returns (Sullivan, 2020). A crucial step in this integration is the identification of key ESG criteria, along with the long-term objectives and the most relevant social and environmental issues.

An emerging trend in the financial sector is sustainable ESG portfolio investments. While embodying key traditional investment principles like diversification of total wealth and selection of company portfolios based on individual investor priorities, these investments incorporate ESG factors. (Alessandrini & Jondeau, 2020; Migliorelli, 2021).

Liquidity preference theory posits that economic agents often favor holding low-risk assets, such as cash, over higher-risk options like bonds and stocks, unless the latter offers significant potential gains (see Pederson, Fitzgibbons, & Pomorski, 2020). Furthermore, economic agents typically do not allocate all their wealth in portfolios as they must also meet transactional demands and daily expenses. Consequently, economic agents who are unable to cover these daily expenses often do not diversify their investment broadly. This scenario results in two types of investors: those who are risk-averse and those who diversify their risks. Regardless of the individual differences in true proportion of wealth invested in portfolios, all investors aiming to diversify risk share a common goal to maintain their overall wealth by balancing liquid assets and portfolio investments.

$$W = M + P \qquad\qquad (3.1)$$

Where:

        W = Total wealth of an economic agent.

        M = Fraction of total wealth held in money.

        P = Fraction of total wealth held in portfolio investment(s) (e.g., shares, stocks, bonds).

Equation 3.1 shows that an individual's wealth can be allocated either solely in money, solely in portfolio investments, or in a combination of both. A risk diversifier will opt for a mix of money and portfolio investments which best suits their preferences (Ogiriki & Andabai, 2014). In applying Equation 3.1, economic agents face the critical task of determining and selecting suitable portfolio investments. This necessitates portfolio screenings to facilitate informed investment decisions. Contrary to traditional economic agents who focus solely on economic returns from portfolio investments, ESG-focused economic agents look beyond the bottom line of profits. They incorporate ESG factors into the construction of their portfolio investments (OECD, 2017). Incorporating ESG in portfolio construction entails ESG investor investors consciously integrating ESG risks and opportunities into the conventional analysis of investment decisions (Dorfleitner, Utz, & Wimmer, 2018).

When incorporating ESG factors into investment decisions, economic engages may employ various methods, including screening, exclusionary, or engagement (Jin, 2022; Plaut, 2022).

1 **The Screening Method**: This approach requires investors to conduct a comprehend information gathering process about the sustainability performance or ESG ratings of companies issuing the portfolios. ESG ratings serve as an essential screening tool, enabling investors to compare ESG performances effectively. This approach guides economic agents in making investment decisions based on their screening criteria, selecting companies that align with their anticipated economic, environmental, social, and governance risk and opportunity factors.

    The screening method can manifest in two forms: best-in-class or thematic investment. The best-in-class screening method involves investors establishing a benchmark performance to include or exclude companies based on their ESG rating. This inclusive approach includes companies with good ESG scores and excludes those with poor scores. However, thematic investment focuses on selecting a specific ESG theme (e.g., water supply) to construct a specialized portfolio of related securities (refer to OECD, 2017).

    Recently, Duan (2023) outlined the creation of an international ESG stock index which encompasses five phases. Duan (2023) delineates the following circular process illustrated in Figure 3.3:

Phase 1: The investor selects a benchmark index to serve as a reference in integrating ESG in portfolio construction.

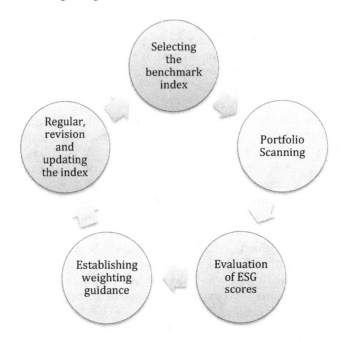

Figure 3.3 The five phases of screening method

Phase 2: The investor scans the portfolios for negative externalities in the business sector(s) of interest. These negative externalities may comprise of human rights violations, environmental concerns, poor governance, or other ESG-related concerns.

Phase 3: This phase is crucial for selecting the final ESG index sample. It involves the evaluation of ESG scores through a process of formulation, ranking, and re-screening based on the investor's ESG factor preferences.

Phase 4: This phase is to establish the weighting guidelines of the index, ensuring that these guidelines align with the objectives of the index design and its compatibility with the investor's goals.

Phase 5: The final phase involves regular and rigorous monitoring to revise and update the composition of the index, reflecting the evolving priorities and the objectives of the investor.

2 **The Exclusion Method**: This investment strategy involves economic agents decisively exclude certain sectors or markets from their target investment population (OECD, 2017). From the pool of targeted companies, they select those in which to invest their portfolio. For instance, an agent might avoid investment in industries, such as fossil fuels, alcohol, and ammunition manufacturing. This method implies that an investor may divest from companies whose practices do not align with sustainability of ESG goals. While this method is generally less costly and simpler to execute compared to the screening method, it is more susceptible to tracking errors regarding

current business operations (Plaut, 2022). For example, excluding the fossil fuel sector from investment considerations does not consider companies that depend on fossil fuels for their operations.

3 **The Engagement Method**: In contrast to screening or divestment strategies, the engagement method involves investors leveraging their ownership rights to influence the company's board of directors to adopt ESG factors or sustainability practices in their business operations. Instead of divesting their portfolios, investors using this method advocate for a shift from unsustainable to sustainable business practices (OECD, 2017). This proactive strategy emphasizes engagement and dialogue with company leadership to foster internal change, rather than excluding the company from the investment portfolio.

After exploring the various methods ESG considerations can be incorporated into investment decisions, we now focus on the practical implications of these strategies on investment dynamics. In particular, we will discuss the scenario in which an individual acquires an ESG portfolio at a specified price. This scenario modifies Equation 3.1, changing the dynamics of wealth allocation between money and portfolio investments. This modification is captured in Equation 3.2:

$$W_R = M\left(r_1 + g_1\right) + P_{\text{esg}}\left(r_2 + g_2\right) \tag{3.2}$$

Where:
W_R = Overall returns from total wealth of the economic agent's portfolios.
M = Fraction of total wealth held in money.
P_{esg} = Fraction of total wealth held in portfolio investments.
r_1 = the expected ESG returns from money.
g_1 = the expected returns from ESG portfolio investments as stipulated by the issuers upon maturity.
r_2 = capital gains or loss associated with holding money.
g_2 = capital gains or loss associated with holding ESG portfolio investment.
The fraction of total wealth kept in money does not attract ESG returns and capital gains/loss. In other words, $r_1 = 0$ and $g_1 = 0$.

$$W_R = M(0+0) + P_{\text{esg}}\left(r_2 + g_2\right) \tag{3.3}$$

$$W_R = P_{\text{esg}}\left(r_2 + g_2\right)$$

Equation 3.3 shows that the fraction of total wealth associated with ESG returns and ESG capital gain/loss is P_{esg}. It is imperative to note that ESG investors can either earn returns from ESG portfolio upon its maturity period or by selling the portfolio to make capital gains. Consequently, the relationship between ESG returns upon maturity and ESG capital gains/loss is mutually exclusive. The occurrence of one will prevent the occurrence of the other.

A situation where an ESG agent waited for maturity to earn returns on its ESG portfolio investments will make $g_2 = 0$:

$$W_R = P_{esg}(r_2) \tag{3.3a}$$

Equation 3.3a reveals that investor is expected to earn interest rate returns as his ESG portfolio investment when it matures. Consequently, the original value of the ESG portfolio investment when it matures. Consequently, the original value of the ESG portfolio purchased can be written as $P_{esg/}(r_2)$.

When the ESG portfolio is sold before maturity, the individual investor can either make a capital gain or loss. This implies that the overall returns from the portfolio investments depend on its capital gains/loss. Consequently, we have:

$$W_R = P_{esg}(g_2) \tag{3.3b}$$

However, capital gains or losses can only be traced to the relationship that exists between the original value and current market value of the ESG portfolio investment. Therefore, we have:

$$g_2 \leftarrow = \left(\frac{(P_{esg}/(r))}{(P_{esg}/(r_2))} \right) - \left(\frac{(P_{esg}/(r_2))}{(P_{esg}/(r_2))} \right) \tag{3.4}$$

Equation 3.4 indicates the relationship between current market value and original market value of ESG portfolio investment.

Where:

P_{esg} = Fraction of total wealth held in portfolio investments.

r_2 = The expected returns from ESG portfolio investments as stipulated by the issuers upon maturity, that is, the original interest rate carried by the ESG portfolio investments.

r = The ruling or current (market) interest rate for the bond.

g_2 = capital gains or loss associated with holding ESG portfolio investment.

P_{esg}/r = The current market value for the ESG portfolio investment.

P_{esg}/r_2 = The original value carries by the ESG portfolio investment.

The simplification of Equation 3.4 becomes:

$$g_2 \leftarrow = (P_{esg}/P_{esg} \times r/r_2) - (P_{esg}/P_{esg} \times r_2/r_2)$$

$$g_2 = \left(\frac{(r_2)}{(r)} \right) - (1) \tag{3.4a}$$

If $r_2 > r$, then $g > 0$ (capital gain).
If $r_2 < r$, then $g < 0$ (capital loss).
If $r_2 = r$, then $g = 0$ (neither gain nor loss).
When Equation 3.4a is multiplied by $P_{esg}(r)$

$$g_2 = P_{esg}(r_2) - P_{esg}(r) \tag{3.4b}$$

Where:

$P_{esg}(r)$ = the overall ESG returns (economic) based on current market value.

$P_{esg}(r_2)$ = the overall ESG returns (economic) original value of the P_{esg} at purchase price.

If $P_{esg}(r_2) > P_{esg}(r)$, the individual investor will earn capital gains on its portfolio investment by selling.

If $P_{esg}(r_2) < P_{esg}(r)$, the individual investor will earn capital loss on its portfolio investment by selling.

If $P_{esg}(r_2) = P_{esg}(r)$, the individual investor neither earns capital gains nor loss on its portfolio investment by selling.

Demand for ESG Portfolio

In addition to considering the relationship between the current market and actual value of ESG portfolio investments, risk-averse investors also aim to maximize their ESG returns at a specific rate. To realize capital gains or absorb losses, these investors may engage in speculative behavior in their investment decisions. These decisions often depend on a critical value rate (r_c), which represents the point at which they anticipate the current market interest rate will deviate from the current market value, either falling below or rising above it. This critical interest rate (r_c) is subjective and varies among ESG investors due to their differing risk tolerances associated with ESG portfolio. Each investor inherently knows their r_c, reflecting their personal risk threshold. Given that g_2 is a random variable, holding ESG portfolio investments involves inherent risks and opportunities. The final outcome, whether a capital gain or loss, is contingent on the market conditions at the time of selling the investment, especially if it occurs before the investment matures.

$$E(g_2) \leftarrow D'_c = \left(\frac{(r)}{(r)}\right) - \left(\frac{(r_c)}{(r)}\right) \qquad (3.4c)$$

Equation 3.4c shows that in establishing investment decision on demanding or holding portfolio investment, the portfolio seller will take cognizance of the current market value in relation to its critical value. The relationship between the critical and the current market value of the ESG portfolio investment determines the investment decision for holding ESG portfolio at the current market price, which is denoted by. Since expectations on capital gains/losses are a random variable, will equal 0 (Expectation of random variable). Equation 3.4c can be simplified into:

$$D'_c = (1) - \left(\frac{(r_c)}{(r)}\right) \qquad (3.4d)$$

By multiplying Equation 3.4d by $P_{esg}(r)$, the equation is modified into:

$$D'_c = P_{esg}(r) - P_{esg}(r_c) \qquad (3.4e)$$

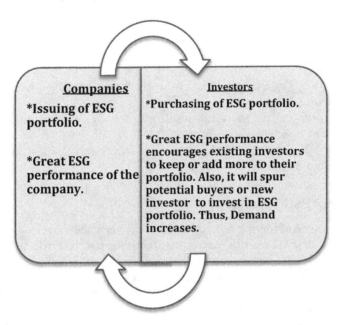

Figure 3.4 The relationship between ESG portfolio performance and its demand

Equation 3.4e shows the relationship between current market values and changes in expectation with regards to the market value of the ESG portfolio investment.

If $P_{esg}(r) > Pesg(r_c)$; then $D'_c > 0$. This means that when current ESG returns are above his/her ESG expectations, the investor will be willing to hold his/her wealth in ESG portfolio investment because the expected ESG returns are greater than additional risks associated with the portfolio investment. In this situation, the risk diversifier is optimistic on holding the bond.

If $P_{esg}(r) < P_{esg}(r_c)$; then $D'_c < 0$. In this situation, the expectation of the risk diversifier on the ESG portfolio investment is gloomy. This implies that when current ESG returns are below his/her ESG expectations, the investor will be willing to hold his/her wealth in money because the expected ESG risks are greater than additional benefits associated with the portfolio investment.

If $P_{esg}(r) = P_{esg}(r_c)$; then $D'_c = 0$. This is the inconclusive region.

The implication of Equation 3.1 to 3.4d is that:

First, an investor will be willing to invest in ESG portfolio when he expects a net positive value of ESG returns at any given interest rate.

Second, as ESG returns (performance) increase, the demand for ESG portfolio will also increase at a given tolerable economic returns (Figure 3.4).

Third, the demand behavior exhibited by ESG investors depends on array of factors. The key factors include the degree of information gathered by the individual investors on companies' ESG ratings or sustainable performances, price of the ESG portfolio investment, his available resources (or total size of wealth) along with how he prioritized his ESG returns (economic, environmental, social, and governance) and investment goals. This implies that risks diversifiers

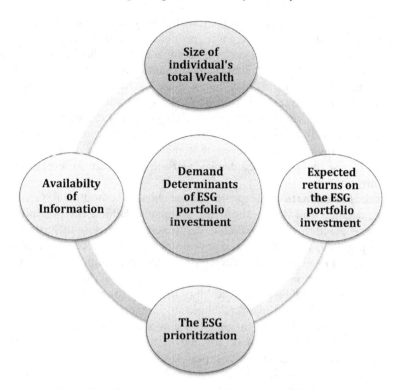

Figure 3.5 Factors influencing the integration of ESG considerations in portfolio construction

exhibit behaviors that encompass at least two theories of sustainable finance in diversifying their total wealth. These factors are key determinants of his ESG integration portfolio investment construction at any given time. Consequently, an individual demand function for ESG investment portfolios is specified as:

$$ESGint = F(tsiw, exESGre, ESGpri, avainfo) \qquad (3.5)$$

Where:

$ESGint$ = ESG integration
$tsiw$ = total size of individual's wealth
$exESGre$ = expected ESG returns on the ESG portfolio investment
$ESGpri$ = ESG privatization
$avainfo$ = available information

The factors influencing the integration of ESG investment portfolios are also the key determinants of demand for ESG portfolio investments as presented in Figure 3.5.

Based on the established model, these factors encompass:

i   **Size of Individual's Total Wealth**: An individual's total wealth plays a crucial role in their ability to incorporate ESG considerations into portfolio construction. A financially stable individual may be more inclined to forgo a portion of their economic gains (profits) to pursue ESG goals, even at the higher cost of ESG portfolios compared to traditional ones. Conversely, an individual with financial constraints, limited savings, and higher necessity-driven demands may demonstrate less interest in ESG goals.

ii   **The ESG Prioritization**: An individual's emphasis on ESG factors significantly influences their integration into portfolio decisions. For example, an individual who values environmental safety may choose ESG factors in their portfolio, even if it means sacrificing some economic gains. These investors often display a strong preference for green portfolio investments.

iii   **Level of Information**: Regardless of the chosen method for ESG integration, detailed knowledge about the companies behind the portfolio and business practices is essential. The depth and reliability of information on ESG portfolio's availability and significance greatly affect the integration process. An investor who understands the global economic importance of ESG is more inclined to incorporate these elements in their strategy. Additionally, the availability and credibility of ESG ratings for companies can significantly influence investors' choice to integrate ESG considerations.

iv   **ESG Returns and Expectations**: Since no business intends to operate at a loss, an investor's outlook on the market conditions of an ESG portfolio is crucial. If investors anticipate a pessimistic (or optimistic) outlook, they may choose to divest if the investment falls below their threshold for overall returns (combining economic and ESG returns). Conversely, robust returns or improved ESG performance in a portfolio can boost its demand.

Conclusion and Policy Implications

This chapter's exploration of ESG considerations in portfolio construction, underscores a paradigm shift in the realm of investment decision-making. The intersection of sustainable development and financial profitability has led to a nuanced understanding of investment, transcending the traditional emphasis on solely financial returns. This chapter has outlined various theoretical frameworks and practical strategies that emphasize the integration of ESG criteria into portfolio construction, signaling a new era of responsible investing.

Central to this discussion is the recognition that ESG integration is a complex, multifaceted process shaped by various factors, including investors' total wealth, ESG goal prioritization access to relevant information, and return expectations. Theories such as Priority Theory, Peer Emulation Theory, Life-Span Theory, System Disruption Theory, Positive Signaling Theory, and the Resource Theory of Sustainable Finance offer a rich tapestry of perspectives on how ESG considerations are perceived and implemented by different economic agents. These theories offer a valuable framework for understanding the dynamics of the rapidly changing field of sustainable finance.

Moreover, the practical approaches to ESG integration – screening, exclusion, and engagement – each represents different methodologies for investors to align their portfolios with ESG principles. For example, the screening method enables investors to choose investments based on comprehensive ESG ratings. In contrast, the exclusion method involves intentionally avoiding investments in sectors that do not align with ESG objectives. Meanwhile, the engagement method focuses on actively influencing corporate practices to enhance ESG compliance.

Furthermore, the integration of ESG factors into investment decisions goes beyond theoretical consideration and significantly impacts investment dynamics. This impact is exemplified by the modifications in investment decision-making processes, as illustrated by the equations discussed in the article. These equations illustrate how ESG considerations alter the traditional investment framework by including variables such as risk preferences and market expectations. It is essential to recognize that incorporating ESG factors into portfolio construction represents not just a trend, but a deeper societal shift toward sustainability and ethical stewardship. As the world grapples with challenges such as climate change, social inequality, and corporate governance issues, the importance of ESG in investment decisions is increasingly crucial. This shift focuses not only on risk mitigation or complying with regulatory requirements but also on seizing new opportunities and creating value that transcends financial returns.

In conclusion, incorporating ESG considerations into portfolio construction represents a significant advancement in the field of investment. This approach not only meets financial goals but also aligns with broader objectives of environmental protection, social responsibility, and ethical governance. As the field of sustainable investment continues to evolve, it will undoubtedly present new challenges and opportunities. The theories and practices outlined in this chapter provide a robust framework for navigating this complex and dynamic landscape. Ultimately, the incorporation of ESG factors into investment strategies is a testament to the growing recognition that economic success and sustainable development are deeply interconnected – a recognition that is vital for the prosperity of both current and future generations.

References

Alessandrini, F., & Jondeau, E. (2020), 'ESG investing: From sin stocks to smart beta', *The Journal of Portfolio Management, 46*(3), 75–94. https://doi.org/10.3905/jpm.2020.46.3.075.

Ben, P., Yong, M., & Darren, R. (2019), 'Three pillars of sustainability: In search of conceptual origins', *Sustainability Science, 14*(3), 681–695. https://doi.org/10.1007/s11625-018-06527-5. ISSN 1862-4065.

Charlin, V., Cifuentes A., & Alfaro, J. (2022), 'ESG ratings: An industry in need of a major overhaul', *Journal of Sustainable Finance and Investment*, 1–19. https://doi.org/10.1080/20430795.2022.2113358.

Correia, M.S. (2019), 'Sustainability: an overview of the triple bottom line and sustainability implementation', *International Journal of Strategic Engineering, 2*(1), 29–38. https://doi.org/10.4018/IJoSE.2019010103.

Ditlev-Simonsen, C.D., & Midttun, A. (2011), 'What motivates managers to pursue corporate responsibility? A survey among key stakeholders', *Corporate Social Responsibility and Environmental Management, 18*(1), 25–38. https://doi.org/10.1002/csr.237.

Dorfleitner, G., Utz, S., & Wimmer, M. (2018), 'Patience pays off – corporate social responsibility and long-term stock returns', *Journal of Sustainable Finance and Investment, 8*(2), 132–157. https://doi.org/10/ggk2kd

Duan, L. (2023), 'ESG index construction and china's ESG system', *BCP Business & Managemment, 38,* 175–180. https://doi.org/10.54691/bcpbm.v38L.3685.

Elkington, J (1994), 'Towards the sustainable corporation: Win-win-win business strategies for sustainable development', *California Management Review, 36,* 90–100. https://doi.org/10.2307/41165746.

Hill, J. (2020). *Environmental, Social, and Governance (ESG) Investing A Balanced Analysis of the Theory and Practice of a Sustainable Portfolio.* London Wall: Academic Press. ISBN: 978-0-12-818692-3

Hummel, K., & Szekely, M. (2021), 'Disclosure on the sustainable development goals – Evidence from Europe', *Accounting in Europe,* 1–38. https://doi.org/10.1080/17449480.2021.1894347

Ioannou, I., & Serafeim, G. (2019), 'Corporate sustainability: A strategy?', *Harvard Business School Accounting and Management Unit,* In SSRN Electronic Journal. https://doi.org/10.2139/ ssrn.3312191.

Jin, I. (2022), 'ESG-screening and factor-risk-adjusted performance: the concentration level of screening does matter', *Journal of Sustainable Finance and Investment, 12*(4), 1125–1145. https://doi.org/10.1080/20430795.2020.1837501.

Korpela, V., Kuusisto, P., Fagerstrom, A., & Kaivo-oja, J (2021), 'Introduction to sustainable portfolio theory', https://doi.org/10.13140/RG.2.2.21287.47528.

Kuhn, B.M. (2020), 'Sustainable finance in Germany: Mapping discourses, stakeholders, and policy initiatives', *Journal of Sustainable Finance and Investment, 12*(2), 1–28. https://doi.org/10.1080/20430795.2020.1783151.

Kumar, S. (2023), 'Exploratory review of ESG factor attribution to the portfolio return in FAMA-FRENCH factor model framework', *Academic of Marketing Studies, 27*(3), 1–20.

Luo, D. (2022), 'ESG, liquidity, and stock returns', *Journal of International Financial Markets Institutions and Money, 78*(2). https://doi.org/10.1016/j.intfin.2022.101526.

Migliorelli, M. (2021), 'What do we mean by sustainable finance? assessing existing frameworks and policy risks', *Sustainability,13*(2), 975. https://doi.org/10.3390/su13020975.

Minoja, M. (2012), 'Stakeholder management theory, firm strategy, and ambidexterity', *Journal of Business Ethics, 109,* 67–82. https://doi.org/10.1007/s10051-012-1980-9

Ngu, S.B., & Amran, A. (2021), 'Materiality disclosure in sustainability reporting: Evidence from Malaysia', *Asian Journal of Business and Accounting, 14*(1), 225–252. https://doi.org/10.22452/ajba.vol14no1.9

OECD (2017), '*Investment governance and the integration of environmental, social and governance factors*', 1–56. https://www.oecd.org/finance/Investment-Governance-Integration-ESG-Factors.pdf.

Ogiriki, T., & Andabai, P.W. (2014), 'Liquidity preference theory: A comparison of William Baumol's and James Tobin's Propositions', *African Research Review, 8*(4), 143–152. https://doi.org/10.4314/afrrev.v8i4.12.

Ozili, P.K. (2021), 'Making sustainable finance sustainable', *Financial Internet Quarterly, 17*(3), 64–70. https://doi.org/10.2478/fiqf-2021-0020.

Ozili, P.K (2023), 'Theories of sustainable finance', *Managing Global transition, 21*(1), 5–22. https://doi.org/10.26493/1854-6935.21.5-22.

Parent, M.M., & Deephouse, D.L. (2007), 'A case study of stakeholder identification and prioritization by managers', *Journal of Business Ethics*, 75(1), 1–23. https://doi.org/10.1007/s10551-007-9533-y

Pedersen, L.H., Fitzgibbons, S., &Pomorski, L. (2020), 'Responsible investing: The ESG efficient frontier', *Journal of Financial Economics*, 14(2), 1–26. https://doi.org/10.1016/j.jfineco.2020.11.001.

Plaut, A. (2022), 'How to build an ESG portfolioo'. https://www.fool.com/investing/stock-market/types-of-stocks/esg-investing/esg-portfolio/&ved=2ahUKEwigh86ourmCAxVuW0FAHcU0C_0QFnoECBMQAQ&usg=AOvVaw05DQFL1N4k2aMCGaV8yTVy

Sandu, D. (2023), 'Is there any effect of ESG scores on portfolio performance in South Africa?', *Proceedings of the International Conference on Business Excellence*, 17(1), 1807–1817. https://doi.org/10.2478/picbe-2023-0160.

Sullivan, D. (2020), Quantifying ESG in Portfolio Construction. Topics of Interest 4Q20, Verus Washington. https://www.verusinvestments.com>Quantifying

Wai-Khuen, W., Boon-Heng, T., & Siow-Hoon, T. (2023), 'The influence of external stakeholders on environmental, social, and governance (ESG) reporting: Toward a conceptual framework for esg disclosure', *Foresight and STI Governance*, 17(2), 9–20. https://doi.org/10.17323/2500-2597.2023.2.9.2.

Wilson, C. (2010), 'Why should sustainable finance be given priority? Lessons from pollution and biodiversity degradation', *Accounting Research Journal*, 23(3): 267–280. https://doi.org/10.1108/10309611011092592.

4 Case Studies in Green Bond Portfolio Management

Best Practices and Lessons Learned

Uzma Kashif and Muhammad Saeed Meo

Introduction

The Green Bond Portfolio, a meticulously curated selection of environmentally responsible investment instruments, serves as a testament to the integration of sustainable finance principles within the global investment landscape (Eldeep & Zaki, 2023). Comprising a diverse range of green bonds issued by reputable entities, this portfolio stands as a powerful embodiment of the commitment to address pressing environmental and social challenges while achieving sound financial returns (Tauseef Hassan et al., 2023). These green bonds finance projects aimed at reducing carbon emissions, promoting renewable energy sources, supporting sustainable agriculture, improving access to education and healthcare, and aiding in disaster relief and reconstruction efforts (Ma et al., 2023). Beyond merely generating financial gains, this portfolio allows investors to actively participate in the transition toward a low-carbon and sustainable global economy, reinforcing the potential for socially responsible investing to make a substantial, positive impact on our world (Anderson & Ponnusamy, 2023). The management of the Green Bond Portfolio is entrusted to a dedicated fund manager, who plays a pivotal role in ensuring that the portfolio aligns with both environmental and financial objectives (Chang et al., 2023). This skilled professional carefully selects green bonds from issuers committed to sustainable projects that adhere to stringent environmental standards. They conduct rigorous due diligence to evaluate the eligibility and impact of green bond projects, ensuring they contribute to carbon reduction, sustainable agriculture, enhanced social services, and disaster resilience (Fatah & Pasławski, 2023). The fund manager monitors the performance of these bonds, ensuring they meet financial targets and remain aligned with sustainability goals (Rahman et al., 2023). Their expertise lies in balancing portfolio diversification while maintaining a strong focus on environmental and social responsibility, driving the portfolio's success in delivering both financial returns and sustainable impact (Kinda et al., 2023).

Case studies are invaluable in portfolio management for various reasons. Firstly, they offer real-world examples that provide practical insights into managing investment portfolios effectively (Wang et al., 2023). These practical

DOI: 10.4324/9781032686844-4

insights are derived from examining the performance of portfolios under different market conditions, thus helping portfolio managers make more informed decisions about asset allocation, diversification strategies, and risk management (Cline, 2023). Secondly, case studies play a crucial role in risk assessment (Yao et al., 2023). By analyzing past cases, portfolio managers can gain a better understanding of various risks associated with different investment strategies (Armoti et al., 2023). This knowledge allows them to make well-informed decisions and develop effective risk management strategies to protect the portfolio from potential losses (Yang et al., 2022). Moreover, case studies serve as benchmarks for evaluating portfolio performance (Wolff & Mykhnenko, 2023). By comparing their portfolios' performance to the cases studied, portfolio managers can identify areas of improvement and make necessary adjustments to enhance returns and manage risks more effectively (Weitzel et al., 2023). Case studies also highlight the impact of market trends, dynamics, and economic events on investment portfolios (Miklian & Hoelscher, 2022). Understanding how different assets react to market changes is vital in making investment decisions that align with the prevailing market conditions (Jin et al., 2023).

These studies often focus on behavioral biases and emotional decision-making in investment outcomes (Yu et al., 2023). By examining such examples,

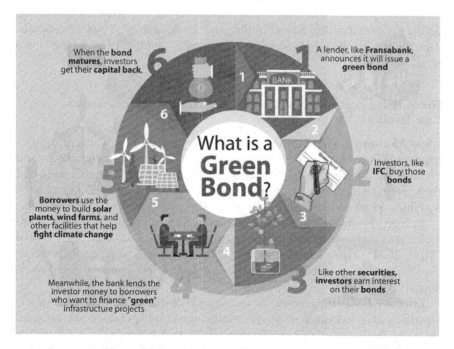

Figure 4.1 Green bonds working
Source: World Bank.

portfolio managers can recognize and counteract cognitive biases that may affect their investment decisions, leading to more rational and strategic choices. Case studies provide insights into sustainable and responsible investing, such as green bonds and ESG-focused portfolios (Miklian & Hoelscher, 2022). They help portfolio managers align their portfolios with environmental, social, and governance goals, addressing the growing importance of socially responsible investing (Yang et al., 2022). Figure 4.1 shows green bonds working.

Best Practices in Green Bond Portfolio Management

The Green Bond Principles (GBP), administered by the International Capital Market Association (ICMA), are a set of voluntary guidelines for "Best Practices" for issuing Green Bonds. The PSP Green Bond Framework aligns with the GBP in the following key areas, the PSP Green Bond Framework specifies how the funds raised through Green Bonds will be used, ensuring that they are dedicated to environmentally and socially responsible projects. The framework outlines a clear process for evaluating and selecting assets or projects that meet the criteria for green investments. This ensures that the projects funded by green bonds have positive environmental and social impacts. The PSP Green Bond Framework provides guidelines on how the proceeds from Green Bonds are managed, ensuring that the allocated funds are used in a responsible and transparent manner. The framework emphasizes the importance of reporting on the performance and impact of the green projects funded by Green Bonds. This aligns with the GBP's focus on transparency and disclosure in the Green Bond Market.

Green Bond Portfolio Management Key Success Factors Across Case Studies

Clear Alignment with Sustainability Goals: Each case study demonstrates a strong alignment between the green bond portfolio management strategy and broader sustainability goals (Edmans, 2023). Successful managers ensure that their investments directly contribute to environmental and social impact, such as reducing carbon emissions or promoting renewable energy.

Robust Frameworks and Guidelines: Implementing clear and comprehensive frameworks and guidelines for green bond investments is crucial (Maiti, 2021). These frameworks help in the selection of appropriate projects, the allocation of proceeds, and the measurement of environmental and social impacts.

Effective ESG Integration: Environmental, Social, and Governance (ESG) integration plays a central role in successful green bond portfolio management (Michael E. Porter & George Serafeim & Mark Kramer, n.d.). Case studies emphasize the importance of incorporating ESG factors into the investment decision-making process to enhance financial returns and sustainability outcomes (Edmans, 2023).

Table 4.1 Critical Success Factors for Green Bond Market Development

Critical Success Factor	Percentage of Identification by Experts
Official Interest Rate of GB	95
Legal Framework of GB	82
Institution Infrastructure	80
International Cooperation in GB	76
Monetary Policy	70
Fiscal Policy	69
Inflation Rate	60
Political Stability	53
Official Exchange Rate	51

Transparency and Reporting: Transparency is a common theme in the case studies. Effective reporting on the use of proceeds and the performance of green projects is essential (Porter et al., 2020). It builds trust with investors, stakeholders, and the public by demonstrating the impact of green bond investments.

Government and Regulatory Support: Government initiatives, such as grant schemes or carbon taxes, can significantly boost the green bond market (Schramade, 2016). Regulatory alignment with international green bond standards, as seen in the Singapore case study, attracts issuers and investors, facilitating market growth (Briand et al., 2011).

Diversification and Risk Mitigation: Case studies highlight the importance of diversifying investments to reduce risks (Roselle, 2016). Combining negative screening with green bond investments, as seen in AP1's case, can provide financial resilience.

Investor Engagement and Activism: The Engine no. 1 case study showcases how investors can use green bond activism to drive positive change within corporations (Chan et al., 2020). This form of engagement encourages companies to reallocate bond proceeds for sustainable projects (Henisz et al., 2019).

Multilateral and Collaborative Approaches: Multilateral institutions and partnerships, like the Global Green Bond Initiative (GGBI) and the European Development Finance Institutions (Kotsantonis et al., 2016), create a collaborative environment for raising green capital and promoting sustainable investments in emerging markets.

Alignment with Sustainable Development Goals (SDGs): Several case studies underscore the significance of green bond investments in contributing to the United Nations Sustainable Development Goals (SDGs) (Aich et al., 2021). Aligning waddles global objectives adds credibility and purpose to green bond portfolios.

Continuous Monitoring and Adaptation: Regularly monitoring the performance of green bond portfolios and adjusting strategies as needed is crucial for ensuring that both sustainability and financial objectives are met (Jacobey, 2017; Table 4.1).

Sustainable Investment Case Studies

AP1's Negative Screening for Fossil Fuels: A Sustainable Investment Approach

AP1, the Swedish national pension fund, is one of the world's largest pension funds, managing assets exceeding SEK 4 trillion. Committed to sustainable investing, AP1 ventured into green bonds as early as 2010 (Declaration et al., 2009). In 2017, AP1 announced its decisive shift away from fossil fuels driven by various factors including financial risks, environmental concerns, and the increasing demand for sustainable investments from its members (Adriani, 2018). AP1's decision to divest from fossil fuels was a manifestation of its commitment to sustainability. By adopting a negative screening approach, AP1 excluded companies from its investment portfolio that derived more than 5% of their revenue from fossil fuel production or distribution. This choice not only signified AP1's dedication to a low-carbon economy but also its proactive role in shaping responsible investment practices. The divestment from fossil fuels was not merely a symbolic gesture; it reflected a strategic allocation of assets. The freed capital was redirected into the green bond market, which was experiencing rapid growth. Green bonds finance projects with positive environmental or social impacts. By engaging in this market, AP1 sought to generate attractive returns while concurrently supporting sustainability initiatives that aligned with its values.

Portfolio Management Strategy: AP1's portfolio management strategy was founded on ethical exclusion, particularly excluding companies heavily involved in fossil fuel-related activities. By reducing exposure to the fossil fuel industry, AP1 aimed to mitigate financial risks associated with declining oil prices, the rise of renewable energy, and increasing government regulations (Declaration et al., 2009). Simultaneously, the asset manager targeted green bonds to capitalize on their potential for financial growth and environmental benefits. AP1 effectively integrated green bonds into its portfolio, creating a balanced investment strategy that aligned with its sustainability goals. The combination of negative screening and green bond investments allowed AP1 to fulfill its ethical, financial, and environmental objectives while maintaining portfolio diversification, risk management, and resilience in the face of economic and environmental changes.

Lessons Learned: AP1's case study provides valuable lessons for investors considering negative screening as an investment approach, clearly defines the motivations behind negative screening. AP1's divestment from fossil fuels was driven by concerns about financial risks, environmental impact, and member demand for sustainable investments (Eppler et al., 2015). Develop straightforward and effective criteria for excluding companies. AP1's 5% revenue rule for fossil fuel production or distribution was easy to implement and proved effective in reducing exposure to the fossil fuel industry. Continuously monitor the portfolio's performance to ensure it aligns with investment objectives (Adriani, 2018). AP1's regular monitoring ensures returns are attractive and

A unique ESG investment process

Multi-stage selection approach

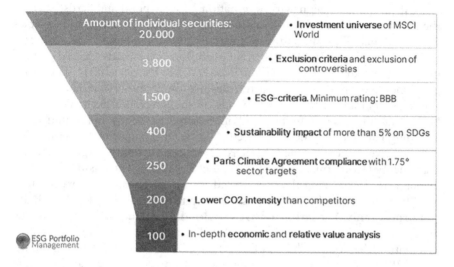

Amount of individual securities: 20.000	• Investment universe of MSCI World
3.800	• Exclusion criteria and exclusion of controversies
1.500	• ESG-criteria. Minimum rating: BBB
400	• Sustainability impact of more than 5% on SDGs
250	• Paris Climate Agreement compliance with 1.75° sector targets
200	• Lower CO2 intensity than competitors
100	• In-depth economic and relative value analysis

ESG Portfolio Management

Figure 4.2 ESG investment process
Source: Christoph Klein

sustainability goals are met. Transparently communicate your commitment to negative screening to stakeholders. AP1's transparent approach has built trust and confidence in its investment process among members and stakeholders. Figure 4.2 shows ESG investment process.

Green Bond Initiatives in Singapore Approaching "Positive Screening"

Singapore has demonstrated its commitment to reducing greenhouse gas emissions by introducing a carbon tax in 2019 and setting ambitious targets for emission reduction, emissions intensity, and renewable energy adoption (Durrani et al., 2020). In alignment with the United Nations Framework Convention on Climate Change (UNFCCC) targets, Singapore aimed to reduce emissions intensity by 36% from 2005 levels by 2030, peak emissions at 65 MtCO2e by 2030, achieve 1 gigawatt-peak (GWp) of solar power beyond 2020, and have 80% of its buildings certified as green by 2030 (Piñeiro-Chousa et al., 2021). These initiatives underscored Singapore's dedication to sustainability. The Monetary Authority of Singapore (MAS) introduced the Green Bond Grant Scheme (GBGS) in 2017, later modified into the Sustainable Bond Grant Scheme (SBGS). GBGS aimed to reduce the issuance costs of green bonds by covering the expenses of external reviews, a prerequisite for labeling bonds as "green." This initiative alleviated a significant barrier to green bond issuance by covering the full reviewing cost, up to S$0.1 million ($0.07 million), until May 2020. Similar green bond subsidies were offered in Hong Kong, China, Japan, and Malaysia.

MAS decided to align with international green bond standards, such as the International Capital Market Association's (ICMA) Green Bond Principles (GBP), Climate Bond Initiative's Climate Bond Standards, and ASEAN Capital Market Forum's (ACMF) ASEAN Green Bonds Standards (ASEAN GBS), instead of introducing national standards (Fatica & Panzica, 2021). This move positioned Singapore as an attractive destination for both local and international issuers looking to list their bonds on the Singapore Exchange (SGX). Several notable issuers participated in Singapore's green bond initiatives, including City Developments Limited (CDL), DBS Bank, Indian Renewable Energy Development Agency (IREDA), Manulife Financial Corporation, and Star Energy Geothermal Limited (Cheng et al., 2023). These issuers played a pivotal role in catalyzing the green bond market in Singapore between 2017 and 2018, with some bonds being issued despite not qualifying for the GBGS.

Purpose and Allocation of Green Bond Proceeds: The green bonds issued in Singapore were instrumental in financing low-carbon projects not only within the country but also in other parts of Asia and North America (Volz, 2018). These projects were diverse and aimed to address a wide range of environmental and sustainability concerns, such as renewable energy, energy-efficient building initiatives, and projects contributing to emissions reduction and the transition to a low-carbon economy (Sangiorgi & Schopohl, 2021). The management of green bonds in Singapore involved a combination of factors, including adherence to international green bond standards and the application of initiatives like the GBGS (Rachello, 2019). The government and central bank's strategy was to create a favorable environment for the issuance of green bonds, attracting both local and international issuers. The focus was on promoting sustainability and environmental responsibility (Ning et al., 2023). Green bonds were seamlessly integrated into the investment landscape in Singapore. The support provided by GBGS and adherence to international standards ensured that green bonds became an attractive and viable investment option for issuers. The portfolio strategy included a diverse range of green bonds that reflected Singapore's commitment to sustainability.

Lessons Learned

Government-led initiatives, such as the introduction of carbon taxes and grant schemes, play a pivotal role in advancing green finance and sustainability goals. Aligning with international green bond standards can attract a broader range of issuers and investors, fostering a more vibrant green bond market (Initiative & the, 2018). A variety of issues, from financial institutions to renewable energy developers, can contribute to the growth and diversity of the green bond market. Green bonds can be a vehicle to finance both local and international low-carbon projects, supporting sustainability objectives beyond

Key Factors in **Positive Screening**

FACTOR	CRITERIA	EXAMPLES
Environmental Considerations	Sustainable Practices	Efficient Resource Use, Waste Reduction, and Pollution Prevention
	Climate Change Mitigation	Greenhouse Gas Reduction and Support for Clean Energy
	Conservation Efforts	Biodiversity and Habitat Conservation, Responsible Land and Water Use
Social Considerations	Human Rights and Labor Practices	Fair Wages, Safe Working Conditions, and Anti-discrimination Policies
	Diversity, Equity, and Inclusion	Fostering Diverse, Inclusive, and Equitable Work Environments
	Community Engagement and Philanthropy	Philanthropy and Volunteer Initiatives
Governance Considerations	Board Diversity and Independence	Diverse and Independent Boards
	Executive Compensation	Transparent, Fair Compensation Linked to Long-Term Company Performance
	Shareholder Rights and Engagement	Prioritizing Shareholder Input and Maintaining Transparent Communication

FINANCE STRATEGISTS

Figure 4.3 Key factors in positive screening
Source: True Tamplin

national borders. Singapore's green bond initiatives exemplify the effectiveness of aligning financial markets with environmental and sustainability goals. The case underscores the significance of government commitment, international alignment, and the role of diverse issuers in promoting sustainable finance and global environmental responsibility (Figure 4.3).

Diversifying Portfolio Risk – Outfoxing the Box

The traditional investment strategy of tilting a portfolio toward specific asset classes or factors, such as value stocks, has come under scrutiny due to extended periods of underperformance (Cagli et al., 2023). This case study explores a reframed perspective on the issue, focusing on the importance of diversifying risk across various asset classes with similar risk-adjusted returns (Díaz et al., 2022). It draws parallels to the efficient market hypothesis, underlining that market efficiency should be a core investment principle. The conventional framing of the issue revolves around the dilemma of adding exposure to value stocks, which may underperform for long periods (Martellini & Vallée, 2021).

Investors planning for retirement express concerns about waiting out a value premium or other factor premium, which could take a decade or more to manifest (Chopra & Mehta, 2023). The traditional approach can be likened to a game with four boxes, each representing a passively managed portfolio holding different asset classes (Baldi & Pandimiglio, 2022). The table presents historical performance data for each box, illustrating that each endures prolonged periods of relatively poor performance. In retirement, sequence risk becomes a significant concern, as losses cannot be easily recovered from assets already spent (Cunningham, 2020).

Diversification as the Solution: "Creating Your Own Box E"

Given these assumptions, the most appropriate strategy is to minimize idiosyncratic risk by diversifying across various asset classes, thereby avoiding an over-concentration of risk (Baldi & Pandimiglio, 2022). This approach eliminates the need to select one particular box (strategy) and acknowledges that no one can predict the future performance of any one of them. Instead of choosing from boxes A, B, C, and D, investors can create their "box E" by diversifying their risks across the different asset classes and factors. This approach reduces the risk of putting all eggs in one basket while acknowledging the impossibility of predicting the "right" basket in advance (Martiradonna et al., 2023). Diversifying across asset classes with similar risk-adjusted expected returns, such as small and value stocks, offers an additional benefit. Their higher expected returns allow investors to hold less overall equity risk, as the equities they do hold have higher expected returns (Yoshino et al., 2023). This enables investors to increase their exposure to safe bonds and term risk, further diversifying their sources of risk and reducing tail risk, including sequence risk.

Tracking Variance: Discipline Over Relative Performance

Diversifying a portfolio across different sources of risk introduces tracking variance, as each asset class may experience variations in performance. While a total market fund perfectly tracks the market's return, a diversified portfolio does not. Nevertheless, the key consideration is discipline over relative performance (Bressan et al., 2022). Investors who prioritize conventional market beta investing may stick with a total market approach due to its predictability. When choosing to diversify, they may experience periods of underperformance, but discipline in adhering to the strategy is more crucial than achieving optimal performance (Horsch & Richter, 2017).

Conclusion: Outfoxing the Box

This case study emphasizes that the decision to diversify a portfolio by adding exposure to various sources of risk should be approached from a standpoint of minimizing idiosyncratic risk and recognizing the unpredictability of future

Investing 101: diversifying your portfolio

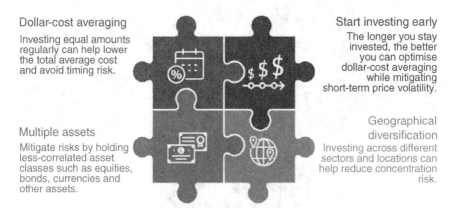

Dollar-cost averaging

Investing equal amounts regularly can help lower the total average cost and avoid timing risk.

Start investing early

The longer you stay invested, the better you can optimise dollar-cost averaging while mitigating short-term price volatility.

Multiple assets

Mitigate risks by holding less-correlated asset classes such as equities, bonds, currencies and other assets.

Geographical diversification

Investing across different sectors and locations can help reduce concentration risk.

Figure 4.4 How to diversify your portfolio

Source: Natalia Kolkowska

performance. By diversifying across asset classes with similar risk-adjusted expected returns, investors can create their own "box E," reducing the risk of putting all their eggs in the wrong basket while gaining the benefits of diversification. It underscores the importance of discipline and adherence to an investment strategy over relative performance. Figure 4.4 shows how to diversify your portfolio.

Key Lessons for Global Future ESG Portfolio Managers

As the world grapples with complex ESG challenges, the role of ESG portfolio managers has become increasingly crucial (Springer et al., 2023). These professionals are tasked with not only generating strong financial returns but also aligning investments with sustainable practices and positive societal impact. In light of this evolving landscape, here are some key lessons for global future ESG portfolio managers:

Deepen ESG Understanding and Expertise: ESG factors are constantly evolving, and portfolio managers must stay abreast of the latest developments and best practices (Zaid & Issa, 2023). This involves continuous learning, engagement with industry experts, and active participation in ESG initiatives.

Integrate ESG into Investment Process: ESG considerations should be seamlessly integrated into the entire investment process, from research and analysis to portfolio construction and risk management (Boisvert, 2022a). This requires a holistic approach that assesses ESG risks and opportunities alongside traditional financial metrics.

Employ Robust ESG Data and Analytics: The quality and availability of ESG data have improved significantly, but portfolio managers need to carefully

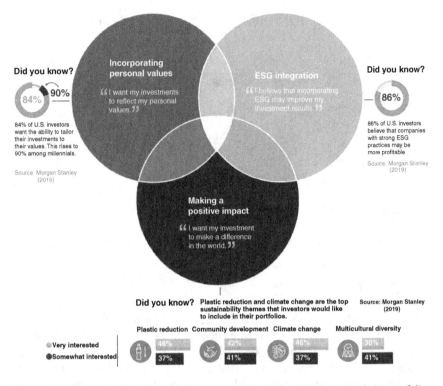

Figure 4.5 Common motivations of investors to include ESG assets in their portfolio
Source: MSCI. COM

evaluate and select data providers and tools that align with their specific needs and investment strategies (Lee, 2021). Advanced analytics can help uncover hidden insights and inform decision-making.

Engage with Companies and Industry Stakeholders: Active engagement with companies and industry stakeholders is essential to drive positive ESG change. Portfolio managers can use their influence to encourage companies to adopt more sustainable practices, improve governance, and address social issues (Boisvert, 2022b).

Collaborate with ESG Experts and Networks: Building strong relationships with ESG experts and networks can provide valuable insights, support, and collaboration opportunities. This can include partnering with ESG research firms, attending industry conferences, and engaging with ESG-focused organizations (Morrow et al., 2017).

Stay Ahead of Regulatory Developments: ESG regulations are becoming increasingly complex and nuanced, and portfolio managers need to stay informed about emerging rules and standards (Daugaard & Ding, 2022). This requires ongoing monitoring and proactive engagement with regulators and policymakers.

Embrace Transparency and Communication: ESG portfolio managers should be transparent about their investment strategies, ESG criteria, and engagement activities (Ailman et al., 2017). Effective communication with investors and stakeholders is crucial for building trust and credibility.

Continuously Adapt and Evolve: The ESG landscape is constantly changing, and portfolio managers need to be adaptable and willing to evolve their approaches. This involves staying up to date with emerging ESG trends, refining investment methodologies, and incorporating new data and analytics tools.

Foster a Culture of ESG Integration: A strong ESG culture within the investment firm is essential for long-term success. This involves embedding ESG principles into the firm's values, mission, and employee training programs (Springer et al., 2023).

Advocate for ESG Leadership: ESG portfolio managers can play a leading role in promoting sustainable investing and encouraging broader adoption of ESG practices across the financial industry (Boisvert, 2022a). This involves advocating for ESG-friendly policies, supporting ESG initiatives, and educating others about the importance of ESG investing. Figure 4.5 shows the common motivations of investors to include ESG assets in their portfolio.

Implications for Future Green Bond Portfolio Management Practices

The green bond market has experienced significant growth in recent years, driven by increasing investor demand for sustainable investments and a growing recognition of the role of green bonds in financing environmentally friendly projects. This expansion has brought about several implications for future green bond portfolio management practices:

Diversification of Green Bond Universe: The expanding green bond universe presents opportunities for portfolio diversification across geographies, sectors, and issuers. This diversification can help mitigate risks and enhance portfolio returns.

Enhanced Green Bond Standards and Transparency: As the market matures, there is a growing emphasis on developing and enforcing robust green bond standards and enhancing transparency around project selection, impact reporting, and use of proceeds. Portfolio managers need to stay informed about these developments and incorporate them into their investment decisions.

Integration of ESG Factors and Impact Measurement: Green bond portfolio managers should consider integrating broader ESG factors into their investment analysis, going beyond the specific environmental impact of the projects financed. This requires a holistic approach that assesses the social and governance implications of green bond investments.

Active Engagement with Issuers and Market Participants: Active engagement with green bond issuers, market participants, and policymakers can help shape the future of the green bond market and promote the development of high-quality green bond instruments. Portfolio managers can use their influence to encourage issuers to adopt stricter green bond standards and promote transparency around impact reporting.

Evolving Green Bond Products and Strategies: The green bond market is constantly evolving, with new products and strategies emerging to meet the diverse needs of investors and address a wider range of environmental challenges. Future green bond portfolio management practices will need to adapt to these innovations.

Thematic and Sector-Specific Green Bonds: Thematic and sector-specific green bonds, such as blue bonds for marine conservation and green bonds for climate adaptation, offer investors targeted exposure to specific environmental themes and sectors. Portfolio managers can use these bonds to align their investments with their specific sustainability goals.

Sustainability-Linked Bonds (SLBs): SLBs are a hybrid form of debt that combines traditional bond features with ESG-linked performance targets. Portfolio managers can use SLBs to encourage issuers to improve their ESG performance while generating financial returns.

Green Bond ETFs and Mutual Funds: Green bond ETFs and mutual funds provide investors with convenient access to diversified green bond portfolios. These products can help lower investment barriers and democratize access to green bond investments.

Technological Advancements and Data Analytics: Technological advancements and the availability of sophisticated data analytics tools are transforming green bond portfolio management practices.

ESG Data and Analytics Platforms: ESG data and analytics platforms provide portfolio managers with access to a wealth of information on the environmental and social impact of green bond projects. This data can be used to assess the impact of green bond investments and make informed investment decisions.

Artificial Intelligence (AI) and Machine Learning (ML): AI and ML techniques are being applied to develop predictive models for green bond performance and risk assessment. These models can help portfolio managers identify promising green bond opportunities and mitigate potential risks.

Natural Language Processing (NLP): NLP is being used to analyze unstructured data, such as corporate disclosures, news articles, and social media feeds, to gain insights into companies' ESG practices and the impact of green bond projects. This information can supplement traditional ESG data sources and provide a more holistic view of a company's ESG performance.

Regulatory Landscape and Investor Expectations: The regulatory landscape surrounding green bonds is evolving rapidly, and investors are increasingly demanding transparency and accountability from issuers and asset managers. Future green bond portfolio management practices will need to align with these regulatory and investor expectations.

Harmonization of Green Bond Standards: Efforts are underway to harmonize green bond standards across jurisdictions, which will provide greater clarity and consistency for investors. Portfolio managers need to stay informed about these developments and incorporate them into their investment processes.

Increased Scrutiny of Green Bond Impact Reporting: Regulators and investors are demanding stricter standards for green bond impact reporting, requiring issuers to provide more detailed and verifiable information on the environmental and social impact of their projects. Portfolio managers should incorporate impact reporting into their due diligence processes and use it to assess the effectiveness of their green bond investments.

Enhanced Disclosure of Green Bond Use of Proceeds: Investors are seeking greater transparency around the use of proceeds from green bond issuances. Portfolio managers should encourage issuers to provide clear and detailed disclosures on how green bond proceeds are allocated to specific environmental projects.

Recommendations for Effective Integration of Green Bonds

Set clear green investment objectives: Clearly define the goals you aim to achieve with your green bond investments, whether it's reducing portfolio carbon emissions, promoting renewable energy projects, or supporting sustainable infrastructure development.

Establish a robust green bond selection framework: Develop a structured approach to identifying and evaluating green bonds, encompassing factors such as project alignment with environmental and social impact goals, issuer credibility, and transparency of use of proceeds.

Conduct thorough due diligence: Engage in in-depth research and analysis of potential green bond investments, scrutinizing issuer disclosures, project documentation, and independent assessments to ensure alignment with your green investment objectives.

Employ impact measurement tools: Utilize impact measurement tools and frameworks to assess the environmental and social impact of green bond investments, enabling informed decision-making and tracking of progress toward sustainability goals.

Engage with issuers and market participants: Actively engage with green bond issuers to encourage transparency, promote best practices, and advocate for higher standards in the green bond market. Collaborate with peers and industry experts to share insights and enhance collective impact.

Leverage technological advancements: Embrace technological advancements in ESG data and analytics to gain deeper insights into green bond opportunities, assess project impact, and inform investment decisions. Utilize artificial intelligence and machine learning tools to refine selection criteria and risk assessment.

Stay informed about regulatory developments: Keep abreast of evolving regulatory frameworks and standards governing green bonds, ensuring compliance and adapting investment strategies accordingly. Engage with policymakers and regulators to promote harmonization of green bond standards across jurisdictions.

Incorporate green bonds into portfolio diversification: Integrate green bonds into your overall investment portfolio to diversify risk and enhance returns while contributing to sustainable development goals. Explore thematic and sector-specific green bonds to target specific environmental themes and sectors.

Promote transparency and accountability: Maintain transparent communication with investors and stakeholders regarding your green bond investment decisions, impact measurement efforts, and engagement activities. Foster a culture of accountability within your organization to ensure alignment with ESG principles.

Continuously refine and adapt: Regularly evaluate and refine your green bond investment strategies in response to market developments, technological advancements, and emerging ESG best practices. Adapt your approach to address new challenges and opportunities in the green bond market.

Conclusions and Policy Implications

Green bonds have emerged as a powerful tool for mobilizing capital toward sustainable investments and addressing environmental challenges. Case studies provide valuable insights into the practices and experiences of green bond portfolio managers, offering lessons for effective green bond investment strategies. Case studies in green bond portfolio management provide valuable lessons for investors and asset managers seeking to navigate the complexities of ESG investing and contribute to a more sustainable future. By adopting a strategic approach, conducting thorough due diligence, embracing transparency, and actively engaging with issuers and market participants, green bond portfolio managers can make informed investment decisions that align with their sustainability goals and generate positive environmental impact. As the green bond market continues to evolve, continuous adaptation and innovation will be crucial for success in this dynamic and rapidly growing field.

References

Adriani, N. (2018). Electronic copy available at : Electronic copy available at: *Grou*, *23529*(2), 1–45.

Aich, S., Thakur, A., Nanda, D., Tripathy, S., & Kim, H.-C. (2021). Factors affecting esg towards impact on investment: A structural approach. *Sustainability*, *13*(19), 10868. https://doi.org/10.3390/su131910868

Ailman, C., Edkins, M., Mitchem, K., Eliopoulos, T., & Guillot, J. (2017). The next wave of ESG integration: Lessons from institutional investors. *Journal of Applied Corporate Finance*, *29*(2), 32–43. https://doi.org/10.1111/jacf.12231

Anderson, K., & Ponnusamy, S. (2023). Structural transformation away from agriculture in growing open economies. *Agricultural Economics*, *54*(1), 62–76. https://doi.org/10.1111/agec.12745

Armoti, A. Al, Ameri, S. Al, & Hammadi, J. Al. (2023). The impact of strategic human resource development on organizational growth. *Journal of Asian Business Strategy*, *13*(1), 1–13. https://doi.org/10.55493/5006.v13i1.4705

Baldi, F., & Pandimiglio, A. (2022). The role of ESG scoring and greenwashing risk in explaining the yields of green bonds: A conceptual framework and an econometric analysis. *Global Finance Journal, 52*, 100711. https://doi.org/10.1016/j.gfj.2022.100711

Boisvert, M. B. (2022a). ESG Poster ESG10: Key lessons in planning for proactive decommissioning – a review of the Thevenard Island decommissioning project. *The APPEA Journal, 62*(4). https://doi.org/10.1071/AJ21435

Boisvert, M. B. (2022b). ESG Poster ESG10: Key lessons in planning for proactive decommissioning – a review of the Thevenard Island decommissioning project. *The APPEA Journal, 62*(4). https://doi.org/10.1071/AJ21435

Bressan, G., Monasterolo, I., & Battiston, S. (2022). Sustainable investing and climate transition risk: A portfolio rebalancing approach. *The Journal of Portfolio Management, 48*(10), 165–192. https://doi.org/10.3905/jpm.2022.1.394

Briand, R., Urwin, R., & Chia, C. P. (2011). Integrating ESG into the investment process. …, *New York, NY, Available at: Www …, August 2011*. https://www.top1000funds.com/wp-content/uploads/2011/08/Integrating_ESG_into_the_Investment_Process_Aug_20111.pdf

Cagli, E. C., Taşkin, D., & Evrim Mandaci, P. (2023). The role of uncertainties on sustainable stocks and green bonds. *Qualitative Research in Financial Markets, 15*(4), 647–671. https://doi.org/10.1108/QRFM-02-2022-0032

Chan, Y., Hogan, K., Schwaiger, K., & Ang, A. (2020). ESG in factors. *The Journal of Impact and ESG Investing, 1*(1), 26–45. https://doi.org/10.3905/jesg.2020.1.1.026

Chang, L., Iqbal, S., & Chen, H. (2023). Does financial inclusion index and energy performance index co-move? *Energy Policy, 174*, 113422. https://doi.org/10.1016/j.enpol.2023.113422

Cheng, L. T. W., Sharma, P., & Broadstock, D. C. (2023). Interactive effects of brand reputation and ESG on green bond issues: A sustainable development perspective. *Business Strategy and the Environment, 32*(1), 570–586. https://doi.org/10.1002/bse.3161

Chopra, M., & Mehta, C. (2023). Going green: Do green bonds act as a hedge and safe haven for stock sector risk? *Finance Research Letters, 51*, 103357. https://doi.org/10.1016/j.frl.2022.103357

Cline, W. (2023). Fighting the pandemic inflation surge of 2021–2022. *SSRN Electronic Journal*. https://doi.org/10.2139/ssrn.4408811

Cunningham, L. (2020). *Quality Shareholders*. Columbia University Press. https://doi.org/10.7312/cunn19880

Daugaard, D., & Ding, A. (2022). Global drivers for ESG performance: The body of knowledge. *Sustainability, 14*(4), 2322. https://doi.org/10.3390/su14042322

Declaration, U., Rights, H., Government, S., Agenda, A., Dignity, P., Persons, E., Robinson, M., Pinheiro, P., Agenda, T., Initiative, S., Dignity, H., Change, C., Human, W., Court, R., & Affairs, F. (2009). *Swiss Initiative to Commemorate the 60th Anniversary of the UDHR Protecting Dignity: An Agenda for Human Rights RESEARCH PROJECT ON CLIMATE CHANGE : "Climate change and Human Rights : The Status of Climate Refugees in Europe" by Margit Ammer, Ludwig B.*

Díaz, A., Esparcia, C., & López, R. (2022). The diversifying role of socially responsible investments during the COVID-19 crisis: A risk management and portfolio performance analysis. *Economic Analysis and Policy, 75*, 39–60. https://doi.org/10.1016/j.eap.2022.05.001

Durrani, A., Rosmin, M., & Volz, U. (2020). The role of central banks in scaling up sustainable finance – what do monetary authorities in the Asia-Pacific region think? *Journal of Sustainable Finance & Investment*, *10*(2), 92–112. https://doi.org/10.1080/20430795.2020.1715095

Edmans, A. (2023). The end of ESG. *Financial Management*, *52*(1), 3–17. https://doi.org/10.1111/fima.12413

Eldeep, C., & Zaki, C. (2023). On the unfinished business of stabilization programs: a CGE model of Egypt. *Middle East Development Journal*, 1–35. https://doi.org/10.1080/17938120.2023.2200727

Fatah, R. H., & Pasławski, J. (2023). Factors affecting labor productivity on construction in Kurdistan of Iraq: Web survey. *Journal of Engineering*, *29*(1), 14–41. https://doi.org/10.31026/j.eng.2023.01.02

Henisz, W., Koller, T., & Nuttall, R. (2019). Five ways that ESG creates value. *McKinsey Quarterly, November*, 1–12.

Horsch, A., & Richter, S. (2017). Climate change driving financial innovation: The case of Green bonds. *The Journal of Structured Finance*, *23*(1), 79–90. https://doi.org/10.3905/jsf.2017.23.1.079

Initiative, I., & the C. B. (2018). Creating Green bond markets. *Creating Green Bond Markets*. https://doi.org/10.1596/30940

Jacobey, L. (2017). *Research Report: Talk Is Not Cheap – The Role of Interpersonal Communication as a Success Factor of Engagements On*. 1–5.

Jin, W., Gao, S., & Pan, S. (2023). Research on the impact mechanism of environmental regulation on green total factor productivity from the perspective of innovative human capital. *Environmental Science and Pollution Research*, *30*(1), 352–370. https://doi.org/10.1007/s11356-022-22120-x

Kinda, T., Sollaci, A., Chai, H., Kido, Y., Qi, F., De Stefani, A., Chahande, K., Chen, Y., & Dabla-Norris, E. (2023). Accelerating innovation and digitalization in Asia to boost productivity. *Departmental Papers*, *2023*(001), 1. https://doi.org/10.5089/9798400224034.087

Kotsantonis, S., Pinney, C., & Serafeim, G. (2016). ESG integration in investment management: Myths and realities. *Journal of Applied Corporate Finance*, *28*(2), 10–16. https://doi.org/10.1111/jacf.12169

Lee, L. E. (2021). What does ESG investing really mean? Measuring materiality. *Sustainable Investment in Retirement …*, *March*. https://pensionresearchcouncil.wharton.upenn.edu/wp-content/uploads/2021/04/LeeCombined_OSM-4.9.21.pdf

Ma, Y., Fan, Y., & Razzaq, A. (2023). Influence of technical efficiency and globalization on sustainable resources management: Evidence from South Asian countries. *Resources Policy*, *81*, 103281. https://doi.org/10.1016/j.resourpol.2022.103281

Maiti, M. (2021). Is ESG the succeeding risk factor? *Journal of Sustainable Finance & Investment*, *11*(3), 199–213. https://doi.org/10.1080/20430795.2020.1723380

Martellini, L., & Vallée, L.-S. (2021). Measuring and managing ESG risks in sovereign bond portfolios and implications for sovereign debt investing. *The Journal of Portfolio Management*, *47*(9), 198–223. https://doi.org/10.3905/jpm.2021.1.290

Martiradonna, M., Romagnoli, S., & Santini, A. (2023). The beneficial role of green bonds as a new strategic asset class: Dynamic dependencies, allocation and diversification before and during the pandemic era. *Energy Economics*, *120*, 106587. https://doi.org/10.1016/j.eneco.2023.106587

Miklian, J., & Hoelscher, K. (2022). SMEs and exogenous shocks: A conceptual literature review and forward research agenda. *International Small Business*

Journal: Researching Entrepreneurship, 40(2), 178–204. https://doi.org/10.1177/02662426211050796

Morrow, D., & Morrow, D. (2020). *Impact Through. January.*

Ning, Y., Cherian, J., Sial, M. S., Álvarez-Otero, S., Comite, U., & Zia-Ud-Din, M. (2023). Green bond as a new determinant of sustainable green financing, energy efficiency investment, and economic growth: A global perspective. *Environmental Science and Pollution Research, 30*(22), 61324–61339. https://doi.org/10.1007/s11356-021-18454-7

Piñeiro-Chousa, J., López-Cabarcos, M. Á., Caby, J., & Šević, A. (2021). The influence of investor sentiment on the green bond market. *Technological Forecasting and Social Change, 162,* 120351. https://doi.org/10.1016/j.techfore.2020.120351

Porter, L., Rickards, L., Verlie, B., Bosomworth, K., Moloney, S., Lay, B., ... & Pellow, D. (2020). Climate justice in a climate changed world. *Planning Theory & Practice, 21*(2), 293–321.

Rachello, V. (2019). *The Green Bond Market in Emerging Market Economies.* 1–154. http://dspace.unive.it/bitstream/handle/10579/15699/845865-1224411.pdf?sequence=2

Rahman, P., Zhang, Z., & Musa, M. (2023). Do technological innovation, foreign investment, trade and human capital have a symmetric effect on economic growth? Novel dynamic ARDL simulation study on Bangladesh. *Economic Change and Restructuring, 56*(2), 1327–1366. https://doi.org/10.1007/s10644-022-09478-1

Roselle, P. (2016). The evolution of integrating ESG analysis into wealth management decisions. *Journal of Applied Corporate Finance, 28*(2), 75–79. https://doi.org/10.1111/jacf.12178

Sangiorgi, I., & Schopohl, L. (2021). Why do institutional investors buy green bonds: Evidence from a survey of European asset managers. *International Review of Financial Analysis, 75,* 101738. https://doi.org/10.1016/j.irfa.2021.101738

Schramade, W. (2016). Integrating ESG into valuation models and investment decisions: The value-driver adjustment approach. *Journal of Sustainable Finance & Investment, 6*(2), 95–111. https://doi.org/10.1080/20430795.2016.1176425

Springer, C., Tang, K., Nedopil, C., Alden, C., & Van Staden, C. (2023). Elevating ESG: Empirical lessons on environmental, social and governance implementation of Chinese projects in Africa. *SSRN Electronic Journal.* https://doi.org/10.2139/ssrn.4562949

Tauseef Hassan, S., Wang, P., Khan, I., & Zhu, B. (2023). The impact of economic complexity, technology advancements, and nuclear energy consumption on the ecological footprint of the USA: Towards circular economy initiatives. *Gondwana Research, 113,* 237–246. https://doi.org/10.1016/j.gr.2022.11.001

Volz, U. (2018). Fostering Green finance for sustainable development in Asia. *SSRN Electronic Journal, 814.* https://doi.org/10.2139/ssrn.3198680

Wang, S., Tian, W., & Lu, B. (2023). Impact of capital investment and industrial structure optimization from the perspective of "resource curse": Evidence from developing countries. *Resources Policy, 80,* 103276. https://doi.org/10.1016/j.resourpol.2022.103276

Weitzel, M., Vandyck, T., Rey Los Santos, L., Tamba, M., Temursho, U., & Wojtowicz, K. (2023). A comprehensive socio-economic assessment of EU climate policy pathways. *Ecological Economics, 204,* 107660. https://doi.org/10.1016/j.ecolecon.2022.107660

Wolff, M., & Mykhnenko, V. (2023). COVID-19 as a game-changer? The impact of the pandemic on urban trajectories. *Cities*, *134*, 104162. https://doi.org/10.1016/j.cities.2022.104162

Yang, H., Huang, X., Westervelt, D. M., Horowitz, L., & Peng, W. (2022). Socio-demographic factors shaping the future global health burden from air pollution. *Nature Sustainability*, *6*(1), 58–68. https://doi.org/10.1038/s41893-022-00976-8

Yao, H., Gu, X., & Yu, Q. (2023). Impact of graduate student expansion and innovative human capital on Green total factor productivity. *Sustainability*, *15*(2), 1721. https://doi.org/10.3390/su15021721

Yoshino, N., Yuyama, T., & Taghizadeh-Hesary, F. (2023). Diversified ESG evaluation by rating agencies and net carbon tax to regain optimal portfolio allocation. *Asian Economic Papers*, 1–16. https://doi.org/10.1162/asep_a_00871

Yu, C., Long, H., Zhang, X., Tu, C., Tan, Y., Zhou, Y., & Zang, C. (2023). Regional integration and city-level energy efficiency: Evidence from China. *Sustainable Cities and Society*, *88*, 104285. https://doi.org/10.1016/j.scs.2022.104285

Zaid, M. A. A., & Issa, A. (2023). A roadmap for triggering the convergence of global ESG disclosure standards: Lessons from the IFRS foundation and stakeholder engagement. *Corporate Governance: The International Journal of Business in Society*, *23*(7), 1648–1669. https://doi.org/10.1108/CG-09-2022-0399

5 Quantifying Portfolio Environmental and Social Impact

Assessing Metrics and Tools with a Focus on Green Bonds

Ferhat Çıtak and Muhammad Saeed Meo

Introduction

In the evolving landscape of finance, there is a growing recognition that the impact of investment decisions extends beyond mere financial returns. Investors are increasingly considering the environmental and social implications of their portfolios, acknowledging the interconnectedness of economic success and broader societal and environmental well-being. This paradigm shift has given rise to the imperative of measuring the environmental and social impact of portfolios, a multifaceted endeavor that involves sophisticated metrics and tools. This topic delves into the intricate realm of responsible investing, where the pursuit of financial gains coexists with a commitment to positive contributions to the environment and society. The integration of environmental and social considerations into portfolio management represents a transformative approach to investment strategies. As investors seek to align their financial goals with ethical values and sustainability objectives, the need for accurate and comprehensive impact measurement becomes paramount.

Over the past decade, green bonds have emerged as a key innovation in the field of sustainable finance. Green bonds play an important role in green finance by channeling investment into environmentally sustainable initiatives, attracting investors that are interested in environmental issues, and supporting the pursuit of sustainable development. In a sense, these bonds have used a private debt instrument explicitly designed to finance efforts consistent with ecological goals. These objectives encompass a wide range of areas, such as developing renewable energy, improving energy efficiency, reducing pollution, and promoting sustainable land management practices (Alamgir and Cheng, 2023).

The importance of green bonds in sustainable finance is manifold. In particular, they act as a catalyst to raise funds for environmentally sensitive projects that are often overlooked by traditional financing channels. Green bonds not only attract environmentally conscious investors by increasing the flow of funds to green initiatives, but also promote transparency and accountability by enforcing strict policies and regulations to ensure that funds flow exclusively

DOI: 10.4324/9781032686844-5

to qualified green projects (Agliardi and Agliardi, 2019; Maltais and Nykvist, 2020; Chen and Zhao, 2021).

The assessment of environmental and social effects, aligned with sustainable development goals (SDGs), involves evaluating both the beneficial and adverse impacts of corporate actions, projects, or policies on environmental and societal aspects (Castellas and Ormiston, 2018). This evaluation has become increasingly crucial as various organizations, including businesses and governments, strive for sustainable and responsible operations (Liang et al., 2022; Giri and Chaparro, 2023). Moreover, portfolios aligned with the United Nations Sustainable Development Goals (SDGs), particularly those focusing on environmental issues, are growing significantly. These sustainability-focused portfolios often focus on environmental sustainability goals, including clean water and sanitation initiatives (SDG 6), combating climate change (SDG 13), and promoting affordable clean energy (SDG 7) (Rizzello, 2022; Shayan et al., 2022; Sadiq, 2023).

The aim of this chapter is to set out the tools and metrics used to measure the environmental and social outcomes of portfolios.

Environmental, Social, and Governance Integration

Environmental, social, and governance (ESG) integration involves incorporating environmental, social, and governance factors into investment analysis and decision-making. ESG factors are non-financial factors that have a significant impact on a company's long-term financial performance and aim to identify the risks and opportunities associated with these factors and ultimately lead to better investment results by promoting sustainable business practices (Aldowaish et al., 2022). However, ESG integration is a complex concept that involves taking into consideration ESG factors alongside conventional financial factors in the investment process. It attempts to gauge the long-term viability and impact of a company's actions, rather than simply focus on the short-term financial gain that can be achieved (Verheyden et al., 2016; Galina, 2022). Overall, ESG integration is a beneficial tool for investors who want to enhance their financial performance, reduce risk, and have a positive impact on the world.

Additionally, governments and other organizations are increasingly recognizing the value of ESG integration, this leads to the implementation of new rules and initiatives intended to promote environmentally responsible investments. ESG integration is crucial to the investment process for many organizations, as it allows them to make decisions that are environmentally responsible and have a positive social impact. By including ESG factors in the analysis of investment possibilities, companies cannot only have a more effective way of managing risks, but also a long-term view of how to create value. This method is essential to achieving long-term development and promoting responsible investment. As the integration of ESG has continued to progress, it is crucial for organizations to understand the complexities and variations associated with ESG factors, as well as the unique specifics of each criterion, and to adopt effective practices and principles for ESG integration and reporting (De Souza Barbosa et al., 2023; De Spiegeleer et al., 2023).

Key Metrics for Environmental and Social Impact

Environmental and social indicators play a key role in tracking and assessing an organization's impact on the environment and society. These indicators are not only critical for identifying areas for improvement in an organization's sustainability performance, but they also serve as a communication medium for communicating sustainability progress and commitments to stakeholders. In this sense, it is the method of evaluating companies' concern for social responsibility or conscientiousness regarding economic development and environmental protection (Escrig-Olmedo et al., 2019; Mengistu and Panizzolo, 2023).

Investors can assess the social and environmental consequences of their investments through various methods, including utilizing social screening tools, creating indices that measure the social and environmental effects of investments, and evaluating the social and environmental performance of investments. These approaches facilitate the identification of areas that need improvement, they help to increase accountability, and they facilitate financial performance. Additionally, understanding how to effectively measure and manage impact is pivotal in ensuring that impact investors achieve the desired results regarding social and environmental issues.

Measuring environmental and social impacts in portfolio management is critical for several reasons. First, it allows investors to identify companies that align with their values and investment objectives, particularly those related to ESG investing. Second, it helps investors understand the true impact of their investment decisions and prioritize investments that create sustainable value. As highlighted by Kocmanová et al. (2016), these indicators include a comprehensive assessment of environmental, social, and governance aspects and provide a model for measuring sustainable value. Third, it allows investors to quantify and assess the impact of their investments, demonstrating their positive impact on society and the environment. Additionally, it provides valuable insights that can inform and improve the investment decision-making process, allowing investors to make more informed decisions that are consistent with their ESG goals and values. Ibáñez-Forés (2022) highlights the usefulness of sustainability reporting as a tool for measuring and monitoring the shift toward sustainable and circular economy practices within organizations. In conclusion, measuring environmental and social impact in portfolio management is important for aligning investments with values and objectives, understanding the real impact of investment decisions, and demonstrating positive impacts on society and the environment.

This chapter delves into the crucial metrics for managing a portfolio with an emphasis on environmental and social impact.

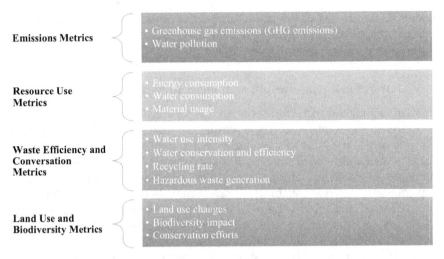

Source: Coton Innovation Cirad[1]

Figure 5.1 Types of environmental metrics
Source: Coton Innovation Cirad

Environmental Metrics

Environmental metrics are a set of measurements that assess the impact and influence of human activities on the natural world. These metrics often encompass variables, such as water and air quality, land use, biodiversity, and carbon emissions. They are used to gauge the effectiveness of environmental policies and initiatives, and to determine if they are meeting their intended goals. Additionally, environmental metrics are used to monitor and track changes in the environment over time, providing critical information for decision makers and stakeholders. Figure 5.1 depicts the categorization of environmental metrics according to their specific areas of focus.

Emissions Metrics

Emissions metrics are concerned with the volume or rate of greenhouse gas emissions (GHGs) or other pollutants produced by human activity. These metrics are used to gauge and measure the consequences of human activity on the environment, as well as to assess the effectiveness of policies and actions intended to reduce emissions. Some common metrics for emissions that are common include the carbon footprint, the amount of carbon dioxide per capita, and the energy-related emissions. These can be determined in different units, such as kilotonnes of CO_2 equivalent or megajoules (MJ) per person per year.

There are different emission metrics available, each offering a different approach. The primary considerations in selecting these metrics include their effects on climate and the duration over which comparisons are made (Aamaas et al., 2013). Emissions metrics can be enumerated as follows:

- **Greenhouse gas emissions (GHG emissions)**
  Greenhouse gas (GHG) emissions, which are important contributors to global warming and climate change, include various pollutants, such as carbon dioxide (CO_2), methane (CH_4), and nitrous oxide (N_2O). These emissions can be measured using different methods, including calculating the total GHGs emitted in relation to economic activity (such as GDP) per capita or per tonne of goods and services produced or consumed.

  Countries are creating national emissions inventories and proposing actions to reduce GHG emissions. Despite international agreements aimed at mitigating climate change, CO_2 emissions, which are the primary contributors to global GHG emissions, continue to rise at a global scale. Total GHG emissions across the world have been steadily increasing. According to a recent GHG emission report released by the Emissions Database for Global Atmospheric Research (EDGAR), the total worldwide GHG emissions for 2022 were reported to be around 57.4 Gigatonnes. This was a 1.2% increase from the previous year, 2021, and broke a new record in global emissions of GHG. Additionally, the average amount of global GHG

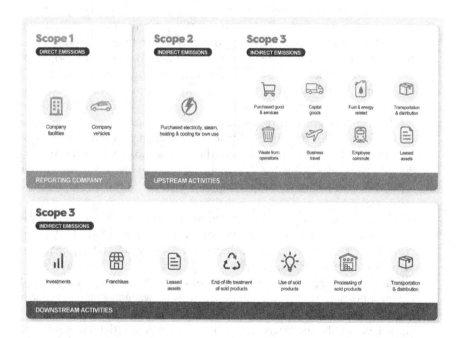

Figure 5.2 Green gas protocol – carbon accounting categories
Source: https://www.brightest.io

emissions per capita increased by 0.4% in 2022, which led to a total increase of 8.3% between 1990 and 2022.

According to the Greenhouse Gas Protocol[1] and ISO 14064, GHG emissions are divided into three categories: Scope 1, Scope 2, and Scope 3. Figure 5.2 illustrates the different categories of carbon accounting that are listed in the Green Gas Protocol.

Scope 1 (direct emissions from owned source): Companies that have ownership or control over their sources of GHGs are required to report these emissions as Scope 1 emissions. These direct GHG emissions primarily originate from activities like generating electricity, heat, or steam via fuel combustion, physical, or chemical processing of substances, transportation of substances and products, and fugitive emissions, which are caused by either intentional or accidental release from sources like equipment failure, chemical pollution from coal mining, hydrofluorocarbon (HFC) emissions during the production of ice, and methane leaking from transportation. These emissions are crucial to the reporting and management of GHGs.

Scope 2 (indirect emissions from the consumption of purchased electricity, steam, heating, and cooling): Companies report the emissions associated with the consumption of purchased electricity that is used in their owned or controlled equipment and operations as Scope 2 emissions, which are classified as indirect emissions. Purchased electricity is often the largest contributor to the release of GHGs for many companies. This represents a significant opportunity to reduce emissions. The tracking scope 2 emissions allows companies to assess the potential dangers and benefits of altering the sources of electricity and GHG emissions. It's also significant in regard to following certain GHG protocols. To lower the release of Scope 2 toxins, companies can devote funds to energy-efficient technology, conservation of energy, exploring power markets for a cleaner electricity source, and considering on-site generation of electricity. Reporting these emissions promotes transparency in the accounting for and quantification of the GHG emissions reported, and the reductions that have been achieved through these initiatives.

Scope 3 (other indirect emissions in a company's value chain): Scope 3 emissions are considered an innovative approach to dealing with GHGs for corporations. This category facilitates the accounting and reporting of activities that are associated with your business's goals and have a significant data component. The variety of categories that can be selected makes it possible to miss direct comparisons between companies regarding Scope 3. Scope 3 includes the extraction and production of purchased materials and fuels, transportation-related activities, employee travel, transportation of products and waste, and other activities that are not covered in Scope 2. Scope 3 emissions are a chance to initiate a comprehensive account of GHGs.

- **Water pollution**
  Water pollution is a significant problem around the world that poses a threat to human health, ecosystems, the environment, and economic development (Li et al., 2019; Hao et al., 2021; Jiang et al., 2023). The United Nations' Sustainable Development Goals (SDGs) recognize the necessity of clean water and sanitation and include several goals that seek to reduce water pollution and improve water quality. SDG 6 focuses on ensuring availability and sustainable management of water and sanitation for all, as well as addressing water pollution. This goal is aimed to achieve the following:

  access to safe drinking water, sanitation, and hygiene,
  water quality,
  sustainability of water resources,
  sustainable management of water-related ecosystem.

Resource Use Metrics

Resource use metrics that are used to evaluate the consumption of natural resources from different sources. There are important metrics used to consume resources:

- **Energy consumption**
  Energy consumption includes the amount of energy used by individuals, institutions, or communities to carry out various activities. This encompasses the use of electricity, gas, water, and other forms of energy in daily life.
- **Water consumption**
  Water consumption includes the total amount of water used by an individual or business. This important resource has multiple uses, such as drinking, food preparation, sanitation, and agricultural irrigation.
- **Material usage**
  Material usage involves the kinds of materials used in different processes and products. Tracking material usage is crucial to monitor the use of these materials to grasp their environmental effects and to find chances to replace them with more eco-friendly options.

Waste Efficiency and Conservation Metrics

Waste efficiency and savings metrics are important tools for companies and organizations to monitor progress toward sustainability goals. These metrics enable companies to identify areas for reducing waste and improving resource efficiency.

- **Water use intensity**

  Water use intensity, also known as water use efficiency, quantifies the amount of water used to produce a given amount of output. This indicator is usually expressed in liters or cubic meters per unit of product, such as liters per kilogram of rice or cubic meters per tonne of steel. It can be determined for a single product, process, or across industries. The importance of water intensity lies in its role as a key indicator of environmental performance, indicating the effectiveness of water use. Lower water intensity means less water is required to achieve the same level of production, which helps conserve water and minimize environmental impact.

- **Water conservation and efficiency**

  Water conservation involves the efficient and responsible utilization of water resources in order to minimize waste, this is accomplished through various strategies that reduce the unnecessary consumption of water and preserve it for future uses. Additionally, water efficiency focuses on completing the same tasks or processes with less water, this further emphasizes the importance of environmentally sustainable and efficient water usage.

- **Recycling rate**

  The recycling rate is the percentage of waste that is wasted away from landfills and repurposed into new products. This rate is crucial to the measurement of environmental efficiency, it demonstrates the effectiveness of material utilization and the degree to which waste is produced.

- **Hazardous waste generation**

  The hazardous waste generation process is the production of materials that are health hazardous or environmentally harmful. These materials can be in the form of solids, liquids, or gases, and they can have a variety of dangerous properties, including flammability, reactivity, toxicity, corrosion, and cancerogenicity.

Land Use and Biodiversity Metrics

The use of land and biodiversity metrics is crucial to the assessment of the effects of human activity on the natural environment. These metrics have a significant impact on the relationship between land use and the health and diversity of ecosystems.

- **Land use changes**

  Land use change is the transformation of one type of land cover or use to another. This procedure has various environmental effects like biodiversity loss, climate change, water pollution, and erosion.

- **Biodiversity impact**

  Biodiversity is the cornerstone of life on Earth, encompassing the vast range of biological diversity in all its manifestations, from the genetic constitution of plants and animals to the richness of cultural diversity.

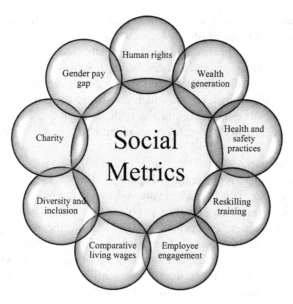

(Source: https://quantive.com/)

Figure 5.3 Classification of Social Metrics

Source: https://quantive.com/

- **Conservation efforts**

  Conservation efforts, such as habitat protection, species restoration, population management, and sustainable land use, are essential in order to preserve species that are endangered, preserve natural habitats, and promote environmentally responsible practices. These initiatives are intended to preserve biodiversity, environmental integrity, and the dependence of life on Earth.

Social Metrics

Social metrics are a subset of ESG metrics that are specifically concerned with the social consequences of an organization's actions or activities. Social metrics can be used in various ways to assess the extent to which the targets of the SDGs have been achieved. For example, measures such as the number of people living in extreme poverty or the number of children out of school can be used to assess the degree of progress toward SDG 1. Measures such as the gender pay gap or the number of people trafficked can be used to assess the degree of progress toward SDG 5. Figure 5.3 illustrates the different subcategories within the social metrics framework.

- **Human rights**

  Human rights are fundamental to sustainable development because they enable individuals and communities to participate in decision-making, hold governments to account and demand equal access to resources and opportunities. When human rights are respected, people are more likely to escape poverty, enjoy good health, and live in peaceful, secure environments. The Sustainable Development Goals and human rights are inextricably linked. Achieving the Sustainable Development Goals requires respecting, protecting, and realizing human rights, which constitute the normative framework for sustainable development, and the realization of the SDGs will in turn promote and enhance the protection of human rights (Kaltenborn et al., 2020).

- **Gender pays gap**
  The gender pay gap is the average disparity in the wages of men and women in the labor force. It is typically expressed as a percentage of the income of men and persistent and pervasive problem that affects women of all ages, races, and ethnicities. The gender pay gap is a significant obstacle that has an effect on various SDGs such as SDG 1 (No Poverty), SDG 4 (Quality Education), SDG 5 (Gender Equality), SDG 8 (decent work and economic growth), SDG 10 (reduced inequalities), SDG 16 (Peace, Justice, and strong institutions) (Rai et al., 2019; Küfeoğlu, 2022). By adopting a comprehensive and integrated approach that focuses on the causes of the gender pay gap, these strategies can have a significant impact on achieving gender equality and promoting economic development that is sustainable in accordance with the SDGs.

- **Charity**
  Charities have a significant role in helping to achieve the SDGs by providing crucial services, advocating for policy changes, and educating people about the importance of issues. Charities and the SDGs have a strong association with one another; both seek to create a more sustainable and equitable world. Charities have a variety of activities that contribute to the attainment of all of the SDGs, this creates positive change on a global scale (Dalby et al., 2019).

- **Diversity and inclusion**
  Diversity and inclusion (D&I) initiatives seek to create environments that value everyone, honor their contributions, and allow them to succeed. Many benefits exist in having a diverse and inclusive workforce, these include increased creativity, innovation, and productivity. D&I are primarily associated with the SDG 4 (Quality Education), the SDG 5 (Gender Equality), the SDG 8 (Decent Work and Economic Growth), and the SDG 10 (Reduced Inequalities). To promote diversity and include policies more effectively, companies and organizations should focus on initiatives intended to include people, increase the number of minorities in the management team, promote actions and behaviors by people (Küfeoğlu, 2022).

- **Comparative living wages**
  The idea of living wages is intrinsically linked to the SDGs, specifically regarding poverty, promoting decent work, reducing inequality, and having a sustainable economic impact. By paying workers a wage that covers their

basic needs, organizations and policy makers can help to achieve multiple goals of the SDGs (i.e., SDG 1, SDG 5, SDG 8, SDG 19) which in turn will lead to a more sustainable and equitable world (Mair et al., 2019).

- **Employee engagement**
  Employee engagement plays a key role in advancing the SDGs by encouraging active engagement in sustainable practices within the organization and fostering a strong commitment to the company's mission, values, and sustainability initiatives. Engaged employees demonstrate greater commitment to their work, greater productivity, and a tendency to innovate. In particular, employee engagement is aligned with key SDGs, including SDG 7 (Affordable and Clean Energy), SDG 8 (Decent Work and Economic Growth), SDG 12 (Responsible Consumption and Production), SDG 13 (Climate Action), and SDG 17 (Partnerships for the Goals). This alignment highlights the positive impact that engaged employees can have on achieving the SDGs (Castellani et al., 2023).

- **Reskilling training**
  Investing in reskilling and education is crucial to creating a successful future. Giving people the basic skills needed for the changing business environment not only supports sustainable development, but also creates a more equal world and a more positive tomorrow for all. The essence of the retraining training methodology in the context of the SDGs is its emphasis on providing new skills and knowledge. This is important to adapt to the dynamic nature of job markets and the challenges associated with environmental changes. The key SDGs that align with reskilling training are *Quality Education* (SDG 4), which ensures people continue to learn and adapt; *Decent Work and Economic Growth* (SDG 8), which focuses on the evolution of jobs and economic advancement; *Industry, Innovation, and Infrastructure* (SDG 9), which promotes progressive and sustainable industrial development; and *Climate Action* (SDG 13), which educates individuals about the dangers of climate change.

- **Health and safety practices**
  Health and safety practices (HSP) are intrinsically tied to the SDGs, as they have a significant role in enhancing well-being and economic sustainability (Magar, 2015). HSP are, specifically, linked with the SDGs including SDG 3 (Good Health and Well-being), SDG 8 (Decent Work and Economic Growth). Including health and safety in sustainable development initiatives that are also intended to preserve workers and contribute to larger social and economic goals increases the probability of success.

- **Wealth generation**
  Wealth generation is crucial to the realization of sustainable development, as it demonstrates the country's capacity to produce and maintain the welfare of both present and future populations (Anger, 2010). Wealth generation, when done sustainably, can have a significant impact on the achievement of the SDGs in several ways including poverty reduction,

improved healthcare, education and skills development, and environmental protection (Sugiawan, 2023).

In summary, integrating these important environmental and social indicators into corporate strategies and policies is not only just a matter of regulatory compliance or corporate responsibility, but also it is a forward-looking approach that recognizes the link between environmental health and social well-being. By carefully tracking and improving these metrics, companies can make a tangible difference in their environmental footprint and social impact. This commitment to sustainable practices is increasingly becoming a cornerstone of corporate image and consumer trust, shaping a future where businesses are valued not just for their financial performance but also for their contribution to a sustainable and equitable world.

Additionally, as the global community continues to struggle with environmental issues and social issues, these metrics serve as essential tools to assess the progress toward a more sustainable and just society. They offer a solid platform on which to align the operations of organizations with the Sustainable Development Goals (SDGs), this will guarantee that the growth of the organization is both environmentally responsible and sustainable. In this manner, the adoption and expansion of environmental and social impact metrics is crucial to the development of a more resilient, equitable, and sustainable future for all.

In conclusion, measuring environmental and social impact in portfolio management is important for aligning investments with values and goals, understanding the true impact of investment decisions, and demonstrating positive effects on society and the environment. It also helps in making informed decisions, improving accountability, and achieving desired impact results in impact investing.

Tools for the Environmental and Social Impact of Portfolios

A growing number of tools are available to help investors assess the environmental and social impacts of their portfolios. These tools can be used to screen companies with strong ESG practices, monitor the ESG performance of individual companies and portfolios, and engage with companies to improve their ESG practices. Some of the most popular ESG investment tools are as follows.

ESG Ratings and Metrics

ESG ratings and metrics are a set of standards used to evaluate a company's ESG performance. ESG metrics are specific measures that companies use to track their sustainability progress, such as GHG emissions, diversity percentages, and tax payments. These metrics help investors and stakeholders understand how a company is managing its ESG risks and opportunities, and how well it aligns with their values and priorities (Berg et al., 2022).

ESG ratings and metrics are measured using both quantitative and qualitative metrics. Quantitative metrics are numbers-based, measurable metrics such as GHG emissions or water consumption. The ESG ratings approach uses quantitative metrics to evaluate a company's ESG performance. Qualitative metrics, on the other hand, are more subjective and rely on expert judgment and analysis. These metrics can include factors, such as employee satisfaction, community engagement, and board diversity. ESG scores are a measure of how well a company addresses risks with respect to ESG issues in its day-to-day operations (Pagano et al., 2018; Clément et al., 2022).

ESG ratings and metrics first emerged in the 1980s as a way for investors to evaluate companies and are becoming increasingly important in investing, as more investors are recognizing the potential financial impact of ESG factors. A strong ESG rating indicates that a company manages its ESG risks well in comparison to its peers, whereas a poor ESG rating indicates that the company may face significant ESG risks that could affect its long-term financial performance (Anquetin et al., 2022). These ratings and metrics can help investors identify and understand financially material ESG risks to a business, making it easier to evaluate the potential risks and returns of an investment (OECD, 2022).

There are various methods available for ESG ratings, such as the MSCI Global Sustainability Indices, the Dow Jones Sustainability Indices (DJSI), RobecoSAM's Corporate Sustainability Assessment (CSA) methodology, the Focus Index (Dow Jones Sustainability World Index) and the FTSE4Good Index Series.

Carbon Footprint Analysis

Carbon footprint analysis is the process of measuring the amount of GHGs emitted by an individual, organization, product, or service. Greenhouse gases such as carbon dioxide (CO_2), methane (CH_4), and nitrous oxide (N_2O) contribute to climate change by trapping heat in the atmosphere. Carbon footprint analysis helps identify sources of GHG emissions and develop strategies to reduce them (Radonjič and Tompa, 2018; Walenta, 2021).

Carbon footprint analysis offers a myriad of benefits across individual, organizational, and societal levels. By meticulously quantifying GHG emissions associated with activities, products, or services, this analysis provides a critical foundation for targeted mitigation strategies. Identifying major emission sources enables individuals and organizations to make informed decisions, fostering the development of effective reduction initiatives. Moreover, carbon footprint analysis facilitates bench marking against industry standards, allowing for the tracking of emission reduction progress and the demonstration of environmental responsibility. Beyond environmental impact, the analysis often leads to cost savings through enhanced energy efficiency, waste reduction, and sustainable practices. Contributing to broader climate change mitigation efforts, carbon footprint analysis aligns with sustainability goals and enhances an entity's reputation, attracting environmentally conscious consumers, partners, and investors. Overall, the systematic evaluation of carbon footprints serves as a powerful tool for fostering environmental stewardship, driving positive change, and promoting a more sustainable future. (Anquetin et al., 2022).

Impact Investing Platforms

Impact investing platforms are online platforms that connect investors with impact investments—investments that aim to create a positive social or environmental impact in addition to financial returns. They provide investors with a range of tools and resources, including investment opportunities, due diligence and transparency, impact measurement, education, and resources (Mendell and Barbos, 2013). Numerous platforms dedicated to impact investing, such as the Investing with Impact platform from Morgan Stanley, the Apollo's Impact Mission Strategy, ImpactBase, Seedrs, and MicroVentures, have all contributed to the growth of impact investing. These platforms provide a variety of accessible and diverse options for investors that are committed to aligning their financial goals with positive environmental and social results.

Sustainable Investing Indices

Sustainable investment indices are metrics that gauge the success of companies in regards to ESG principles. These metrics are intended to assist investors in making educated decisions about their finances by concurring with their financial objectives regarding values. There are numerous types of sustainable investment indices, each of which is dedicated to a specific aspect of ESG.

Environmental indices focus on companies that have a robust environmental performance, they take into account factors like GHG emissions, energy conservation, and water usage.

Social indices concern companies that have a strong social reputation, they evaluate aspects like labor practices, human rights, and community involvement.

Governance indices concern companies that have effective corporate leadership, they assess aspects like the composition of the board, executive compensation, and shareholder rights.

Sustainable investment indices are intended to provide transparency and guidance regarding responsible investment by categorizing companies based on their adherence to ESG principles. The most commonly recognized sustainable investing indices are MSCI ESG Leaders Indexes, FTSE Russell ESG Indexes, and S&P DJI Sustainability Indices, all of which are intended to focus on specific criteria that companies should utilize in order to assess their efforts toward sustainability.

Socially Responsible Investment Screeners

Socially Responsible Investment (SRI) scanners are tools that can be used by investors to assess and eliminate investment possibilities based on ESG. These screeners have a significant role in responsible investing by allowing investors to associate their portfolios with moral and environmental principles (Friedman and Miles, 2001).

SRI screeners are invaluable tools for investors who want to align their investments with their ethical principles. These instruments facilitate the recognition of companies that specialize in sustainability and social responsibility, this allows investors to assess the ESG quality of potential investments. Additionally, SRI investors can observe the evolution of companies toward addressing ESG concerns over time. By providing comprehensive information, these screeners enable investors to make informed and responsible decisions about investment that are in line with their values, this will lead to a more ethical and sustainable approach to financial management (Sparkes, 2003; Hallerbach et al., 2004).

Two primary types of SRI screeners exist: negative screens and positive screens. Negative screens exclude companies from investment consideration based on specific criteria, such as involvement in tobacco production, weapons manufacturing, or fossil fuel extraction. Conversely, positive screens concentrate on identifying companies exhibiting robust ESG performance. These screens employ various criteria, including a company's dedication to renewable energy, its ethical labor practices, or its active involvement in the community. Together, these screening approaches enable investors to shape their portfolios in alignment with their ethical values and sustainability objectives.

Several well-known SRI screeners are Morningstar Sustainability Rating, Sustainalytics ESG Risk Ratings, MSCI ESG Indexes, CDP Carbon Footprint, and GRI (Global Reporting Initiative) Sustainability Reporting Standards. These diverse screeners equip investors with valuable tools to align their portfolios with ethical and sustainability considerations.

Conclusion and Policies

Integrating environmental and social metrics into portfolio management offers a multitude of benefits for both companies and investors. One notable advantage is the capacity to identify and effectively manage risks linked to environmental and social factors. When ESG factors are considered in investment decisions, investors gain a more comprehensive insight into the risks and opportunities associated with various companies. This holistic approach often translates into enhanced long-term financial performance, as companies prioritizing ESG factors tend to demonstrate greater resilience and are better poised for success. Furthermore, investing in companies with robust ESG performance not only aligns with investors' values but also contributes to fostering positive social and environmental outcomes (Poveda and Young, 2015; Lee and Suh, 2022).

However, the utilization of environmental and social metrics in the management of portfolios is not without significant obstacles. One of the greatest barriers is the lack of universal metrics and reporting standards. This lack of uniformity is unable to be overcome, which makes it difficult to assess the performance of ESG in different companies and industries and leads to potential problems in reporting. Additionally, there may be a deficiency of understanding or awareness regarding ESG issues among investors or managers in charge of portfolios, this is problematic because it prevents the smooth implementation of ESG metrics. Ultimately, the incorporation of ESG factors into investment decisions is resource-intensive and requires significant expertise, this is particularly true of smaller companies, which have a more complex approach to taking on this transformative approach (Fagarasan et al., 2023).

In spite of these hurdles, valuable lessons emerge from the implementation of environmental and social metrics in portfolio management. First, there is a critical need to develop a clear understanding of the material ESG issues specific to the industry or sector at hand. This understanding aids in prioritizing ESG metrics, ensuring alignment with the company's strategic objectives. Second, the establishment of clear and consistent reporting standards is paramount to guaranteeing comparability of ESG data across companies and sectors. Third, active engagement with companies on ESG issues emerges as a powerful tool for fostering positive change and motivating improvements in ESG performance. Lastly, a continuous process of reviewing and evaluating the effectiveness of ESG metrics and reporting frameworks, with adjustments made as needed, is imperative. Through assimilating these lessons, both companies and investors can more adeptly integrate environmental and social metrics into portfolio management, contributing substantively to positive social and environmental outcomes (Lee and Suh, 2022; Fagarasan et al., 2023).

Lastly, precision in impact measurement stands as a crucial element for comprehending the efficacy of programs and interventions. This process entails a systematic evaluation and analysis of an organization's social, environmental, and economic impact. Impact measurement serves as a valuable tool, offering insights into the outcomes and changes induced by an intervention, encompassing both positive and negative aspects. Through a comprehensive understanding of program impact, organizations gain the ability to make well-informed decisions regarding resource allocation, program design, and implementation strategies. Additionally, impact measurement serves as a diagnostic tool, pinpointing areas for enhancement and fostering the development of more effective and efficient programs.

Note

1 GHG Protocol establishes comprehensive global standardized frameworks to measure and manage GHG emissions from private and public sector operations, value chains, and mitigation actions (https://ghgprotocol.org/).

References

Aamaas, B., Peters, G., & Fuglestvedt, J. (2013). Simple emission metrics for climate impacts. *Earth System Dynamics Discussions*, *4*, 145–170. doi:10.5194/ESD-4-145-2013

Agliardi, E., & Agliardi, R. (2019). Financing environmentally-sustainable projects with green bonds. *Environment and Development Economics*, *24*(6), 608–623. doi:10.1017/S1355770X19000020

Alamgir, M., & Cheng, M.C. (2023). Do green bonds play a role in achieving sustainability? *Sustainability*, *15*(13), 10177. doi:10.3390/su151310177

Aldowaish, A., Kokuryo, J., Almazyad, O., & Goi, H.C. (2022). Environmental, social, and governance integration into the business model: Literature review and research agenda. *Sustainability*, *14*(5), 2959. doi:10.3390/su14052959

Anger, B. (2010). Poverty eradication, millennium development goals and sustainable development in Nigeria. *Journal of Sustainable Development*, 3(4), 138–144. Retrieved from: https://dlc.dlib.indiana.edu/dlc/handle/10535/6830

Anquetin, T., Coqueret, G., Tavin, B., & Welgryn, L. (2022). Scopes of carbon emissions and their impact on green portfolios. *Economic Modelling*, *115*, 105951. doi:10.1016/j.econmod.2022.105951

Berg, F., Koelbel, J.F., & Rigobon, R. (2022). Aggregate confusion: The divergence of ESG ratings. *Review of Finance*, *26*(6), 1315–1344. doi:10.1093/rof/rfac033

Castellani, P., Rossato, C., Giaretta, E., & Vargas-Sánchez, A. (2023). Partner selection strategies of SMEs for reaching the Sustainable Development Goals. Review of Managerial Science, 1–36. doi:10.1007/s11846-023-00656-7

Castellas, E.I., & Ormiston, J. (2018). Impact investment and the sustainable development goals: Embedding field-level frames in organisational practice. In *Entrepreneurship and the Sustainable Development Goals* (pp. 87–101). Emerald Publishing Limited.

Chen, Y., & Zhao, Z.J. (2021). The rise of green bonds for sustainable finance: Global standards and issues with the expanding Chinese market. *Current Opinion in Environmental Sustainability*, *52*, 54–57. doi:10.1016/j.cosust.2021.06.013

Clément, A., Robinot, É., & Trespeuch, L. (2022). Improving ESG scores with sustainability concepts. *Sustainability*, *14*(20), 13154. doi:10.3390/su142013154

Dalby, S., Horton, S., Mahon, R., & Thomaz, D. (Eds.). (2019). *Achieving the sustainable development goals: Global governance challenges*. Routledge.

de Souza Barbosa, A., da Silva, M.C.B.C., da Silva, L.B., Morioka, S.N., & de Souza, V.F. (2023). Integration of Environmental, Social, and Governance (ESG) criteria: their impacts on corporate sustainability performance. *Humanities and Social Sciences Communications*, *10*(1), 1–18. doi:10.1057/s41599-023-01919-0

De Spiegeleer, J., Höcht, S., Jakubowski, D., Reyners, S., & Schoutens, W. (2023). ESG: A new dimension in portfolio allocation. *Journal of Sustainable Finance & Investment*, *13*(2), 827–867. doi:10.1080/20430795.2021.1923336

Escrig-Olmedo, E., Fernández-Izquierdo, M.Á., Ferrero-Ferrero, I., Rivera-Lirio, J.M., & Muñoz-Torres, M.J. (2019). Rating the raters: Evaluating how ESG rating agencies integrate sustainability principles. *Sustainability*, *11*(3), 915–938. doi:10.3390/su11030915

Fagarasan, C., Cristea, C., Cristea, M., Popa, O., & Pisla, A. (2023). Integrating sustainability metrics into project and portfolio performance assessment in agile software development: A data-driven scoring model. *Sustainability, 15*(17), 13139. doi:10.3390/su151713139

Friedman, A.L., & Miles, S. (2001). Socially responsible investment and corporate social and environmental reporting in the UK: An exploratory study. *The British Accounting Review, 33*(4), 523–548. doi:10.1006/bare.2001.0172

Galina, K. (2022). Potential Effects of ESG (Environmental, Social, and Governance) policies on the returns of an investment portfolio. *Review of Business and Economics Studies, 10*(2), 21–55. doi:10.26794/2308-944X-2022-10-2-21-55

Giri, F.S., & Chaparro, T.S. (2023). Measuring business impacts on the SDGs: A systematic literature review. *Sustainable Technology and Entrepreneurship, 2*(3), 100044. doi:10.1016/j.stae.2023.100044

Hallerbach, W., Ning, H., Soppe, A., & Spronk, J. (2004). A framework for managing a portfolio of socially responsible investments. *European Journal of Operational Research, 153*(2), 517–529. doi:10.1016/S0377-2217(03)00172-3

Hao, X., Ruihong, Y., Zhuangzhuang, Z., Zhen, Q., Xixi, L., Tingxi, L., & Ruizhong, G. (2021). Greenhouse gas emissions from the water–air interface of a grassland river: A case study of the Xilin River. *Scientific Reports, 11*(1), 2659. doi:10.1038/s41598-021-81658-x

Ibáñez-Forés, V., Martínez-Sánchez, V., Valls-Val, K., & Bovea, M.D. (2022). Sustainability reports as a tool for measuring and monitoring the transition towards the circular economy of organisations: Proposal of indicators and metrics. *Journal of Environmental Management, 320*, 115784. doi:10.1016/j.jenvman.2022.115784

Jiang, S., Li, E., Wei, Y., Yan, X., He, R., Banny, E.T., & Xin, Z. (2023). Measurement and influencing factors of carbon emission efficiency based on the dual perspectives of water pollution and carbon neutrality. *Science of the Total Environment*, 168662. doi:10.1016/j.scitotenv.2023.168662

Kaltenborn, M., Krajewski, M., & Kuhn, H. (2020). *Sustainable development goals and human rights* (p. 239). Springer Nature. doi:10.1007/978-3-030-30469-0

Kocmanová, A., Pavláková Dočekalová, M., Škapa, S., & Smolíková, L. (2016). Measuring corporate sustainability and environmental, social, and corporate governance value added. *Sustainability, 8*(9), 945. doi:10.3390/su8090945

Küfeoğlu, S. (2022). SDG-5 Gender equality. In: *Emerging Technologies.* Sustainable Development Goals Series. Cham: Springer. doi:10.1007/978-3-031-07127-0_7

Lee, M.T., & Suh, I. (2022). Understanding the effects of environment, social, and governance conduct on financial performance: Arguments for a process and integrated modelling approach. *Sustainable Technology and Entrepreneurship, 1*(1), 100004. doi:10.1016/j.stae.2022.100004

Li, J., See, K.F., & Chi, J. (2019). Water resources and water pollution emissions in China's industrial sector: A green-biased technological progress analysis. *Journal of Cleaner Production, 229*, 1412–1426. doi:10.1016/j.jclepro.2019.03.216

Liang, H., Fernandez, D., & Larsen, M. (2022). Impact assessment and measurement with sustainable development goals. *Handbook on the Business of Sustainability: The Organization, Implementation, and Practice of Sustainable Growth*, 424.

Magar, V. (2015). Gender, health and the sustainable development goals. *Bulletin of the World Health Organization, 93*(11), 743–743. doi:10.2471/BLT.15.165027

Mair, S., Druckman, A., & Jackson, T. (2019). Higher wages for sustainable development? Employment and carbon effects of paying a living wage in global apparel supply chains. *Ecological Economics, 159*, 11–23. doi:10.1016/j.ecolecon.2019.01.007

Maltais, A., & Nykvist, B. (2020). Understanding the role of green bonds in advancing sustainability. *Journal of Sustainable Finance & Investment*, 1–20. doi:10.1080/20 430795.2020.1724864

Mendell, M., & Barbosa, E. (2013). Impact investing: A preliminary analysis of emergent primary and secondary exchange platforms. *Journal of Sustainable Finance & Investment*, 3(2), 111–123. doi:10.1080/20430795.2013.776258

Mengistu, A.T., & Panizzolo, R. (2023). Metrics for measuring industrial sustainability performance in small and medium-sized enterprises. *International Journal of Productivity and Performance Management*. doi:10.1108/IJPPM-04-2022-0200

OECD (2022). ESG ratings and climate transition: An assessment of the alignment of E pillar scores and metrics, OECD Business and Finance Policy Papers, OECD Publishing, Paris, doi:10.1787/2fa21143-en.

Pagano, M.S., Sinclair, G., & Yang, T. (2018). 18. Understanding ESG ratings and ESG indexes. *Research Handbook of Finance and Sustainability*, 339.

Poveda, C.A., & Young, R. (2015). Potential benefits of developing and implementing environmental and sustainability rating systems: Making the case for the need of diversification. *International Journal of Sustainable Built Environment*, 4(1), 1–11. doi:10.1016/j.ijsbe.2014.12.003

Radonjič, G., & Tompa, S. (2018). Carbon footprint calculation in telecommunications companies–The importance and relevance of scope 3 greenhouse gases emissions. *Renewable and Sustainable Energy Reviews*, 98, 361–375. doi:10.1016/j.rser. 2018.09.018

Rai, S.M., Brown, B.D., & Ruwanpura, K.N. (2019). SDG 8: Decent work and economic growth–A gendered analysis. *World Development*, 113, 368–380. doi:10.1016/j.worlddev.2018.09.006

Rizzello, A. (2022). Green Finance and SDGs: Emerging trends in the design of Green Investment Portfolios. *Green Investing: Changing Paradigms and Future Directions*, 85–105.

Sadiq, M., Ngo, T.Q., Pantamee, A.A., Khudoykulov, K., Ngan, T.T., & Tan, L.P. (2023). The role of environmental social and governance in achieving sustainable development goals: evidence from ASEAN countries. *Economic research-Ekonomska istraživanja*, 36(1), 170–190. doi:10.1080/1331677X.2022.2072357

Shayan, N.F., Mohabbati-Kalejahi, N., Alavi, S., & Zahed, M.A. (2022). Sustainable development goals (SDGs) as a framework for corporate social responsibility (CSR). *Sustainability*, 14(3), 1222. doi:10.3390/su14031222

Sparkes, R. (2003). *Socially responsible investment: A global revolution*. John Wiley & Sons.

Sugiawan, Y., Kurniawan, R., & Managi, S. (2023). Assessing the United Nations sustainable development goals from the inclusive wealth perspective. *Scientific Reports*, 13, 1601. doi:10.1038/s41598-023-28540-0

Verheyden, T., Eccles, R.G., & Feiner, A. (2016). ESG for all? The impact of ESG screening on return, risk, and diversification. *Journal of Applied Corporate Finance*, 28(2), 47–55. doi:10.1111/jacf.12174

Walenta, J. (2021). The making of the corporate carbon footprint: the politics behind emission scoping. *Journal of Cultural Economy*, 14(5), 533–548. doi:10.1080/175 30350.2021.1935297

6 Green Bonds

Mitigating Risk and Diversifying Portfolios for a Sustainable Future

Calvin Cheong Wing Hoh, Alade Ayodeji, ADEMOKOYA, Lianne Lee Mei Quin, and Ayesha Zahid

Introduction

In the rapidly changing landscape of global finance, green bonds have emerged as a pivotal instrument in mobilizing resources for environmental sustainability. These bonds represent a significant evolution in funding ecological initiatives, linking financial returns with ecological responsibility. Green bonds are essentially debt securities issued by corporations, financial institutions, or governments with the specific purpose to raise funds for environmentally driven projects (Azhgaliyeva, Kapoor, & Liu, 2020; Climate Bonds Initiative, 2023). These projects cover a broad spectrum, from renewable energy initiatives and sustainable waste management to clean transportation and water preservation (Azhgaliyeva & Liddle, 2020).

The concept of green bonds originated in 2007 when the European Investment Bank launched the Climate Awareness Bond. This was a response to investors' growing interest in supporting climate-friendly projects, and it successfully raised approximately 600 million Euros for renewable energy and energy efficiency initiatives (World Bank, 2018). The following year, the World Bank issued the first instrument to be labeled as a 'green bond', targeting Swedish pension funds keen on investing in projects that reduced greenhouse gas emissions (Oguntuase & Windapo, 2021). This pivotal moment catalyzed the green bond market growth, setting a precedent for future issuances. Over time, the green bond market has witnessed remarkable growth, reflecting a burgeoning interest in sustainable investment. According to the Climate Bonds Initiative, the green bond issuance surged from $87 billion in 2016 to $350 billion in 2020 (World Bank Group, 2021). This uptrend underscores a significant shift in investor priorities, now increasingly focused on environmental impact as well as financial return. Presently over 50 countries around the world have issued green bonds, marking their global acceptance and importance in financing sustainable development, with the United States leading the way, followed closely by China and France.

Green bonds stand out from traditional bonds due to their dedicated use of funds for environmentally beneficial projects. This earmarking of funds is

DOI: 10.4324/9781032686844-6

a fundamental attribute, assuring investors of their direct contribution to sustainable development. A key aspect of green bonds is the need for transparency and accountability. Issuers are often required to regularly report on the use of funds and the environmental impact of the projects financed (Climate Bonds Initiative, 2023). The unique appeal of green bonds lies in meeting two investor goals: financial return and social responsibility. They offer a tangible solution for investors seeking to align their portfolios with their environmental values without sacrificing profitability. Moreover, green bonds often offer with tax incentives to both issuers and investors.

However, the green bond market faces challenges, notably the absence of uniform standards for qualifies as a 'green' project. This lack of clarity raises concerns about 'greenwashing' where the environmental benefits of a project are exaggerated or falsely presented to attract investment. To address this, several international standards, and certifications, such as the Green Bond Principles and the Climate Bonds Standard, have been established to ensure transparency and integrity in the green bond market.

Green bonds represent a significant stride toward a sustainable financial future. They are more than financial instruments; they symbolize a growing awareness of the environmental impact of investments. As the market continues to evolve, green bonds are poised to play an increasingly important role in funding a more sustainable future. In the following sections of this chapter, we offer insights into the dynamics of green bonds, the benefits in their use, challenges to their proliferation, as well as profound implications for their future.

Maximizing Benefits with Green Bonds

Green bonds have revolutionized the landscape of environmental finance, offering a unique blend of ecological responsibility and financial with financial pragmatism. In this section, we delve into the multifaceted benefits of green bond investments, appealing to investors who prioritize both environmental and financial goals, and examine the incentives that make these bonds attractive.

The primary allure of green bonds is their role in funding environmentally positive projects. For investors, this represents an opportunity to support sustainable initiatives in areas like renewable energy, energy efficiency, sustainable agriculture, and clean transportation. Investing in green bonds allows individuals and institutions to actively participate in fighting climate change and fostering environmental sustainability, aligning their investments with their ecological values.

In addition to aiding broader ecological goals, research indicates that issuing or investing in green bonds offers direct, observable advantages. These include an improved reputation and image, the opportunity to tap into new markets and attract different investors, and the potential for risk mitigation and cost reduction. Furthermore, these bonds contribute to an organization's or society's transition toward a low-carbon future (Zhao, Chau, Tran, Sadiq, Xuyen & Phan, 2022). We discuss these in turn below:

a **Reputation and Image**: By issuing or investing in green bonds, entities underscore their commitment to sustainability and environmental stewardship, improving their brand value. This can translate into greater customer loyalty in an increasingly eco-conscious society (Maltais & Nykvist, 2020).

b **Access to New Markets**: Issuers of green bonds gain access to an expanding pool of capital from investors drawn to environmentally friendly projects. Additionally, green bonds open door into new markets and sectors prioritizing sustainability. This diversification is beneficial as it enables investors to distribute their across different sectors, thereby lowering the total risk of their investment portfolio (Chang et al., 2022. Furthermore, due to the growing regulatory emphasis on sustainability, sectors financed by green bonds are expected to receive ongoing support, enhancing their long-term stability and profitability.

c **Risk Mitigation and Cost Reduction**: Green bonds generally exhibit lower default rates and receive higher credit ratings compared to conventional bonds. This results in lower borrowing costs for issuers. The green bond market has experienced significant growth, leading to better liquidity, and further reducing costs. Moreover, green bonds are often accompanied by tax incentives, including credits, exemptions, and rebates, as the government globally promotes investment in these bonds. These incentives aim to enhance the appeal of green bonds to investors, decreasing borrowing costs for issuers and increasing returns for investors. Li et al. (2020) highlight that green bonds can also help investors minimize their exposure to environmental and social risks, such as climate change, pollution, and human rights violations. In an economy increasingly attentive to environmental factors, investments neglecting these aspects are poised to become more hazardous. By financing environmentally responsible projects, green bonds offer a potential safeguard against such risks, providing greater stability and protection for investors' portfolios.

d **Supporting the Low-Carbon Transition**: By issuing or investing in green bonds, organizations and individuals play an important role in global initiatives to mitigate climate change and fulfill the sustainable development goals. They achieve this by financing projects focused on reducing greenhouse gas emissions, enhancing energy efficiency, and advancing clean technologies. This approach benefits both the environment and society at large. Additionally, it positively impacts the profits of the organization or investors involved, as it demonstrates their commitment to values that resonate with the public. This alignment not only attracts goodwill but also reinforces their social legitimacy.

Navigating the Challenges in Green Bond Investment

While green bonds are a promising option for sustainable investment, they come with their own set of challenges. Both issuers and investors have to deal with various obstacles, including issues with standardization and market liquidity. In this section, we identify and address the common obstacles faced in green bond investment and offer insights for overcoming these challenges.

A significant challenge in the green bond market is the absence of a universally recognized definition for green bonds, a standardized criterion for what qualifies as a 'green' project, and a mandatory requirement for independent verification or certification of green bonds. This lack of standardization leads to uncertainty and can result in 'greenwashing', where the environmental benefits of a green bond issue are overstated or falsely presented. To counteract this, investors should conduct extensive due diligence, carefully evaluating the environmental impact of the project and the issuer's dedication to sustainability. While existing standards like the Green Bond Principles and Climate Bonds Standards are beneficial, further efforts are required, especially in environmental auditing and assurance, to address these challenges effectively.

The pricing of green bonds presents another significant challenge. Issuing green bonds can be costlier than traditional bonds due to the extra requirements for reporting and certifications, potentially leading to lower yields for investors. Additionally, accurately assessing the risk-return profile of green bonds is challenging. Green projects often face greater uncertainties compared to conventional projects, such as regulatory hurdles, technological disruptions, or environmental shocks. Furthermore, existing bond valuation models indicate that bonds in high demand generally offer lower yields. With the increasing popularity of green bonds, their typically lower yields may not be sufficiently enticing for issuers, especially if they have access to more affordable financing from other sources. This aspect, explored by Kapraun, Latino Scheins, and Schlag (2021), highlights the complexities in the green bond market related to pricing and investor incentives.

The evolving regulatory landscape surrounding green bonds presents challenges, particularly in terms of transparency, reporting standards, and quality. As the regulatory framework for green bonds is still developing in many markets, inconsistencies and uncertainties in market practices are common. The scarcity of reliable data and research on the characteristics, performance, and impact of green bonds hinders investors' ability to make informed decisions. It is essential for investors to have access to up-to-date and trustworthy information about the usage of funds and environmental impact achieved. Therefore, to improve the accountability and trustworthiness of both issuers and investors, there is a pressing need for standardized, transparent reporting standards and a clear disclosure requirement for green bonds (Agliardi & Agliardi, 2021; Baldi & Pandimiglio, 2022).

Lastly, a significant issue with investing in green bonds is the limited diversity in the types of projects being funded. Currently, the majority of green bond-funded projects are concentrated in the energy and transport sectors and are primarily located in Europe. While this focus is not inherently problematic, it does limit the broader appeal of green bonds because: (1) it fails to represent the diverse range of global environmental opportunities and challenges, and (2) it may inadvertently increase concentration risk in portfolios that are heavily invested in green bonds. In other words, there is a need for a wider variety in the types of projects, industry sectors, and geographical regions financed by green bonds. Expanding this diversity would enhance the attractiveness and accessibility of green bonds to both issuers and investors (Ehlers & Packer, 2017 Mejía-Escobar, González-Ruiz, & Franco-Sepúlveda, 2021).

While investing in green bonds presents certain challenges, these can be navigated with due diligence, informed decision-making, and a proactive approach to market developments. By understanding and addressing these obstacles, investors and issuers can effectively capitalize on the opportunities presented by green bonds, contributing to a sustainable financial future while safeguarding their investments.

The Environmental Footprint: Green Bonds in Climate Action Green bonds have emerged as a key element in the global effort toward environmental sustainability and climate action. They play a crucial role in financing a variety of projects that positively impact the environment. These projects, which include renewable energy, energy efficiency, sustainable agriculture, and waste management, represent significant progress in addressing climate change and promoting sustainable development (Bhutta, Tariq, Farrukh, Raza, & Iqbal, 2022; Dai & Chen, 2023). The growing issuance of green bonds, increasingly acknowledged by investors and government alike, reflects a shared dedication to fighting climate change. These financial tools are specifically designed to support projects that lower greenhouse gas emissions and facilitate a shift toward a low-carbon economy(Torvanger, Maltais, & Marginean, 2021; Afshan et al., 2023). For example, funding for renewable energy infrastructure, such as wind farms and solar panel plants, directly contributes to reducing reliance on fossil fuel-based power generation. This not only cuts down carbon dioxide emissions but also encourages innovation in green technologies.

Furthermore, green bonds also make a substantial contribution to environmental conservation by financing projects that support the preservation of natural resources and biodiversity. This includes initiatives in sustainable forestry, land management, and those aimed at ensuring clean water and air, demonstrating the wide-ranging environmental benefits of these bonds (Ning, Cherian, Sial, Alvarez-Otero, Comite, & Zia-Ud-Din, 2023). Furthermore, the specific allocation of green bonds to energy efficiency projects, like retrofitting buildings and modernizing industrial processes, highlights their role in reducing energy use and associated emissions. These activities showcase the effectiveness of green bonds in addressing various aspects of environmental sustainability (Sartzetakis, 2021).

The administration of green bonds is founded on principles of credibility and transparency. Issuers of these bonds comply with established frameworks like the Green Bond Principles, Climate Bond Standards, and Sustainability Bond Guidelines. This compliance ensures that the environmental integrity of their projects is not only maintained but also transparently reported(Sartzetakis, 2021). This compliance ensures that the environmental integrity of their projects is not only maintained but also transparently reported. Such adherence boosts investor confidence and highlights the alignment of the bonds with international climate objectives, including the goals of Paris Agreement. Beyond just financing environmental projects, green bonds play a crucial role in promoting awareness about sustainable financing. They emphasize the importance of responsible corporate behavior and environmental stewardship in the investment community. The varied success stories of green bonds, which include projects like upgrading national power grids and restoring mangrove forests, demonstrate their significant impact worldwide, benefiting both developing and developed countries.

Nevertheless, it is important to acknowledge that while green bonds are vital, they are not a complete solution to the climate crisis. They represent just one component within a wider array of strategies needed for climate mitigation, requiring collective action from government, businesses, and individuals (Chen & Zhao, 2021). Essentially, green bonds serve as channels for directing capital toward sustainable projects. These projects not only contribute to building a more resilient world, but also provide a profitable opportunity for investors. The effectiveness of green bonds reflects a shifting paradigm in which financial returns and environmental sustainability are increasingly intertwined, heralding a new era in responsible investing.

Social Impact: How Green Bonds Foster Community Development

Green bonds, as an emerging financial instrument, significantly impact social welfare and community development, with their benefits reaching beyond just environmental sustainability. These bonds fund a wide array of projects, including public infrastructure improvements and sustainable agriculture, each making a meaningful contribution to social equity and the well-bringing of communities (Fonash & Baba, 2013; Bhutta et al., 2022). A notable advantage of investing in green bonds is job creation. Green bond-funded projects, such as renewable energy installation and the development of sustainable infrastructure, require skilled labor. This demand helps stimulate employment growth in local communities, contributing positively to economic health. Beyond job creation, this also helps support skill development and capacity building, fostering a skilled workforce for the future (McHugh, Biosca, & Donaldson, 2023).

Green bonds are also instrumental in improving public infrastructure, such as transportation systems, clean water facilities, and affordable housing. By investing in these areas, they help to improve the quality of life and resilience of communities, making them more livable. For example, housing projects financed by green bonds often feature energy-efficient designs. This not only reduces utility costs but also increases the sustainability of living spaces (Baptista et al., 2021; Sartzetakis, 2021). Consequently, and perhaps unintentionally, these investments in green bonds also have a direct positive effect on community health and well-being. Projects that focus on clean energy and reducing pollution lead to cleaner air and water, which in turn improve public health and lower the healthcare costs related to pollution-induced illnesses (Sartzetakis, 2021). Additionally, green bonds support initiatives in sustainable agriculture, fostering food security and promoting sustainable livelihoods within farming communities.

Moreover, green bond projects typically involve active community engagement and consultation. This ensures that the initiatives funded are in line with community's needs and values. Such an inclusive approach promotes a sense of belonging and ownership among community members, leading to a more equitable distribution of the benefits derived from these projects(Baptista et al., 2021). Focusing on greater social inclusion, particularly in marginalized or underserved areas, plays a crucial role in bridging social inequalities. It enhances fairness and equity in accessing resources and opportunities (Fonash & Baba, 2013; Chishti, Arfaoui, & Cheong, 2023). By fostering communities that are collective and inclusive rather than individualistics, green bonds contribute to improved climate resilience and disaster mitigation. This is because the risks associated with environmental and climate challenges are shared across the community, united by a common commitment to environmental stewardship. This collective approach, fueled by funding from green bonds, aids in mitigating the impact of climate-related risks (Tian, Yu, Xue, Zhuang, & Shan, 2022).

In the long run, the influence of green bonds on community development becomes apparent through the rise in property values and the attraction of additional investments. Initiatives in sustainable development and green infrastructure invigorate local economies. This economic boost enhances the equity of homeowners and contributes to the stability and growth of communities. By funding projects that tackle a wide range of social challenges, green bonds exemplify the potential of investments to serve societal benefits. They play a significant role in fostering more equitable, resilient, *and* sustainable communities, thus demonstrating that financial instruments can indeed align with and support broader social objectives.

Regulatory and Policy Support for Green Bonds Investment

The rise of green bonds as a key tool for sustainable financing is closely linked to the regulatory and policy frameworks that support their growth and effectiveness. Governments and regulatory authorities around the world have been instrumental in nurturing the green bond market. They have implemented various strategies to promote green bond investments and ensure their integrity and transparency. A crucial strategy in this context is the provision of tax incentives. Governments offer exemptions or reduced tax rates to green bond issuers or investors, making these bonds more attractive and financially viable. These incentives are key in spurring investments and increasing demand for green bonds, thereby strengthening their presence in the market (Banga, 2019; Babon-Ayeng et al., 2022; Lin & Hong, 2022).

Regulatory agencies also play a crucial role in the green bond market by setting labeling and reporting standards, which mandate transparency and verification for the use of process. These standards are essential in assuring investors that their funds are genuinely allocated to environmentally beneficial projects. Alongside this, industry-led initiatives like the Green Bond Principles offer voluntary guidelines for issuers and investors. These guidelines encourage best practices in disclosure and reporting, further reinforcing investor confidence reporting (Babon-Ayeng et al., 2022; Lin & Hong, 2022). However, establishing standards alone is not enough to ensure the financial viability of green bonds. Like all financial instruments, the liquidity of green bonds is a primary concern. To address this, government and financial institutions have developed dedicated green bond funds and indices. These tools are designed to promote price transparency and enhance the liquidity of green bonds, thereby making them more attractive to institutional investors and supporting market growth. To this end, governmental efforts in creating regulatory frameworks that simplify issuance procedures, reduce administrative burdens, and improve market liquidity are vital for the development of green bond markets. Such efforts create a more favorable investment environment and lower transaction costs, which in turn encourages greater market participation. These comprehensive measures are crucial for the continued growth and success of the green bond market (Babon-Ayeng et al., 2022).

In addition, international collaboration plays a key role in standardizing green bond practices, facilitating cross-border investments, and boosting investor confidence. This cooperation, often spearheaded by global organizations and coalitions, is crucial in broadening the base of potential issuers and investors, and in aligning international efforts toward sustainable finance (Babon-Ayeng et al., 2022). However, it is important to recognize that regulatory and policy support for green bonds is not fixed but continually evolving. Policymakers must persistently adapt and refine regulations to stay in step with market changes and new challenges. This dynamic approach is essential to tackle issues like greenwashing and to ensure that green bonds make a real impact on the environment. A robust framework for issuing green bonds is vital. This framework should guarantee transparency and compliance, and when combined with fiscal incentives, it creates a conducive environment for the growth of green bonds. Such a comprehensive support system not only stimulates investment but also upholds the credibility and integrity of green bonds. Consequently, it effectively channels capital toward sustainable projects and aids in transitioning to a green economy.

Enhanced Reputation and Stakeholder Engagement in Green Bonds Investment

Green bonds have become a dynamic force in sustainable finance, acting as key instruments for environmental and social change and as powerful catalysts for enhancing corporate reputation and engaging various stakeholders. Both investing in and issuing green bonds are seen as significant indicators of a company's commitment to sustainability. This commitment resonates strongly with eco-conscious consumers, investors, and the broader public, demonstrating the growing importance and influence of green bonds in today's market.

Regulatory frameworks and policies are crucial in enhancing the credibility and trustworthiness of green bond investments. These standardized frameworks guarantee that the investments are truly sustainable, reinforcing the image of investors as responsible and progressive. The certainty that funds are being utilized for sustainable projects boosts investor confidence and emphasizes a company's dedication to environmental stewardship. This relationship between regulation, investor trust, and corporate responsibility highlights the importance of a solid regulatory foundation for the success of green bonds (Lee, 2020; Kawabata, 2020; Amoah, Dzeha & Arun, 2022).

The transparency and reporting obligations enforced by regulatory agencies play a vital role in improving accountability in the realm of green bonds. These clear reporting standards allow stakeholders to evaluate the environmental impact of their investments accurately. This level of transparency is essential in building trust and facilitating informed investment decisions. It is particularly appealing to ethical investors who focus on Environmental, Social and Governance (ESG) criteria (Lu, 2021; Sangiorgi & Schopohl, 2021; Pavlidis, 2022).

Additionally, green bonds can also provide organizations with a competitive advantage in acquiring capital. By showcasing their commitment to sustainability, these organizations can attract investors who prioritize environmentally responsible businesses. This alignment with investor values can potentially lead to a lower cost of capital and improved access to funding. These financial benefits are often bolstered by regulatory incentives, which further enlarge the pool of available capital for sustainable projects. This synergy between an organization's sustainability initiatives and favorable financial conditions underscores the strategic value of green bonds in sustainable finance (Maltais & Nykvist, 2020).

Investing in green bonds also brings the significant advantage of enhancing public perception. When a company associates itself with environmentally friendly projects through green bonds, it boosts its public image, generates goodwill, and position itself as a leader in sustainability. This improved public perception can lead to tangible benefits, such as increased customer loyalty and stronger relationships with regulatory bodies. These advantages under-score the value of green bonds not just in financial terms, but also in terms of corporate reputation and stakeholder relations (Torvanger et al., 2021).

Green bond investments have a notable effect on stakeholder engagement. Companies that issue green bonds have the opportunity to interact with a diverse set of stakeholders, including environmental groups and community organizations. This engagement fosters a deeper understanding of stakehold-ers' concerns and helps align the company's strategies with societal needs. Such interactions not only build trust but also promote a sense of shared ownership and partnership in sustainability initiatives, highlight the role of green bonds in strengthening corporate-stakeholder relationships (Weber & Saravade, 2019).

Green bonds are more than just financial instruments; they play a signifi-cant role in building and improving corporate reputation and relationships with stakeholders. By strategically utilizing green bonds, companies can posi-tion themselves as leaders in sustainability. This enhances their reputation and earns the trust and loyalty of stakeholders, contributing to the collective aim of a sustainable future. Additionally, the regulatory and policy support for green bond investments promote market growth and ensures the integrity and effectiveness of these investments. This makes green bonds a fundamen-tal component in the shift toward a sustainable financial system, highlighting their importance in both the financial and environmental landscapes (Yadav, Mishra, & Ashok, 2023).

Diversification and Risk Mitigation in Portfolios

In the evolving landscape of investment, green bonds have established them-selves as a strategic instrument for diversifying portfolios and reducing risks, particularly with respect to ESG factors. These bonds present investors with a chance to balance their portfolios by including assets that have unique ben-efits and are in line with long-term sustainability objectives. This role of green bonds underscores their value in modern investment strategies, offering both financial and environmental advantages.

Green bonds offer investors a way to diversify their portfolios beyond con-ventional stocks and bonds. By incorporating green bonds, investors intro-duce assets that typically do not move in direct correlation with the standard market trends. This helps in reducing the overall risk of the portfolio by dis-tributing investments across various asset classes and sectors (Bao & Zhang, 2021). Such diversification becomes especially valuable during times of eco-nomic uncertainty when traditional markets are underperforming, as green bonds often exhibit different behavior compared to standard financial assets. This characteristic of green bonds enhances their appeal as a component of a well-rounded investment strategy.

Moreover, green bonds can serve as a protective measure during periods of crisis. They offer a measure of stability against the volatility often seen in renewable energy stocks and carbon markets. In scenarios where other investments in a portfolio might be suffering losses, green bonds can help balance these downturns, acting as a stabilizing factor. This attribute of green bonds makes them a valuable addition to investment portfolios, particularly for mitigating risks in times of market instability as these bonds can help offset these losses, providing stability (Bao & Zhang, 2022; Chen & Zhang, 2022; Stankevičienė & Bao, 2023).

Additionally, investing in green bonds aligns with ESG principles, reflecting the increasing focus on climate change and social responsibility. Green bonds fund projects that are environmentally and socially beneficial, thereby lowering the investor's exposure to risks associated with ESG factors. These investments often support critical initiatives, such as renewable energy and energy efficiency improvements, which are key in transitioning to a low-carbon economy. This approach also provides a safeguard against the potential decline of industries heavily reliant on carbon, positioning green bonds as a proactive choice for investors concerned with sustainable and responsible investing.

Green bonds are generally characterized by lower volatility compared to traditional bonds. This is attributed to the predictable nature of cash flows from green projects and strong demand from a varied investor base, which further bolsters their role in risk mitigation. However, it is important for investors to be aware of the inherent risks associated with green bonds. Challenges such as limited liquidity, lower yields, and the possibility of greenwashing are important factors to consider. These risks underscore the need for careful evaluation and thoughtful integration of green bonds into a comprehensive investment strategy. Investors should balance these risks with the benefits, keeping in mind their personal investment goals, tolerance for risk, and investment timeframe. This careful consideration is crucial for maximizing the potential of green bonds within an investment portfolio (Brown Advisory, 2023; Gola, 2023).

Ultimately, green bonds present a valuable option for investors seeking to diversify their portfolios and mitigate risk, especially in relation to ESG factors. By incorporating green bonds in an investment portfolio not only enhances its resilience but also supports sustainable development initiatives. Despite their benefits, it is crucial for investors to adopt a balanced approach that acknowledges the potential risks associated with green bonds. Effectively integrating these bonds into investment strategies requires ensuring that they are in line with the investor's broader financial goals and risk tolerance. This balanced approach is key to leveraging the advantages of green bonds while managing potential challenges.

The Potential for Competitiveness in Financial Returns

Green bonds have become a notable force in the financial markets, offering an investment option that is sustainable and competitive with traditional financial instruments in terms of returns. The appeal of green bonds in the financial landscape is driven by several factors. These include the growing emphasis on global environmental priorities, the establishment of supportive regulatory frameworks, shifting investor preference toward sustainability, and ongoing innovations in the market. This combination of elements contributes to the rising prominence and attractiveness of green bonds as a viable financial option.

The increasing emphasis on environmental sustainability and the pressing need to address climate change have led to a robust market for green bonds. Governments and investors alike are striving to shift toward a low-carbon economy, fueling increased demand for green bonds. This surge in demand enhances their financial appeal and challenges the previously held belief that sustainable investments typically yield lower returns. This shift in perception indicates a broader recognition of the financial viability of green bonds in addressing global environmental concerns (Li et al., 2022).

The support from regulatory and policy frameworks has been crucial in boosting the competitiveness of green bonds. Various incentives, including tax benefits and subsidies, have been introduced to stimulate investments in green bonds. These measures not only foster green finance but also reduce investment risks, potentially leading to more attractive financial returns (Asl, Rashidi, Tiwari, Lee, & Roubaud, 2023). Consequently, green bonds have become increasingly popular among investors who focus on ESG factors. This trend aligns investor values with sustainable investment opportunities, broadening the investor base and heightening demand, which could result in higher financial returns. Additionally, the green bond market has experienced significant diversification in recent years, offering a wider array of investment options in areas like green infrastructure, green efficiency, and sustainable real estate. This diversification has enhanced the appeal and potential profitability of green bonds in the financial market (Huynh, Hille, & Nasir, 2020).

In the context of market performance, green bonds have demonstrated notable resilience during periods of economic decline and have maintained stability under varying market conditions. This stability is largely attributed to the nature of the projects funded by green bonds, which frequently encompass essential services and infrastructure characterized by secure revenue streams. Furthermore, the escalating demand for sustainable investment options has enhanced the pricing efficiency of green bonds. This improvement in pricing efficiency often results in competitive, and occasionally superior yields in comparison to traditional bonds (International Monetary Fund, 2009; Bao & Zhang, 2022). This factor contributes to the long-term stability of green bonds, a characteristic that is particularly attractive to investors. The projects financed through green bonds generally have prolonged operational lifespans, offering predictable and consistent returns over extended periods. This attribute is particularly attractive to institutional investors who are oriented toward long-term investment strategies (Chen & Zhang, 2022; Stankevičienė & Bao, 2023). However, it is imperative to recognize and consider the inherent risks associated with green bonds. These risks include market volatility, uncertainties in valuation, and potential regulatory changes, all of which must be factored into investment decisions involving green bonds.

Ultimately, green bonds offer a distinct opportunity for investors who aim to achieve competitive returns while also contributing to environmental and social benefits. As the market for green bonds matures, these instruments are expected to become increasingly integral to investment portfolios. They uniquely blend financial stability with sustainable impact. The potential for green bonds to yield competitive financial returns is rooted in several key factors: the escalating global demand for sustainable investments, robust regulatory support, shifting investor preferences toward sustainability, and ongoing innovations in the financial markets. These elements collectively underpin the growing appeal and potential profitability of green bonds in the evolving investment landscape.

Conclusion and Policies

Throughout this chapter, we have seen that green bonds are more than just an innovative financial instrument; they are a critical driver for a sustainable financial future. Green bonds represent a transformative approach to investment, one that seamlessly merges financial goals with environmental and social responsibility. Since their inception, green bonds have undergone rapid evolution, mirroring the growing global awareness of environmental sustainability and an increasing appetite for sustainable investment opportunities. The evolution of green bonds from a specialized market to a mainstream financial instrument highlights a profound shift in investor priorities. This shift transcends the pursuit of financial returns, emphasizing the alignment of investments with the pressing need for environmental conservation and proactive climate action.

Investing in green bonds offers a range of benefits. Financially, they offer yield returns comparable to traditional bonds, while also offering added perks like tax incentives and increased market liquidity. From an environmental perspective, green bonds are crucial for financing projects that directly reduce carbon emissions, boost energy efficiency, and encourage sustainable land use. Socially, they fund initiatives that enhance community well-being. This includes supporting sustainable housing and clean water projects, improving public transportation, and creating job opportunities. These multidimensional benefits make green bonds an attractive option for investors looking to combine financial returns with environmental and social impact.

Yet, the path of green bonds is not free from challenges. Challenges like the absence of standardization, concerns over market liquidity, and the risk of greenwashing require careful due diligence and an active approach from investors. In this scenario, regulatory and policy support is crucial, providing a strong framework that promotes transparency, credibility, and growth in the green bond market. As these regulatory frameworks evolve, they are expected to strengthen the role of green bonds as a dependable and impactful tool for sustainable investment.

Lastly, the potential for green bonds goes beyond just offering financial return. They are a vital component in the pursuit of sustainable development, bridging investors' interests with the wider goals of environmental conservation and social equity. In the face of global challenges like climate change and the need for sustainable development, green bonds emerge as a beacon of hope. They offer a practical and effective means to channel capital toward building a greener and more sustainable future. The evolution of green bonds to date reflects a changing investment landscape, where financial success and sustainability are not seen as separate goals but as interconnected objectives. As the green bond market continues to mature, its role in shaping a sustainable financial landscape and driving positive environmental and social changes is expected to grow increasingly significant.

References

Afshan, S., Cheong, C. W., & Sharif, A. (2023). Modelling the role of energy price movements toward economic stability in Malaysia: New evidence from wavelet-based analysis. *Environmental Science and Pollution Research*, 30(38), 88861–88875.

Agliardi, E., & Agliardi, R. (2021). Corporate green bonds: Understanding the greenium in a two-factor structural model. *Environmental and Resource Economics*, 80(2), 257–278.

Amoah, L., Dzeha, G. C. O., & Arun, T. (2022). Sustainable finance and banking in Africa. In *The Economics of Banking and Finance in Africa: Developments in Africa's Financial Systems* (pp. 405–429). Cham: Springer International Publishing.

Asl, M. G., Rashidi, M. M., Tiwari, A. K., Lee, C. C., & Roubaud, D. (2023). Green bond vs. Islamic bond: Which one is more environmentally friendly? *Journal of Environmental Management*, 345, 118580.

Azhgaliyeva, D., Kapoor, A., & Liu, Y. (2020). Green bonds for financing renewable energy and energy efficiency in South-East Asia: A review of policies. *Journal of Sustainable Finance & Investment*, 10(2), 113–140.

Azhgaliyeva, D., & Liddle, B. (2020). Introduction to the special issue: Scaling up green finance in Asia. *Journal of Sustainable Finance & Investment*, 10(2), 83–91.

Babon-Ayeng, P., Oduro-Ofori, E., Owusu-Manu, D. G., Edwards, D. J., Kissi, E., & Kukah, A. S. K. (2022). Socio-political factors underlying the adoption of green bond financing of infrastructure projects: The case of Ghana. *Journal of Capital Markets Studies*, 6(3), 304–319.

Baldi, F., & Pandimiglio, A. (2022). The role of ESG scoring and greenwashing risk in explaining the yields of green bonds: A conceptual framework and an econometric analysis. *Global Finance Journal*, 52, 100711.

Banga, J. (2019). The green bond market: A potential source of climate finance for developing countries. *Journal of Sustainable Finance & Investment*, 9(1), 17–32.

Bao, T., & Zhang, Y. (2021). The impact of green bonds on corporate innovation. *Journal of Corporate Finance*, 69, 101895. doi:10.1016/j.jcorpfin.2021.101895

Bao, T., & Zhang, Y. (2022). Risk connectedness between green and conventional assets with portfolio implications. *Journal of Risk and Financial Management*, 15(6), 313. doi:10.3390/jrfm15060313

Baptista, F., Lourenço, P., da Cruz, V. F., Silva, L. L., Silva, J. R., Correia, M., ... & Papadakis, G. (2021). Which are the best practices for MSc programmes in sustainable agriculture? *Journal of Cleaner Production*, 303, 126914.

Bhutta, U. S., Tariq, A., Farrukh, M., Raza, A., & Iqbal, M. K. (2022). Green bonds for sustainable development: Review of literature on development and impact of green bonds. *Technological Forecasting and Social Change*, 175, 121378.

Brown Advisory. (2023, October 5). Income and impact: Adding Green Bonds to investment portfolios. *Brown Advisory*. Link to the article.

Chang, L., Taghizadeh-Hesary, F., Chen, H., & Mohsin, M. (2022). Do green bonds have environmental benefits?. *Energy Economics*, 115, 106356.

Chen, Y., & Zhang, Y. (2022). Diversification and hedging strategies of green bonds in financial asset portfolios during the COVID-19 pandemic. *Applied Economics*, 54(47), 11797–11810. doi:10.1080/00036846.2022.2128178

Chen, Y., & Zhao, Z. J. (2021). The rise of green bonds for sustainable finance: Global standards and issues with the expanding Chinese market. *Current Opinion in Environmental Sustainability*, 52, 54–57.

Chishti, M. Z., Arfaoui, N., & Cheong, C. W. (2023). Exploring the time-varying asymmetric effects of environmental regulation policies and human capital on sustainable development efficiency: A province level evidence from China. *Energy Economics*, 126, 106922.

Climate Bonds Initiative. (2023). Green bonds. Retrieved from https://www.climatebonds.net/

Dai, Y., & Chen, X. (2023). Evaluating green financing mechanisms for natural resource management: Implications for achieving sustainable development goals. *Resources Policy*, 86, 104160.

Ehlers, T., & Packer, F. (2017). Green bond finance and certification. *BIS Quarterly Review September*.

Fonash, S., & Baba, M. (2013). Implications: People and Physical Infrastructure.

Gola, M. (2023, September 21). Opportunities and Risks of Green Bond Investing. *Investopedia*.

Huynh, T. L. D., Hille, E., & Nasir, M. A. (2020). Diversification in the age of the 4th industrial revolution: The role of artificial intelligence, green bonds and cryptocurrencies. *Technological Forecasting and Social Change*, 159, 120188.

Kapraun, J., Latino, C., Scheins, C., & Schlag, C. (2021, April). (In)-credibly green: Which bonds trade at a green bond premium? In *Proceedings of Paris December 2019 Finance Meeting EUROFIDAI-ESSEC*.

Kawabata, T. (2020). Private governance schemes for green bond standard: Influence on public authorities' policy making. *Green Finance*, 2(1), 35–54.

Lee, J. W. (2020). Green finance and sustainable development goals: The case of China. *Journal of Asian Finance Economics and Business*, 7(7), 577–586.

Li, Z., Tang, Y., Wu, J., Zhang, J., & Lv, Q. (2020). The interest costs of green bonds: Credit ratings, corporate social responsibility, and certification. *Emerging Markets Finance and Trade*, 56(12), 2679–2692.

Lin, L., & Hong, Y. (2022). Developing a green bonds market: lessons from China. *European Business Organization Law Review*, 23(1), 143–185.

Lu, S. S. (2021). The green bonding hypothesis: How do green bonds enhance the credibility of environmental commitments? (Doctoral dissertation, The University of Chicago).

Maltais, A., & Nykvist, B. (2020). Understanding the role of green bonds in advancing sustainability. *Journal of Sustainable Finance & Investment*, 1–20.

Mejía-Escobar, J. C., González-Ruiz, J. D., & Franco-Sepúlveda, G. (2021). Current state and development of green bonds market in the Latin America and the Caribbean. *Sustainability*, 13(19), 10872.

McHugh, N., Biosca, O., & Donaldson, C. (2023). *Social Finance and Health*. Taylor & Francis.

Ning, Y., Cherian, J., Sial, M. S., Álvarez-Otero, S., Comite, U., & Zia-Ud-Din, M. (2023). Green bond as a new determinant of sustainable green financing, energy efficiency investment, and economic growth: A global perspective. *Environmental Science and Pollution Research*, 30(22), 61324–61339.

Oguntuase, O. J., & Windapo, A. (2021). Green bonds and green buildings: New options for achieving sustainable development in Nigeria. *Housing and SDGs in Urban Africa*, 193–218.

Pavlidis, G. (2022). The digital transformation of the global green bonds market: New-fashioned international standards for a new generation of financial instruments. *Data Governance in AI, FinTech and LegalTech* (pp. 263–278). Edward Elgar Publishing.

Sangiorgi, I., & Schopohl, L. (2021). Why do institutional investors buy green bonds: Evidence from a survey of European asset managers. *International Review of Financial Analysis*, 75, 101738.

Sartzetakis, E. S. (2021). Green bonds as an instrument to finance low carbon transition. *Economic Change and Restructuring*, 54(3), 755–779.

Stankevičienė, J., & Bao, T. (2023). Analysis of success factors, benefits, and challenges of issuing green bonds in Lithuania. *Economies*, 14(12), 589. doi:10.3390/economies14120589

Tian, J., Yu, L., Xue, R., Zhuang, S., & Shan, Y. (2022). Global low-carbon energy transition in the post-COVID-19 era. *Applied Energy*, 307, 118205.

Torvanger, A., Maltais, A., & Marginean, I. (2021). Green bonds in Sweden and Norway: What are the success factors? *Journal of Cleaner Production*, 324, 129177.

World Bank. (2018, September 17). *Launch of the Global Green Bond Partnership*. Retrieved March 29, 2024, from https://www.worldbank.org/en/news/press-release/2018/09/13/launch-of-the-global-green-bond-partnership

Yadav, M., Mishra, N., & Ashok, S. (2023). Dynamic connectedness of green bond with financial markets of European countries under OECD economies. *Economic Change and Restructuring*, 56(1), 609–631.

Zhao, L., Chau, K. Y., Tran, T. K., Sadiq, M., Xuyen, N. T. M., & Phan, T. T. H. (2022). Enhancing green economic recovery through green bonds financing and energy efficiency investments. *Economic Analysis and Policy*, 76, 488–501.

7 Evolutionary Perspective of Green Bond Financing under the Shadow of ESG Readiness

Priyanka Sahu, Orhan Şanli, Laeeq Razzak Janjua and Nouman Maqbool Rao

Introduction

Environmental degradation has been considered the main obstacle to achieving sustainable growth because it has several ecological difficulties, such as global warming, climate change, water scarcity, deforestation, high global temperatures, and emission of GHG. Most emerging and developed countries have been concerned about combating environmental challenges aggravated by individual human actions (Ozcan et al., 2019). Because unmitigated climate change hinders economic growth and increases global inequality, especially for developing countries, it will lead the world toward a more chaotic situation on the achievement of sustainable development goals (Sachs and Sachs 2021). Although a low level of carbon dioxide emission was recorded in 2020, due to the lockdown and slow down of economic growth caused by the pandemic crises of COVID-19 (Khan et al., 2021), the year 2020 was recorded as one of the warmest. Therefore, scientists warn that if current policies remain unaltered, global temperatures might rise by another 2°C–5°C by the end of the century, potentially causing catastrophic economic harm across the globe.

Furthermore, low-carbon technology and sustainable and resilient infrastructure can help to boost development and economic recovery, reduce inequities, and expedite the transition to climate-resilient economies. However, such investment will not be sufficient, and successful climate mitigation and adaptation would require a combination of policies, particularly carbon pricing, including eliminating fossil fuel subsidies, a persistent investment push, and supporting renewable energy research and development. To maximize the synergies of economic, environmental, and social policies, national and international policy settings must be reinforced. International assistance for developing countries will also be required to enable a fair and just transition for all and avoid a "lost decade." Another important aspect of the quest for sustainability is the rise of "green finance," which is funding allocated to eco-friendly projects and initiatives. Products such as "green bonds" and "loans linked to sustainability" have become popular, providing financial incentives to companies that embrace sustainable practices. Governments and financial institutions across the globe are adopting green finance as a way to expedite the

DOI: 10.4324/9781032686844-7

shift to a low-carbon economy. Green bonds have emerged as an important financing mechanism to fund sustainable development projects and advance the environmental, social, and governance (ESG) framework. However, challenges remain in scaling up green bond markets, especially in developing countries. While developed countries have taken the lead in green bond issuance, developing countries face limitations in ESG readiness that constrain market growth. Factors like weak institutional capacity, lack of common standards, underdeveloped capital markets, and limited awareness create hurdles in leveraging green bonds. At the same time, developing countries stand to benefit immensely from sustainable finance instruments to meet their climate goals and large infrastructure gaps. This presents an opportunity for developing countries to build ESG readiness, engage development banks and investors, and create enabling policy environments to grow green bond markets. With targeted capacity building, harmonization with international standards, supportive regulations, and clear political signals, developing countries can overcome structural weaknesses. Regional cooperation can also foster shared learning and scale. Appropriate use of credit enhancements and de-risking instruments can help attract investment. Thus, green bonds, if properly leveraged, can channel private capital toward bankable sustainable projects in developing countries. But strategic efforts are needed to address ESG investment barriers, build robust project pipelines, and create vibrant markets. The growth of green bonds in developing countries will require close coordination between governments, regulators, issuers, verifiers, investors, and other stakeholders within a conductive framework.

Research Synthesis

There are studies that indicate that green bonds could help promote sustainability goals in developing nations. Looking up the recent studies on green bond financing, Zhang and Umair's (2023) study investigates interconnectivity in green finance by analyzing spillover effects among green bonds, renewable energy stocks, and carbon markets from 2010 to 2020. Using vector autoregressive and time-varying parameter models, it finds significant dynamic spillovers between green bonds and renewable stocks, and between carbon markets and renewable stocks. The results also suggest a complementary relationship between green bonds and carbon markets. Overall, the research reveals the interdependence of green financial instruments and their role in enabling sustainable development through informed policymaking and investment. Similarly, Nguyen et al.'s (2023) work explores the evolution of green bonds in Southeast Asian countries, highlighting regulatory and other difficulties that must be resolved.

Likewise, Nurgaliyeva et al.'s (2022) study underlines the prospect of utilizing green bonds to finance eco-friendly projects in Kazakhstan; however, strengthening knowledge transfer, institutional capabilities, and government backing are imperative, whereas Ning et al.'s (2022) study uses fuzzy decision modeling to test the impact of green bond financing on energy efficiency investment and economic growth. It finds bank loans are currently the primary financing source for energy efficiency projects, but green bonds could replace project-based financing and Energy Performance Contracts to spur investment. Similarly, Tuhkanen and Vulturius's (2022) study examines the linkage between corporate green bonds and climate targets amid transition risks and polycentric climate governance. Analyzing the 20 largest European issuers in 2018, it finds discrepancies between issuers' climate goals and green bond frameworks, plus reporting shortcomings. There appears minimal pressure on issuers to achieve science-based targets through green bonds. The results indicate risks of green washing and a need to situate the green bond market within planetary boundaries through policy action. Bohner's (2022) study examines the rise of green bonds post-Paris Agreement as a climate finance instrument to fund mitigation and adaptation projects. Though needed financial flows exceed actual contributions, cumulative green bond issuance since 2007 has hit major milestones, predominantly from the US, China, and Europe. Despite climate exposure, Latin America and Africa lag in issuances. An unorganized green transition could spur instability across prices, populations, and natural resources. Though nascent, standardized green bonds can channel private capital toward climate-resilient, low-carbon development globally. Li et al. (2022) study empirically estimate the relationship between green bond financing and renewable energy indices in OECD countries from 2011 to 2019 using unit root tests, FMOLS, and DOLS techniques. It finds green bond financing has significant positive effects on renewable energy indices. Green bonds increased renewable energy efficiency by 9.4% in OECD countries over the sample period. The results suggest efficient renewable energy regulation can convert financial uncertainty into opportunities. Investing in renewable stocks can help diversify portfolios. The study provides implications for enhancing renewable energy generation and efficiency through alternative sources.

Additionally, there are studies that analyze the emerging green bond market and its potential to advance sustainability. Citing a few, Silva's (2021) study examines the global green bond landscape, emphasizing the need to adapt issuance to local contexts, employ risk mitigation tactics, build capacities, and ensure transparency. Shakizada et al.'s (2021) study examines the growing popularity of green bonds among investors. It outlines the features of green bonds and studies their development in Europe. Figures depict the global distribution of green bonds in 2018, the types of European green bond issuers in 2019, and green bond issuance volumes in select European countries in early 2020. The analysis highlights the rapid expansion of the European green bond market driven by increasing investor demand for sustainable investments. Cortellini et al. (2021) highlight green bonds' appeal to environmentally conscious investors. Flammer (2021) finds investors respond positively to corporate green bond issuance, suggesting a signaling effect. MacAskill et al. (2021) explore the "green premium" for bonds with strong green credentials. These studies emphasize green bonds' growing role in sustainable finance. Gibon et al.'s (2020) study uses life cycle assessment (LCA) to estimate the environmental impacts of renewable energy green bonds from the European Investment Bank. It finds wide variation in avoided greenhouse gas emissions, indicating inefficient fund allocation as impacts are unclear to investors initially. Linking impacts to SDGs reveals trade-offs, with bonds performing well on emissions but negatively on waste or land use. While LCA for green bonds has added costs versus current reporting, existing LCA infrastructure can provide necessary tools as EU taxonomy and impact reporting standards evolve. Overall, LCA enables robust, consistent measurement of green bonds' sustainability.

There are studies which have analyzed the impact of green bond financing post-Paris Agreement as well, citing a few of them, Tolliver et al.'s (2020) study assessed how countries' Paris Agreement commitments affect green bond financing for renewable energy. Using a difference-in-differences analysis of $25 billion in green bond allocations across 66 countries from 2008 to 2017, it found more robust climate commitments strongly increased renewable energy investments through green bonds after 2015. The results suggest climate pledges can drive emissions reductions by spurring greater green bond financing for renewable energy projects critical for meeting emissions targets. Fatica and Panzica's (2020) study investigates whether corporate green bond issuance reduces emissions, using matched bond-issuer data. Comparing green issuers to conventional issuers with similar finances and environmental ratings, green bonds are associated with decreased asset carbon intensity, especially for project bonds without refinancing. Emissions reductions are more significant and lasting for externally reviewed bonds and post-Paris Agreement bonds. The results indicate green bonds can effectively engage issuers to lower emissions through new climate-friendly projects.

Agliardi and Agliardi's (2019) study develops an economic model to analyze the pricing and yield dynamics of green bonds compared to conventional bonds. The study aims to explain the "greenium" yield difference and examine what drives green bond value, whether they improve issuer credit quality, and if they are cost-effective for sustainable investment funding. The model also assesses the impact of investor environmental preferences on portfolio choices and credit quality could reduce capital costs for green bond issuers, and government incentives combined with greater investor green awareness can help scale up the green bond market. Banerjee's (2019) study examines how climate bonds can help bridge the climate finance gap to meet Paris Agreement goals and advance sustainable development. Although interest is growing among investors to consider environmental values, many hesitate due to lack of universal frameworks and guidelines for green bonds. The chapter suggests that green bonds can channel needed capital to environmentally friendly projects. It provides a framework to overcome barriers hindering robust climate bond markets in emerging economies. Mobilizing this financial tool is critical for transitioning to a sustainable global economy. Kiseleva's (2019) study examines the impact of green bonds as a new investment tool on emerging financial markets. Using Environmental Finance's database, it analyzes green bond volume, issuing countries, exchanges, currencies, and other indicators.

The results show green bonds can communicate issuers' sustainability priorities and demonstrate risk management and long-term thinking. The study finds significant green bond growth is tied to legislative initiatives in major financial markets. It estimates Russia's lost benefits from lacking green bond issuance.

There are research that demonstrates green bonds' potential for signaling sustainability commitments and driving growth in emerging markets. Banga's (2019) study discusses the ability of green bonds to mobilize climate funding in emerging economies, though barriers like inadequate frameworks and high expenses need addressing. Ng's (2018) study explores how national policies and market forces enable emerging financial centers to develop green financing systems. Using Hong Kong as a case study, it suggests top-down policy legitimacy and market-based financing can mutually reinforce each other. Through multiple case studies of large, listed companies, it reveals varied approaches to risk, accounting, and green bond issuance. The study proposes a framework on policy-market convergence toward robust green financing systems and discusses implications for sustainability controls. Horsch and Richter's (2017) study examine green bonds as a structured finance tool to attract private and institutional investment for closing the clean energy funding gap. By analyzing market-labeled green bonds, it identifies issuance patterns, issuers, and market dynamics. Using monthly bond price data, the drivers of green bond prices and correlations with other assets are assessed. The mixed risk-return findings suggest that non-economic factors currently drive green bond investments. Flaherty and Semmler's (2016) study build on Sachs' proposal for intergenerational burden sharing of climate action costs. It suggests green bonds allow current generations to fund immediate mitigation investments, with future generations repaying the debt from reduced damages. Using a continuous time overlapping generations model, it shows climate bonds issued now can be repaid sustainably within a finite horizon. Numerous studies highlight the influential role of regulatory institutions in reducing carbon dioxide emissions. Abbas et al. (2021) empirically analyze the nexus between FDI inflow, institutional quality, and carbon dioxide emission in Asian countries. Their findings suggest that energy consumption harms the environment in the long run, whereas greenhouse gases are significantly reduced in the presence of environmental quality regulations. A similar study conducted by Sarkodie and Adams (2018) highlighted in their research work that effective political institutions positively decrease carbon dioxide emissions in South Africa, thus improving environmental quality. Other studies that also indicate institutional quality positively improves the environment are conducted by (Ibrahim and Law, 2016; Godil et al., 2020).

Section A: Finance for Sustainability

It is true to argue that when it comes to guiding the world toward sustainability, finance is essential (Jeucken, 2010). Our world is facing numerous challenges (Rogers & Tough, 1996). However, with the world facing more and more difficult environmental and social issues, financial systems must be aligned with sustainable goals in order to effect positive change. This combination of sustainability and finance is not just a fad; it is a requirement for maintaining long-term prosperity and protecting the environment (Dixon, 2019). In addition, financial institutions are reassessing their operations in order to be in line with sustainability objectives. Investment firms and banks are incorporating ESG metrics into their risk assessment models, integrating sustainability into their core strategies, and creating frameworks for sustainable finance in order to meet the growing demand from investors for ethical investments. This change helps to reduce the risks associated with social and environmental factors, which in turn promotes long-term financial stability.

The role that financial literacy plays in advancing sustainability cannot be emphasized (Lusardi, 2008). People can be empowered to make decisions that support sustainability goals by learning about sustainable investment options, responsible financial practices, and the environmental impact of their financial decisions. This education should be provided to a range of audiences, from individual consumers to corporate executives, in order to create a shared understanding of the role that finance plays in constructing a sustainable future.

Collaboration among stakeholders can lead to the development of creative financial mechanisms and standards that further promote sustainability across sectors (Louman et al., 2020). Policymakers must create regulatory environments that are supportive of sustainable finance while guaranteeing transparency and accountability. Collaboration among governments, financial institutions, businesses, and civil society is also essential. On the other hand, obstacles still stand in the way of attaining finance for sustainability. One such obstacle is the requirement for standardized metrics and reporting frameworks in order to precisely evaluate and contrast the sustainability performance of businesses and investments. Creating generally recognized standards can improve openness and enable improved decision-making in the financial industry. Furthermore, getting past short-term financial incentives is still a challenge. To strike a balance between short-term financial gains and long-term sustainability goals, market players must adopt a new way of thinking that values sustainable practices in producing long-term social and economic benefits. Yes, finance is a powerful tool that can help shape a sustainable future. It is about more than just profits; it is about people and the planet. Putting money into sustainable ventures encourages innovation and helps companies adopt responsible practices. It is not just a business opportunity but also a moral imperative to incorporate sustainability into financial systems. In doing so, we are protecting the environment, building resilience, and promoting equity. Incorporating sustainability benefits entire communities and guarantees a more equitable allocation of resources and opportunities.

Finance can change people's lives (Johnson et al., 2005). Increasing financial literacy gives people the information they need to make sustainable decisions.

It is about giving everyone, from all walks of life, the ability to invest in a future that is both environmentally and financially sound. Working together is essential to increasing the impact of sustainable finance. By bringing together governments, corporations, financial institutions, and communities, we can establish guidelines, impose rules, and motivate collective action toward a common objective of sustainability. Creating innovative financial tools, supporting environmentally friendly technology, and promoting sustainable initiatives are crucial measures to ensure that finance serves as a positive force, effectively balancing economic growth with ecological responsibility (Schmidheiny & Zorraquin, 1996).

A brighter, more prosperous future is possible when finance and sustainability come together. This is a journey that calls for dedication, creativity, and a common vision. As we travel this path, it is important to keep in mind that every financial decision we make today shapes the world we live in tomorrow. Finance can be a catalyst for positive change when it is applied with commitment and teamwork, leading us toward a future where prosperity and environmental stewardship coexist peacefully.

Section B: Essence of Green Bond Financing in Current Era

Green bonds are specifically designated to fund projects that have positive environmental impacts, like renewable energy, clean transportation, sustainable agriculture, and more (Tolliver et al., 2019; Zhao et al., 2022). They play a crucial role in addressing climate change by channeling investments toward initiatives that promote sustainability and reduce carbon footprints (Alamgir & Cheng, 2023). Green bond financing is an effective financial tool that aims to back environmental projects and attract investments from environmentally conscious investors. Nowadays, the primary goal of green bonds, which are issued by governments, businesses, or financial institutions, is to achieve a low-carbon and sustainable economy by raising capital and also give long-run returns to the investors (Sartzetakis, 2021). The money raised from the sale of green bonds is only used for projects that satisfy certain environmental requirements; this explicit earmarking guarantees accountability and transparency in the use of funds, assuring investors about the environmental impact of their investments (Rouhelo & Kepsu, 2022).

The demand for green bonds has been driven by institutional investors, pension funds, and even retail investors seeking opportunities to align their investment portfolios with sustainability goals. The ability of green bond financing to draw in a wide range of investors is one of its main advantages. Both conventional and environmentally concerned investors are attracted to these bonds due to their potential to generate competitive financial returns and good environmental impacts (Bhutta et al., 2022).

Green bonds are an appealing investment option because they have the dual benefit of supporting sustainable development and earning a financial return. Companies and governments that demonstrate a dedication to sustainability by issuing green bonds can enhance their reputation within the investing industry and among consumers. This can result in enhanced financial accessibility and enhanced brand reputation, which can be especially beneficial in the current environmentally aware market (Alsayegh et al., 2020). Furthermore, green bonds have the potential to enhance the image of the issuer and attract fresh investors.

The green bond market is not without its challenges, though. One major issue is the lack of universally accepted standards and frameworks (Weber & Saravade, 2019). Although many organizations and initiatives offer principles and guidelines for the issuance of green bonds, there is no universally accepted standard. This can cause confusion and lead to different interpretations of what constitutes a green project, which could result in green-washing—the practice of labeling projects as green even though they have minimal environmental benefits. Furthermore, there are still issues with tracking and verifying the environmental impact of funded projects. Investors need to be assured that projects financed by green bonds actually contribute to environmental sustainability. However, it is true to argue that transparency and credibility must be ensured through robust reporting and verification mechanisms, which in turn keeps investor confidence in the market (Naveed et al., 2021). But even with these obstacles, there is no denying the potential impact of green bonds. Their ability to combine financial returns with positive environmental change draws investors and propels real progress in sustainability initiatives, this two-fold advantage positions green bonds as a critical driver in our quest for a more sustainable world. The attraction of green bonds is not only their high yield on investment but also their ability to bring about tangible transformations (Gyura, 2020). Through allocating funds to initiatives that reduce greenhouse gas emissions, support renewable energy sources, and advance environmentally friendly infrastructure, these bonds act as a pivot in the shift to a more sustainable global economy (Figure 7.1).

Section C: Economics, Social, and Governance Readiness

A nation's preparedness in these areas frequently determines its capacity to navigate challenges, foster growth, and sustain progress. Thus, economic, social, and governance readiness are crucial pillars that support the stability, development, and resilience of nations in a rapidly evolving global landscape. Let us delve into each dimension to understand their significance and interplay.

Economic Readiness: This relates to a nation's ability to generate new ideas, adjust to changes, and prosper in the worldwide economy. It encompasses elements like commercial activities, infrastructure construction, financial strategies, and technical progress. An economically prepared nation has robust institutions facilitating investment, innovation, and corporate expansion. Furthermore, it is also referred as economic assets, such as roads, railways and airports and all other assets which are directly or indirectly under the control of the government (Moteff et al., 2004). An adequate infrastructure, including

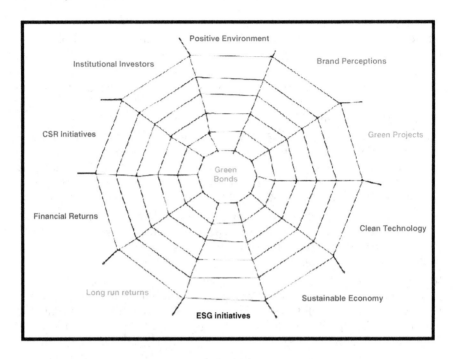

Figure 7.1 Essence of green bond financing
Source: Author's own

energy, digital, transportation, and communication, is the fundamental basis for economic progress. Investments in these sectors enhance overall economic efficiency, productivity, and interconnectedness. Economic diversification refers to expanding economic activity in producing and distributing commodities and services. While it may not directly result in increased output, broadening the financial foundation of countries can promote their stabilization. Economic diversification should be examined through the lens of sustainable development to guarantee the enduring stability of the economy (Anyaehie & Areji, 2015). Countries that place a high priority on R&D and technological developments have an advantage in the international marketplace. Innovation promotes economic growth, productivity gains, and advancement. A strong financial system is essential for economic preparedness because it promotes investment, entrepreneurship, and financial inclusion for all societal groups. It also guarantees stability and credit availability.

Social Readiness: This refers to a country's ability to guarantee the health, equality, and cohesiveness of its citizens. It includes social safety nets, healthcare, education, and cultural diversity. An adept and well-informed labor force fosters economic expansion and ingenuity. Access to a reasonably priced, superior education equips individuals with the necessary skills to make a substantial economic impact. Human development has a significant impact on economic progress. Every component of human progress, in particular, is expected to have a different effect on economic growth. For example, education significantly impacts labor productivity; furthermore, labor productivity positively impacts economic growth in the long run. On the other hand, higher education directly impacts the economic growth process via increased productivity and creativity of local companies (Foster & Rosenzweig, 1995. The education of managers and business executives is bound to influence and impact business performance in the effective use of business capital and policies. Besides this, the volume of domestic and foreign investment directly impacts rates of total factor productivity, which will undoubtedly be higher when the education level of involved labor is higher . In addition to directly impacting economic growth, human capital can help obtain new and foreign knowledge and is a critical factor in whether positive FDI spillovers will occur. As a result, human capital plays a vital role in facilitating international technology transfer from innovative to copycat countries, allowing these countries to catch up to industrialized countries. Similarly, the health of involved labor has shown favorable implications for economic growth. Behrman and Wolfe (1987) endorsed in their research work that education and health may have substantial indirect effects on economic growth due to their effects on income distribution, with education having an even more substantial impact due to its impact on health. Furthermore, people from developing countries are better able to seek economic opportunities once education and health improve. Healthcare facilities that are easily reachable contribute to an efficient workforce and the overall welfare of society. A robust healthcare system ensures the welfare of residents and reduces the economic strain caused by health-related issues. Strong social safety nets, such as welfare payments, pensions, and unemployment insurance, aid marginalized populations and foster stability and social unity. Promoting tolerance, understanding, and peace among different groups, and accepting diversity and fostering inclusion throughout society, contributes to enhancing social preparedness.

Governance Readiness: An effectively managed nation creates an environment conducive to economic advancement, social unity, and stability. Preparedness for effective governance: The pillars of governance preparation include efficient institutions, transparent policies, adherence to the rule of law, and accountability. A society benefits from having strong legal frameworks and ensuring adherence to the rule of law, since this promotes predictability, stability, and transparency. Clear and explicit regulations foster trust among the general public and investors. Transparent governance methods cultivate trust between the government and its stakeholders. Efficient governance requires the implementation of accountability protocols and robust measures to mitigate corruption. Countries with robust political systems are more capable of implementing enduring programs and attracting investments. Political stability is a crucial prerequisite for achieving long-term and sustained economic expansion. Inclusive governance involves actively including individuals in decision-making processes to ensure that policies accurately reflect the needs and objectives of the population.

Concurrently, the state of governance preparation is critical, guaranteeing efficient institutions, accountability, and openness. Robust governance frameworks build public-authority confidence, facilitating responsive decision-making and effective resource distribution. These factors are interconnected; social inclusivity is necessary for a thriving economy to be sustainable, and good governance connects these domains. Governments, businesses, and communities must work together to share resources, knowledge, and viewpoints; businesses must conduct themselves morally, and communities must take an active role in creating policies that support these factors.

They work together to create a society that is resilient and able to take advantage of opportunities as well as overcome obstacles. This reinforces the foundation for a prosperous, equitable, and sustainable future and makes sure that no one is left behind in the pursuit of progress. Considering the fact, responsible investment thus eco-friendly is a crucial element of sustainable finance. Investors now take into account ESG aspects when making investment decisions, enabling them to provide resources to firms that promote sustainable practices. This signifies a shift away from the traditional focus solely on financial profits to a more inclusive evaluation of a company's influence on society and the environment.

Section D: Evolutionary Perspective—Nexus between Green Bond Financing and ESG Readiness

From an evolutionary standpoint, the increasing emphasis on ESG criteria has led to the emergence of green bond financing as a crucial financial tool. The driving force behind this evolution has been the pressing need to address environmental issues while satisfying the market for sustainable investment options. Fundamentally, green bonds are a type of financial instrument intended to raise funds expressly for eco-friendly projects. They are based on the idea of sustainable finance and are in line with the overarching objective of moving toward an economy that is both low-carbon and climate-resilient. The World Bank issued the first green bond in the early 2000s, which was a landmark event in the history of sustainable finance.

Evolutionary speaking, the rise in green bond financing can be attributed to the increasing awareness of environmental risks around the world and the urgency of taking immediate action. As investors' perceptions of ESG factors become more and more important when making investment decisions, the market for sustainable financial instruments grows. Green bonds are a reflection of this shift in investor sentiment toward ethical and responsible investing. ESG readiness is a key factor in determining how green bond financing develops. Organizations that want to issue green bonds have to show that they have a strong ESG framework in place, which guarantees accountability, transparency, and adherence to environmental standards. Investors then examine these elements to determine the legitimacy and veracity of green bond offerings. As a result, the growth of the green bond market and ESG readiness are mutually dependent (Figure 7.2).

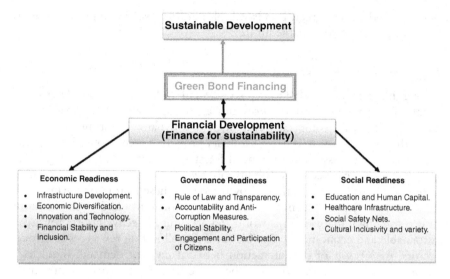

Figure 7.2 Evolutionary perspective

Source: Author's own

Initiatives like the Green Bond Principles and the Climate Bonds Initiative have provided guidelines and certifications, establishing benchmarks for green bond issuers. These frameworks help to standardize green bond practices, enhance market integrity, and bolster investor confidence. Moreover, regulatory frameworks and industry standards have evolved to support the growth of green bond financing. Even with its steady upward trajectory, the development of green bond financing is confronted with persistent obstacles. One of these is the requirement for uniform and widely recognized definitions and standards for what qualifies as a "green" project. Inconsistencies in standards and interpretations of green projects can cause confusion, which makes it more difficult for investors to evaluate the actual environmental impact of these investments.

Furthermore, there is an ongoing examination of the viability and implications of financing for green bonds. Although the market has experienced significant expansion, there is an ongoing search for greater issue volumes in order to adequately address urgent environmental issues. Future prospects for green bond financing indicate that the growing emphasis on sustainability and the urgent need to address climate change will only serve to accelerate this evolution. As ESG factors become increasingly ingrained in investment strategies, green bonds will be increasingly important in directing capital toward environmentally beneficial projects. Finally, the evolution of green bond financing can be seen as a reflection of the evolution of sustainable finance, driven by the interaction of investor demand, regulatory frameworks, ESG readiness, and the need to address environmental challenges. As the market develops and grows, green bonds will play an increasingly important role in promoting a more sustainable future.

Conclusion and Policies

Strong integration of economic, social, and political systems determines a nation's capacity to endure crises and grow sustainably. The capacity of a nation to deal with complexity and adapt to a dynamic environment is built upon these foundations. The extraordinary growth of green bonds is not without its challenges; issues like the need for standardization and effect verification remain unresolved. The validity of these financial instruments, such as green bonds will be strengthened by removing these restrictions, which will help the maintenance of investor trust and transparency and to invest more in eco-friendly initiatives. This world requires our collective efforts toward a sustainable and economically feasible future by allocating resources to critical sectors. As a result of the interaction between investor demand, regulatory frameworks, ESG preparation, and the desire to address environmental challenges, green bond financing has emerged as a kind of sustainable finance. As the green bond market grows and changes, it will play an ever-larger role in promoting a future that is less harmful to the environment.

References

Abbas, H. S. M., Xu, X., & Sun, C. (2021). Role of foreign direct investment interaction to energy consumption and institutional governance in sustainable GHG emission reduction. *Environmental Science and Pollution Research*, *28*(40), 56808–56821.

Agliardi, Elettra, and Rossella Agliardi. 'Financing Environmentally-Sustainable Projects with Green Bonds'. *Environment and Development Economics*, vol. 24, no. 6, Dec. 2019, pp. 608–623.

Alamgir, Muhammad, and Ming-Chang, Cheng. 'Do Green Bonds Play a Role in Achieving Sustainability?'. *Sustainability*, vol. 15, no. 13, 2023, p. 10177.

Alsayegh, Maha Faisal, Rashidah Abdul Rahman, and Saeid Homayoun. 'Corporate Economic, Environmental, and Social Sustainability Performance Transformation through ESG Disclosure'. *Sustainability*, vol. 12, no. 9, 2020, p. 3910.

Anyaehie, Michael Chugozie, and Anthony Chukwudi Areji. 'Economic Diversification for Sustainable Development in Nigeria'. *Open Journal of Political Science*, vol. 5, no. 2, 2015, p. 87.

Banerjee, Arindam. 'Financing the Climate Change through Green (Climate Sustainable) Bonds'. 2019 Advances in Science and Engineering Technology International Conferences (ASET), IEEE, 2019, pp. 1–4.

Banga, J. (2019). The green bond market: a potential source of climate finance for developing countries. *Journal of Sustainable Finance & Investment*, *9*(1), 17–32.

Bhutta, Umair Saeed, Adeel, Tariq, Muhammad, Farrukh, Ali, Raza, and Muhammad Khalid, Iqbal. 'Green Bonds for Sustainable Development: Review of Literature on Development and Impact of Green Bonds'. *Technological Forecasting and Social Change*, vol. 175, 2022, p. 121378.

Bohner, Santiago. 'Green Bonds: Quick Insight into One of the Most Implemented Sustainable Debt Instrument to Tackle Climate Change'. *Ciencias Administrativas*, Dec. 2022, p. 117.

Cortellini, Giuseppe, and Ida Claudia Panetta. 'Green Bond: A Systematic Literature Review for Future Research Agendas'. *Journal of Risk and Financial Management*, vol. 14, no. 12, Dec. 2021, p. 589.

Dixon, F. (2019). Sustainable Finance. *Cadmus*, vol. 4, no. 1, 2019, pp. 47–64.

Fatica, Serena, and Roberto Panzica. 'Green Bonds as a Tool against Climate Change?' *SSRN Electronic Journal*, 2020.

Foster, A. D., & Rosenzweig, M. R. (1995). Learning by doing and learning from others: Human capital and technical change in agriculture. *Journal of political Economy*, *103*(6), pp. 1176–1209.

Flaherty, Michael, and Willi Semmler. 'Financing Climate Policies through Climate Bonds A Three Stage Model and Empirics'. *SSRN Electronic Journal*, 2016.

Flammer, Caroline. 'Corporate Green Bonds'. *Journal of Financial Economics*, vol. 142, no. 2, Nov. 2021, pp. 499–516.

Gibon, Thomas, et al. 'Shades of Green: Life Cycle Assessment of Renewable Energy Projects Financed through Green Bonds'. *Environmental Research Letters*, vol. 15, no. 10, Oct. 2020, p. 104045.

Gyura, Gabor. 'Green Bonds and Green Bond Funds: The Quest for the Real Impact'. *The Journal of Alternative Investments*, vol. 23, no. 1, 2020, pp. 71–79.

Horsch, Andreas, and Sylvia Richter. 'Climate Change Driving Financial Innovation: The Case of Green Bonds'. *The Journal of Structured Finance*, vol. 23, no. 1, Apr. 2017, pp. 79–90.

Ibrahim, M. H., & Law, S. H. (2016). Institutional quality and CO2 emission–trade relations: evidence from S ub-S aharan A frica. *South African Journal of Economics*, *84*(2), pp. 323–340.

Jeucken, Marcel. *Sustainable Finance and Banking: The Financial Sector and the Future of the Planet*. Routledge, 2010.

Johnson, Susan, David, Hulme, and Orlanda Ruthven. *Finance and Poor People's Livelihoods* (pp. 277–303). Edward Elgar, 2005.

Kiseleva, Elena. 'Green Bonds as a Tool for Sustainable Development on Emerging Markets'. *SSRN Electronic Journal*, 2019.

Khan, I., Shah, D., & Shah, S. S. (2021). COVID-19 pandemic and its positive impacts on environment: an updated review. *International Journal of Environmental Science and Technology*, *18*, pp. 521–530.

Li, Na, et al. 'Impact of Financial Inclusion and Green Bond Financing for Renewable Energy Mix: Implications for Financial Development in OECD Economies'. *Environmental Science and Pollution Research*, vol. 29, no. 17, Apr. 2022, pp. 25544–25555.

Louman, Bas, Alexandre Meybeck, Gerhard Mulder, Michael Brady, L. Fremy, H. Savenije, V. Gitz, and E. Trines. *Innovative Finance for Sustainable Landscapes* (Vol. 7). CIFOR, 2020.

Lusardi, Annamaria. *Household Saving Behavior: The Role of Financial Literacy, Information, and Financial Education Programs* (No. w13824). National Bureau of Economic Research, 2008.

MacAskill, S., et al. 'Is There a Green Premium in the Green Bond Market? Systematic Literature Review Revealing Premium Determinants'. *Journal of Cleaner Production*, vol. 280, Jan. 2021, p. 124491.

Moteff, John. D., Paul, Parfomak, and Resources, Science, and Industry Division. (2004, October). Critical Infrastructure and Key Assets: Definition and Identification. Washington: Congressional Research Service, Library of Congress.

Naveed, Muhammad, Maya F., Farah, and Muhammad Junaid Shahid Hasni. 'The Transformative Role of Firm Information Transparency in Triggering Retail Investor's Perceived Financial Well-Being'. *International Journal of Bank Marketing*, vol. 39, no. 7, 2021, pp. 1091–1113.

Ng, Artie W. 'From Sustainability Accounting to a Green Financing System: Institutional Legitimacy and Market Heterogeneity in a Global Financial Centre'. *Journal of Cleaner Production*, vol. 195, Sept. 2018, pp. 585–592.

Nguyen, Anh Huu, et al. 'The Development of Green Bond in Developing Countries: Insights from Southeast Asia Market Participants'. *The European Journal of Development Research*, vol. 35, no. 1, Feb. 2023, pp. 196–218.

Ning, Yiyi, et al. 'Green Bond as a New Determinant of Sustainable Green Financing, Energy Efficiency Investment, and Economic Growth: A Global Perspective'. *Environmental Science and Pollution Research*, vol. 30, no. 22, Jan. 2022, pp. 61324–61339.

Nurgaliyeva, Aliya Miyazhdenovna, et al. 'Opportunities for Using Green Bonds to Finance Environmental Projects in Developing Countries: Experience of the Republic of Kazakhstan'. *Journal of Environmental Management and Tourism*, vol. 13, no. 7, Dec. 2022, p. 1918.

Ozcan, B., Ulucak, R., & Dogan, E. (2019). Analyzing long lasting effects of environmental policies: evidence from low, middle and high income economies. *Sustainable Cities and Society*, *44*, pp. 130–143.

Shakizada, Niyazbekova, et al. '"Green" Bonds - A Tool for Financing "Green" Projects in Countries'. E3S Web of Conferences, edited by V. Breskich and S. Uvarova, vol. 244, 2021, p. 10060.

Rogers, Martha, and Allen Tough. 'Facing the Future Is not for Wimps'. *Futures*, vol. 28, no. 5, 1996, pp. 491–496.

Rouhelo, Kiia, and Mikko Kepsu. Are Green Bonds Delivering on Their Green Promise? 2022.

Sachs, J. D., & Sachs, L. E. (2021). Business alignment for the "Decade of Action". Journal of International Business Policy, 4(1), 22–27.

Sarkodie, S. A., & Adams, S. (2018). Renewable energy, nuclear energy, and environmental pollution: accounting for political institutional quality in South Africa. *Science of the total environment*, *643*, 1590–1601.

Sartzetakis, Eftichios S. 'Green Bonds as an Instrument to Finance Low Carbon Transition'. *Economic Change and Restructuring*, vol. 54, no. 3, 2021, pp. 755–779.

Schmidheiny, Stephan, and Federico J. Zorraquin. *Financing Change: The Financial Community, Eco-efficiency, and Sustainable Development*. MIT press, 1996.

Silva, K. F. D. (2021). Green bonds no Brasil: reação do preço das ações à emissão de títulos verdes.

Tolliver, Clarence, Alexander Ryota Keeley, and Shunsuke Managi. 'Green Bonds for the Paris Agreement and Sustainable Development Goals'. *Environmental Research Letters*, vol. 14, no. 6, 2019, p. 064009.

Tolliver, Clarence, et al. 'Policy Targets behind Green Bonds for Renewable Energy: Do Climate Commitments Matter?' *Technological Forecasting and Social Change*, vol. 157, Aug. 2020, p. 120051.

Tuhkanen, Heidi, and Gregor Vulturius. 'Are Green Bonds Funding the Transition? Investigating the Link between Companies' Climate Targets and Green Debt Financing'. *Journal of Sustainable Finance & Investment*, vol. 12, no. 4, Oct. 2022, pp. 1194–1216.

Weber, Olaf, and Vasundhara Saravade. Green Bonds: Current Development and Their Future. 2019.

Wolfe, B. L., & Behrman, J. R. (1987). Women's schooling and children's health: Are the effects robust with adult sibling control for the women's childhood background?. *Journal of health Economics*, 6(3), pp. 239–254.

Zhang, YaFei, and Muhammad Umair. 'Examining the Interconnectedness of Green Finance: An Analysis of Dynamic Spillover Effects among Green Bonds, Renewable Energy, and Carbon Markets'. *Environmental Science and Pollution Research*, vol. 30, no. 31, June 2023, pp. 77605–77621

Zhao, Linhai, Ka Yin, Chau, Trung Kien, Tran, Muhammad, Sadiq, Nguyen Thi My, Xuyen, and Thi Thu Hien, Phan. 'Enhancing Green Economic Recovery through Green Bonds Financing and Energy Efficiency Investments'. *Economic Analysis and Policy*, vol. 76, 2022, 488–501.

8 Optimizing Portfolios with Sustainable Finance

A Comparative Approach to Green Bonds and Green Sukuk

Md. Mahmudul Haque and Muhammad Saeed Meo

Introduction

Bonds are categorized as fixed-income securities because they commit to a sequence of set payments to the security holder at predetermined dates, usually to use a specific calculating process (; Fabozzi, 2006). The other type of fixed-income security is ownership in a corporation for which holders receive fixed dividend payments in preference to common stockholders (Fabozzi, 2006). According to the World Bank, sukuk is an Islamic bond that may provide profits for investors while being consistent with Islamic Shariah law, which forbids interest. A sukuk is a certificate that is sold, and the profits are used to purchase an asset that is owned jointly by the buyer and seller. Green sukuk are sukuk that are used to fund ecologically beneficial activities. For example, support renewable energy generation, waste management, sustainable agriculture, the construction of energy-efficient buildings, natural resource management, or other initiatives that improve the environment or reduce climate change risks. Green bonds are classified bonds that are meant to finance eco-friendly projects that aim to encourage efficient energy usage, pollution control and prevention, greener agriculture, fish farming, forestry, protection of aquatic and terrestrial ecosystems, sustainable transportation, clean water management, and the development of environmentally friendly technology. Green bond financing has a clear goal of solving climate change and is available to anybody who can achieve those goals (Humphries and Humphries ,2015). Additionally, the World Bank says that a green bond is a "plain vanilla fixed income product that provides investors with the opportunity to participate in the financing of green projects that help countries adapt to the effects of climate change and mitigate climate change." The World Bank published its first green bond in November 2008. The International Capital Market Association has formed the Green Bond Principles (GBP), which are created to make it easier for issuers to raise money for projects that have a positive impact on the environment. Environmental issues like climate change, the depletion of natural resources, the extinction of animal species, air, water, and soil pollution are

DOI: 10.4324/9781032686844-8

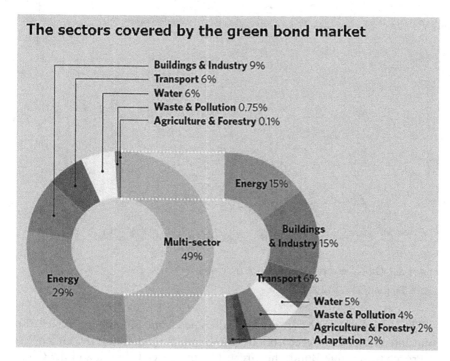

The sectors covered by the green bond market

Buildings & Industry 9%
Transport 6%
Water 6%
Waste & Pollution 0.75%
Agriculture & Forestry 0.1%

Energy 15%

Buildings & Industry 15%

Multi-sector 49%

Transport 6%

Energy 29%

Water 5%
Waste & Pollution 4%
Agriculture & Forestry 2%
Adaptation 2%

Figure 8.1 The sectors covered by the green bond market

Source: World Economic Forum

solved through green bonds. Figure 8.1 shows the sectors that are covered by the green bond market.

The green bond is the first financial product to support corporate governance, which has frequently focused on effects on shareholders. The European Investment Bank released the first green bond in history in 2007 under the title "Climate Awareness Bond." Since then, the green bond market has expanded, and investors' and issuers' assets have become more diverse. The International Capital Market Association released the GBP, which are voluntary procedure rules for issuing green bonds, in 2014 (GBP). Principles are periodically updated with the goal of "supporting the integrity in the green bond market by principles that promote transparency, disclosure, and reporting." The usage of green bonds has some benefits. From the issuer's perspective, it can attract investment for low-carbon assets, indicating the issuer's commitment to sustainability and being green, as well as providing potential access to a larger investor base. Meanwhile, the investor receives transparent information, is protected from environmental and carbon-related risks, and has an improved ESG profile. Specifically, green bonds have become a promising tool to open up green financing and provide money for environmental projects around the globe.

D.Y. Tang, Y. Zhang   *Journal of Corporate Finance xxx (xxxx) xxx–xxx*

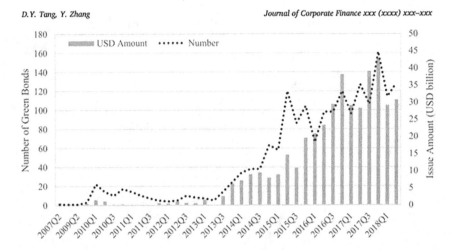

Figure 8.2 Global green bond issuance over time

Source: Tang and Zhang (2020a)

The information used in this article comes from Bloomberg, which lists four different kinds of green bonds: the Green Project Bond, the Green Use of Proceeds Revenue Bond, the Green Use of Proceeds Bond, and the Green Securitized Bond. According to Bloomberg, "green projects" are programs and activities that support climate change or other environmental sustainability goals. Figure 8.2 shows global green bond issuance.

This figure shows the number and USD amount of green bond issuance on a quarterly basis from 2007 to 2018. This figure was merged with the climate bond initiative (CBI) database with the Bloomberg green bond dataset to construct an international green bond dataset. The merged dataset contains 1510 bonds worldwide during the 2007–2018 sample period.

Green Bonds and Green Sukuk-Related Research

The literature review serves as the basis for the structuring of the rest of the work. The approach is discussed in future depth in the following contents in this chapter.

According to Alam et al.(2016), green sukuk are a new asset class that combines Islamic mutual funds, socially responsible investment (SRI), and sukuk. The emergence of Islamic mutual funds has provided Islamic investors with new investing choices on a variety of stock markets. Islamic mutual fund components are selected using qualitative and quantitative filters based on screening procedures comparable to those used for SRI mutual funds. SRI is one sector of financial bonds that focuses on environmental and social welfare crisis protection. On the worldwide SRI market, it is also highly regarded as a green bond that complies with the United Nations' sustainable development goals (SDGs) without sacrificing fiscal revenues. SRI has become one of the most crucial financial challenges. Reflecting the significance of SRI and environmentally friendly financing in particular, interest in "green finance" and the market for green bonds has increased almost exponentially. According to Cheong and Choi (2020), SRI has become one of the most crucial financial challenges. Reflecting the significance of SRI and environmentally friendly financing in particular, interest in "green finance" and the market for green bonds has increased almost exponentially. This rapid market expansion highlights the instrument's significance to SRI and underscores the need for policymakers and regulators to comprehend the extent to which green bond financing impacts market participants, issuers, and stakeholders, as well as the broader economy and the natural environment.

According to Sasongko and Sakti (2020), the green sukuk risks are determined by investors in marketplaces. The study shows that the risks encountered by green sukuk, and nature maintain sustainability in order to break the risk evaluation green sukuk. The classification to accept a green financing contract or a non-green contract is facilitated by the establishment of a green mode of financing. A more balanced economic and financial system, including Islamic investing, could be subsidized in significant part by valued instruments like social-impact sukuk and green sukuk (Delle Foglie, 2020). The green sukuk, which merges the green bond's environmental tenets with the sukuk's financing decisions that complies with Shariah, is a key turning point for Islamic and sustainable finance. The role of green sukuk in realizing the SDGs insists on the implementation of SDG and factors influencing the elements and systematic risk sharing analyses.

Evolution of Sukuk

During the classical Islamic period, a sakk (which is short for sukuk and means "deed" or "instrument") was any document that showed a financial liability. The Organization of the Islamic Conference and the International Islamic Fiqh Academy, an institute for the advanced study of Islam based in Jeddah, Saudi Arabia, issued a statement in 1988 saying that "any combination of assets (or the usufruct of such assets) can be represented in the form of written financial instruments that can be sold at a market price as long as the conditions are met." This statement set the stage for the growth of the sukuk market. The first sukuk was issued in 1990 under the name "Shell MDS Sdn Bhd MYR 125 million Bai Bithaman Ajil," shortly after the Fiqh Academy published the above-mentioned pronouncement. Kumpulan Guthrie Bhd, a Malaysian plantation company, issued the first international sukuk denominated in US dollars in 2001. This sukuk was worth $150 million. In 2001, the first government related entity sukuk was issued by the Bahrain Monetary Authority (currently the Central Bank of Bahrain). Several sovereign countries, including Qatar, Pakistan, and the United Arab Emirates, issued sukuk in Malaysia, garnering international attention for sukuk and paving the way for the market's extraordinary international expansion.

Between late 2007 and early 2009, the sukuk market got a little weaker. This was mostly because of two separate events: the debate over whether some sukuk structures follow Shariah law and the global financial crisis, which caused borrowing costs to go up and investors to lose faith in capital market securities in general.

In the subsequent years, the global sukuk market has rebounded, with issuances exceeding.

$116.4 billion in 2014. The sukuk market is currently a key source of funding for numerous firms, sovereigns, and GREs in Southeast Asia, the Middle East, and North Africa, countries with rapidly expanding Muslim populations. Malaysia continues to dominate the sukuk issuance market, accounting for roughly 60% of all sukuk issuances worldwide. As of November 2014, the global outstanding sukuk market was expected to be $300 billion, up 11.4% from US$269.4 billion at the end of 2013. In addition, the sukuk market has been the second-fastest growing section of Islamic finance, with an average annual growth rate of 41.6% from 2005 to 2012.

In the past, the complexities of structuring sukuk transactions caused many organizations that may have otherwise issued sukuk to continue seeking financing through the bond market or conventional bank loans from European and American banks. In addition, sukuk pricing was typically less advantageous than that of conventional loan and bond markets. However, the credit crunch in Europe and the United States, as well as the Eurozone crisis, altered the environment and prompted an increasing number of firms to turn to the sukuk market.

Global sukuk issuances will likely be primarily driven by continued demand from Islamic investors (particularly Islamic banks) in both the Middle East and Asia. Sukuk have traditionally been acquired by investors who plan to keep the investment certificates until maturity, resulting in a modest degree of performance variation on the secondary market despite widespread global economic turmoil. As the sukuk market matures, potential sukuk issuers are able to obtain more favorable pricing in this market compared to a comparable offering on the conventional bond market. As a result of these and other factors, several market participants anticipate that global sukuk issuances will exceed $250 billion by 2020.

Moreover, sukuk instruments are well-suited to infrastructure finance due to their risk-sharing characteristics, thereby assisting developing nations to cover financing shortfalls. Despite the significant and expanding demand for sukuk, neither supply nor secondary market liquidity have increased. About 0.25% of the global bond market is made up of sukuk. However, because there aren't many Shariah-compliant securities, sukuk are oversubscribed and less liquid because investors choose to "buy and hold" them. Despite the fact that there is limited systematic worldwide research on sukuk features, tenor, and yields, recent sukuk defaults have revealed gaps in understanding the nature of risks connected with sukuk investing. During the global financial crisis, significant sukuk defaults and restructurings exacerbated this, resulting in unexpected outcomes for investors.

Potential of Green Sukuk

The rapidly expanding global sukuk market is perfectly adapted to channel cash to fund renewable energy and ecologically friendly projects in developed Islamic finance territories as well as on western coasts. Sukuk are tradable Islamic financial instruments that can be issued by both sovereigns and corporations to fund significant infrastructure development projects. Sukuk are similar to conventional bonds, but they have Shariah-compliant elements related to Islamic banking and finance. Sukuk are distinguished by the fact that they grant holders ownership rights in underlying assets or earnings from such assets.

Growing global concerns for environment-friendly and sustainable development have led to a growing interest in initiatives that go by the name "green projects." The World Bank, United Nations environmental efforts, and other international organizations have all advocated for a cleaner and more sustainable global ecosystem. Along with this, there was a larger demand for increased access to financing to undertake such green projects. The World Bank pioneered the concept of "green bonds" in 2008, providing investors with a new approach to supporting clean energy and other low-carbon initiatives. Since then, interest in financial instruments backing green initiatives has grown among both issuers and investors. As a result, Islamic finance offers a significant opportunity to create instruments that can support the global surge in demand to launch green initiatives. Islamic finance also has synergies with the concept of sustainability and fits well with its ethical criteria. As a result, environmental conservation fits well with the overarching goals of Islamic finance, which strive to improve society's overall well-being.

Green sukuk are Shariah-compliant investments in renewable energy and other environmental assets, and they satisfy Shariah's concern with environmental protection. Green sukuk proceeds may be used to finance development or the payment of a government-granted green subsidy. As illustrated in Figure 8.3, the structure of green sukuk incorporates the securitization of future revenue cash flows from ring-fenced projects or assets with particular conditions attached.

The majority of the funds raised through sukuk issuances are used towards Shariah-compliant green initiatives. After deducting the expenses of the special purpose vehicle (SPV), the sukuk investors receive the remaining portfolio profits. The Obligor additionally agrees to purchase the portfolio from the special purpose vehicle at maturity. The purchase price will be equal to the sum of the total nominal amount of trust certificates and unpaid accrued distributions.

Green sukuk can be backed by assets like solar parks, biogas plants, wind farms, big plans to make energy use more efficient, renewable transmission

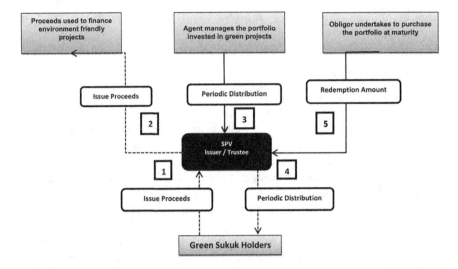

Figure 8.3 Green sukuk structure

and infrastructure, electric cars, and light rail, as described by limate bond standards certification.

Role of Green Sukuk

Sukuk is an interest-free Islamic financial product that delivers profits for investors without violating the norms of Shariah law. Green sukuk adheres to the green framework, which requires the use of the issuance proceeds, a second opinion report or "green certification" by an independent reviewer, and a post-issuance impact report that details the use of the funds and the environmental impact accomplished. Additionally, the green sukuk is attractive to a broad range of investors, including Shariah-compliant investors. The green sukuk must also adhere to specific issuing procedures. As indicated in Figure 8.4, nine (9) phases should serve as a guideline for the issuance. The total amount of green sukuk issued in 2019 is $3.5 billion. The global issuance of green sukuk in 2020 was $ 6.1 billion. This indicates a 74% increase in interest in the green initiative. The issuers were required to use green sukuk to raise roughly four different currencies (EUR, IDR, MYR, and USD). It is one of the SRIs that could help advance the Islamic financial sector.

In comparison to other asset classes, the green sukuk market is relatively tiny and illiquid due to its restricted supply. Investors prefer to hold onto their green sukuk because they believe they will be unable to replace any they sell. Using Islamic financial tools, green sukuk addresses environmental and climate change issues. This concept should be the government's top priority in order to justify the perfect green project that will benefit the people and preserve the environment. According to Morea and Poggi, the institution that issues a green sukuk and successfully reduces government-mandated GHG emissions should be handsomely rewarded. Green sukuk can serve as a bridge

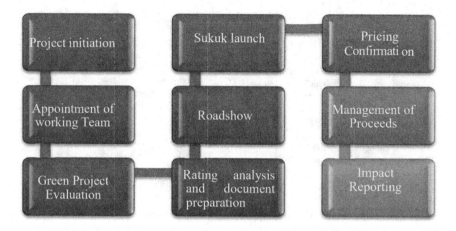

Figure 8.4 Green sukuk issuance process in Malaysia
Source: World Bank (2020)

between an organization in need of financing and those interested in constructing green infrastructure or launching green initiatives.

In Malaysia, the issuance of green sukuk is classified into numerous categories, including renewable energy and green building. Renewable energy, energy efficiency, pollution prevention and control, environmentally sustainable management of living natural resources and land use, terrestrial and aquatic biodiversity conservation, clean transportation, sustainable water, and wastewater management, climate change adaptation, ecoefficient production technologies, green building with recognized standards and certification, and ecoefficient production technologies. The qualifying green sectors of Indonesia and Malaysia are compared in Figure 8.5.

Green projects that qualify for green sukuk issuance vary considerably. With the exception of Aquatic Biodiversity Control, Green Tourism, Pollution Control, and Prevention Control, most of the sectors are identical. According to the Securities Commission (SC), the purpose of green sukuk is to encourage and inspire more issuers to finance green, social, and sustainability projects using sukuk issued under the Securities Commission's Sustainable Responsible Index (SRIN) Sukuk Framework or bonds issued in Malaysia under the ASEAN Green, Social, and Sustainability Bond Standard. Securities Commission offers an incentive consisting of five years of income tax exemption, which claims the sum of 90% of actual external review costs up to a maximum of RM300,000.

Green Sukuk and Socially Responsible Investment

Green sukuk are Shariah-compliant investment instruments that support environmental activities. Financial bonds that deal with protecting the environment and solving social welfare problems are known as SRI instruments. Additionally, it is well-known as a green bond in the worldwide SRI market,

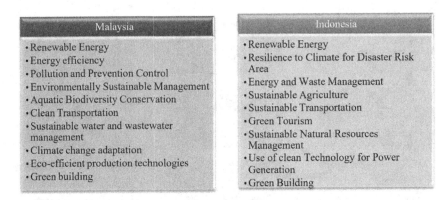

Malaysia	Indonesia
• Renewable Energy	• Renewable Energy
• Energy efficiency	• Resilience to Climate for Disaster Risk Area
• Pollution and Prevention Control	• Energy and Waste Management
• Environmentally Sustainable Management	• Sustainable Agriculture
• Aquatic Biodiversity Conservation	• Sustainable Transportation
• Clean Transportation	• Green Tourism
• Sustainable water and wastewater management	• Sustainable Natural Resources Management
• Climate change adaptation	• Use of clean Technology for Power Generation
• Eco-efficient production technologies	• Green Building
• Green building	

Figure 8.5 Malaysia and Indonesia qualifying green sectors

Source: Abubakar and Handayani (2020) and World Bank (2020)

which complies with the goals of the SDGs without sacrificing fiscal revenues (The World Bank, 2017). It has been observed that SRI sukuk, which also has great potential in Malaysia, has developed as a significant stream of investment options on the international financial markets. In addition to their focus on straightforward financial gains, SRI and Islamic finance both stick to a universal concept that protects investors' ethical code and promotes socio-economic development. These investors are willing to sacrifice their profits for the benefit of societal welfare in order to objectively evaluate their conventional risks and benefits (The World Bank, 2017).

Relationship between Islamic Financial Product (Sukuk) and Socially Responsible Investment

According to Dusuki and Abdullah (2007), the Shariah promotes the well-being of all humans by protecting their money (nasl), intellect ('aql), human self (din), and human self (nafs) (mal). Islamic finance encourages investors to share risks and benefits equally and prohibits all forms of risky investments. Similarly, SRI investors care about both their social and financial returns. The majority of SRI products are considered as equity investments as opposed to fixed-income investments. Sukuk has SRI traits implanted into it. Five fundamental principles underlie Islamic finance are the prohibition of usury (Riba), speculation (Maysir), excess uncertainty (Gharar), and investing in prohibited businesses; the fifth principle encourages the sharing of risk and profit (Hayat and Kraeussl, 2011). In the classical Islamic era, any document reflecting a financial liability was referred to as a sakk (singular of sukuk, literally meaning "deed" or "instrument"). Sukuk are comparable to conventional bonds but have additional features that are compliant with Islamic banking and finance laws according to Shariah. Sukuk are known for giving their holders ownership rights to the underlying assets or income from those assets. The sukuk funds can be utilized for a specific development project, such as a renewable energy project, vaccination program, educational project, or low-cost housing program, which will appeal to SRI investors whose ethics and values match with the welfare of the community (Bennett and Iqbal, 2013). The creation and use of SRI sukuk supports local economies and communities. Tadau Energy Sdn Bhd, a Malaysian company, issued the first green sukuk on July 27, 2017, for 250.0 million Ringgit to finance a large-scale solar project using the SRI sukuk framework.

Moreover, green sukuk are investments in renewable energy and other environmental assets that are compliant with Shariah and that address the environmental protection concern. The money earned from the sukuk issuances is mostly used for environmentally friendly projects that comply with Shariah law. According to Climate Bond Standards certification, assets that can be used for green sukuk include, among other things, solar parks, biogas plants, wind farms, ambitious plans to enhance energy efficiency, renewable transmission and infrastructure, electric cars, and light rail. Comparing green sukuk instruments to other private funding sources, there are various benefits. First and foremost, they stand for a transferable and simple exit-capital market instrument that may be traded. Second, risk diversification is made possible by the possibility of basing green sukuk on a collection of portfolio projects. This might be a solution to the existing problems with economic viability in the location of renewable energy sources.

Green Bond in China as an Example

China is the second-largest green bond market in the world, and green bonds are growing very rapidly. Green bonds are important to the growth of China's ecological construction since a significant amount of the funds raised are used for pollution prevention and environmental protection. In 2015, China launched its first green bond. China's participation in the global green bond market was hardly noticeable in 2015, but within a year, it quickly rose to account for nearly one-quarter of the total. In 2021, of all the major markets, China's green bond issuance increased the highest. The first year after China declared that carbon dioxide will peak by 2030 and become carbon neutral by 2060. The nation's rise of its green bond market during the year reflected its efforts to increase the reduction of carbon pollution. China wants to boost the usage of non-fossil fuels from 15.9% in 2020 to roughly 20% by 2025. According to estimates made by the International Energy Agency, if the nation achieves its short-term energy objectives, carbon emissions would likely peak around 2030 (Figures 8.6 and 8.7).

Figure 8.7 Amount of green bonds issued by China between 2016 and 2020 (in billion USD). The authors compiled the data using the CBI's green definition and China's domestic green definition. It is also based on data from the CBI, Lianhe Equator Environmental Impact Assessment, and China Bond Rating. CBI and CCDC Research (2017, 2018, 2019, 2020)).

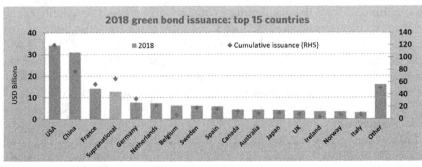

Source: Climate Bonds Initiative

Figure 8.6 Shows the green bond in the top 15 countries in the year 2018. The first place was recorded by the country USA followed by China in the second place, and then France. The least green bond is issued by the country Italy

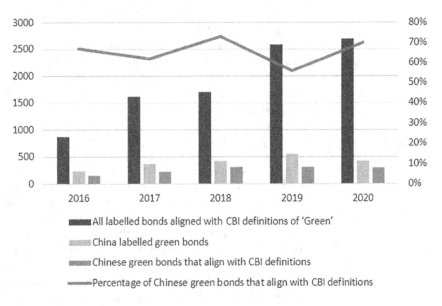

Figure 8.7 Amount of green bonds issued by China between 2016 and 2020 (in billion USD). The authors compiled the data using the CBI's green definition and China's domestic green definition. It is also based on data from the CBI, Lianhe Equator Environmental Impact Assessment, and China Bond Rating. CBI and CCDC Research (2017, 2018, 2019, 2020)).

Challenges and Issues of Green Sukuk

Green sukuk shows prominent results and evolved in many countries. The sustainability of green sukuk became support systems to infrastructure financing during the occurrence of climate change and satisfied the social needs. While technically a sukuk viable instrument contributing SDG goals. An Islamic bond known as a "green sukuk" is used to fund projects that protect the environment. The definition, certification, and reporting of green projects are not standardized, investors and issuers are not well informed about the disadvantages of green sukuk, and there is little historical data available for evaluating the performance and impacts of green sukuk projects. According to a research by the Islamic Development Bank and the Accounting and Auditing Organization for Islamic Financial Institutions titled "Green Sukuk: A New Frontier in Islamic Finance" (2016), the shortage of standardization and registration of development construction in addition to a precise definition of what constitutes a "green" project can make it difficult for consumers to evaluate the ecological effect of a specific sukuk and make prudent investment choices.

There are features that cause financial advisors to pay any attention to sukuk price fluctuations which reflect organizational volatility. The evolution of green sukuk bonds is not supported by governance and lack of support in green securities. According to Taghizadeh-Hesary and Yoshino (2020), most green technologies are still in their immaturity and are less consistent, hazardous, and economically feasible than non-green technologies. Green projects on a large scale require long-term financing. Major financing organizations, such as state financial institutions, must be constructed in order to core capability investment. In addition to the need for government welfare, the sukuk crowdfunding process features an intricate system for putting ethical firms first and averting any undertakings that might have negative repercussions (Rahman et al., 2020). The green sukuk is a significant turning point for Islamic and sustainable finance because it combines the ethical values of a green bond with the financially secure Shariah-compliant structure of a sukuk. Green sukuk are acknowledged to adhere to high morals and ethics and to reflect the Islamic ideas of Maqasid al-Shariah (higher purposes of the Shariah) and Maslahah, thanks to the rising significance of sustainable finance (public interest) (Delle Foglie and Keshminder, 2022). In addition, the facility would address the difficulties of low-yield investments and long-term funding. As a result, the government must assist the Islamic finance sector in advancing a pro-environmental agenda by funding eco-friendly projects and other emission efforts. The sovereign green sukuk, for which investors and analysts must analyze its environmental risks and costs, is the subject of the discussion that follows (Sasongko and Sakti, 2020).

The sociocultural sukuk is the subsequent level of SRI sukuk. Technically speaking, a "pay-for-performance contract" based on the sukuk structure is what is meant by a "social-impact sukuk," which strives to advance a society's social advantages and sustainable environment (Raghibi and Oubdi, 2021). A multi-stakeholder relationship encompassing the public, corporate, and social sectors helps to simultaneously mitigate costly and hazardous societal challenges, such as unemployment, good education system, homelessness, and poverty. The projects are subsidized by socially conscious investors, and their rates of return and any specified gets back based on the positive outcome of the project (Delle Foglie, 2022).

The green and social-impact sukuk are two of the main goods covered by SRI sukuk. The "sukuk" is a certificate of equal value representing undivided shares in the ownership of projects or specific investment activities. The risk-sharing characteristics of the sukuk match infrastructure financing (Kammer et al., 2015), making it suitable for financing new green technologies exhibiting high-risk exposures. "Green" defines the financing of any portfolio that generates various environmental benefits such as renewable energies, biodiversity protection, and climate change adaptation. Green sukuk issues which lead in Malaysia in the way of a new generation of GS for the industry of renewable energy were just issued (2020) (RM 260 million). Ten GS were issued to reduce elements that damage the green environment since it appears that Malaysia is experiencing considerable challenges brought on by these two areas.

Green Sukuk Contribution in SDG goals

Financial tools called green sukuk, usually referred to as Islamic green bonds, are used to raise funds for programs that support the environment. By providing financial support to initiatives that support renewable energy, lower carbon emissions, and protect the environment, they can achieve the SDGs of the United Nations. Green sukuk can be utilized to fund a range of initiatives, such as wildlife conservation, sustainable transportation infrastructure, and renewable energy projects. Goals like Goal 7 (Affordable and Clean Energy), Goal 13 (Climate Action), and Goal 14 can all be attained with the help of green sukuk by funding these kinds of projects (Life Below Water).

Green Sukuk Scenarios in Malaysia

The Malaysian government is encouraging splitting green sukuk initiatives, which redirect sukuk for investments targeted on the environment and so assist in bridging infrastructure and green finance. Green sukuk can aid in the achievement of the SDGs for good health and well-being, quality education, clean water and infrastructure, affordable and clean energy, decent work and economic growth, industry, innovation, and infrastructure, sustainable cities and communities, responsible consumption and production, and climate action (SDG13). For example, Malaysia had also taken an enormous step by issuing GS for RM 250 million and RM 1 billion in the renewable energy industry in just one year. Additionally, RM two billion for the green real estate concepts was approved (Rahman et al., 2022). It emphasizes the need for investments in green real estate and renewable energy in order to have environmental protection. Additionally, two GS for the Renewable energy sector were issued in 2018 for RM 245 million and RM 240 million, respectively. The possibility to engage in green initiatives, the ability to diversify funds, the ability to decrease waste, and the capacity to encourage cooperative elements of society are the primary benefits received from the issue of economic sukuk.

- The next construction permit for the 50 MW photovoltaic power plant in Kudat, Sabah, was granted to Tadau Energy Sdn. Bhd. A total of 250 million were allotted from the whole fund.
- The building of a 50 MW photovoltaic plant project, estimated to cost RM 1 billion, is the subject of the Quantum Solar Park Malaysia Sdn. Bhd. GS.

The company has an AA3 grade already (RAM rating). Tadau energy faces some critical issues in producing their operation as compared to thermal plant operators and suffers less construction risk because solar plants are easier to deploy according to their modularization (Rahman et al., 2022). Due to the lack of mechanical components and an ignition function, solar energy systems like Tadau have a lower operating sophistication than thermal plants. The impact of this operation leads to resourcing renewable energy as disaster risk reduction, and something invented through solar which focuses on nature and also reducing construction and financing cost. Moving to the Quantum Solar Park Malaysia Sdn. Bhd, this historic green SRI sukuk issue, according to QSPM ED and MD Lee Choo Boo, heralds a fresh start for the country's renewable energy industry. The three solar PV projects have a combined land size of over 600 acres and are expected to cost about RM1.25 billion to construct (242.8ha). With a total capacity of 150 MW (AC), or 197 MW peak, this solar energy facility is the biggest of its kind in Southeast Asia. As a result, Malaysia will be one step closer to attaining the carbon reduction goals set forth in the Paris Climate Agreement. To empower circular firms driven by the overall objective of maqasid shariah, green sukuk utilizes compassionate contracts, equity-like investments, and risk-sharing finance solutions. Green sukuk additionally offers a wider variety of finance choices for ventures essential to accomplishing the SDGs.

Green Sukuk Issuance in Indonesia

According to Fitrah and Soemitra (2022) , the Indonesian government has published three green sukuk-structured bond packages through the Ministry of Finance. Using Islamic Shariah law as a guide, green sukuk are green bond securities. Global sukuk of USD 1.25 billion was the first green sukuk, issued in 2018. Green sukuk through the ST-006 series were released for retail use in November 2019. Regarding the utilization, "Eligible Green Projects" or "Eligible Green Projects" refers to expenditures directly related to "Eligible Green Projects" that are funded or remortgage completely through the issue of green sukuk. The GBP, which are forms of input that encourage the switch to low-emission economic development and climate resilience, are explicitly mentioned in the Green Project Criteria. Various ministries or agencies will use the findings of this book to fund projects in five sectors, including renewable energy, resilient to climate change for disaster-prone areas, sustainable transportation, energy and waste management, environmental sustainability, and sustainable forestry. Based on this, the Indonesian government utilizes green framework to produce a sustainability community, supporting more green projects, and development of economy persistence of climate change. In this case, Indonesia management covers the nine sectors in the green sukuk framework as waste management, renewable energy, sustainable agriculture, sustainable transportation, and sustainable management of natural resources, green tourism, and resilience to the effects of climate change (Ramdansyah and Andri, 2022).

Conclusion and Policies

Overall, green sukuk bonds the context and analysis provide a comprehensive content performance of green sukuk. In order to assist the preponderance of the Muslim countries, who have a vital role to play in accomplishing a greener world, green sukuk has received considerable cooperation from the Islamic Finance Sector. To empower circular firms driven by the overall objective of maqasid shariah, green sukuk utilizes compassionate contracts, equity-like investments, and risk-sharing finance solutions. Green sukuk additionally offers a wider variety of finance choices for ventures essential to accomplishing the SDGs. By examining the elements of evolution and challenges of SRI sukuk in Malaysia, this study adds to the body of knowledge on sukuk. It will increase the policy implications in upcoming SRI sukuk guidelines to increase its appeal to local and international investors, issuers, and arrangers.

Thus, the governance support is significant in order to achieve green sukuk goals and the technology revolution playing an important roles in this term. To conclude, green sukuk improves the quality of human life and nature, supporting SDG goals. The government should be concerned in bringing up new technology in order to implement the green sukuk plan and mitigate more plans such as Tadau and Quantum in developing green financing. In my opinion the government should allocate a lump sum amount in the Annual Budget of Malaysia where it will create a good impression among people who can get support from the society. Technically speaking green sukuk developing the economist growth meantime maintains the sustainability of the country. And nature.

Furthermore, the facility would solve the challenges of low-yield investments and long-term funding. As a result, the government must assist the Islamic finance sector in advancing a pro-environmental agenda by funding eco-friendly projects and other carbon-conscious efforts. The sovereign green sukuk, for which investors and analysts must analyze its environmental risks and costs, is the subject of the discussion that follows.

References

Abubakar, L., & Handayani, T. (2020). *Green Sukuk: Sustainable Financing Instruments for Infrastructure Development in Indonesia*. Retrieved from: https://doi.org/10.2991/assehr.k.200529.206

Alam, N., Duygun, M., & Ariss, R. T. (2016). Green sukuk: An innovation in Islamic capital markets. In *Energy and finance: Sustainability in the energy industry* (pp. 167–185). Cham: Springer International Publishing.

Cheong, C., & Choi, J. (2020). Green bonds: A survey. *Journal of Derivatives and Quantitative Studies:* 선물연구, *28*(4), 175–189.

Delle Foglie, A., & Keshminder, J. S. (2022). Challenges and opportunities of SRI sukuk toward financial system sustainability: A bibliometric and systematic literature review. *International Journal of Emerging Markets*.

Fabozzi, F. J., Davis, H. A., & Choudhry, M. (2006). Introduction to structured finance. John Wiley.

Fitrah, R., & Soemitra, A. (2022). Green Sukuk for sustainable development goals in Indonesia: A literature study. *Jurnal Ilmiah Ekonomi Islam*, 8(1), 231–240.Malek, N. H. A. (2017, October 9). Quantum Solar Park to issue RM1b green SRI sukuk.

Raghibi, A., & Oubdi, L. (2021). A Proposed Model for Social Impact Sukuk. *Turkish Journal of Islamic Economics, 8(2)*.

Rahman, M., Isa, C. R., Dewandaru, G., Hanifa, M. H., Chowdhury, N. T., & Sarker, M. (2020). Socially responsible investment sukuk (Islamic bond) development in Malaysia. *Qualitative Research in Financial Markets, 12*(4), 599–619.

Rahman, Z. A., Jensen, D. & Lim A. (2022, September 7). *Facilitating SDGs with Islamic Finance (Part 1) Malaysia's Leadership in Sukuk*. IFAC.

RAM Ratings: Malaysia's First Solar Sukuk to Be Issued by Tadau Rated AA3. (2017, June 8). RAM Holdings Berhad. Retrieved January 14, 2023, from https://www.ram.com.my/pressrelease/?prviewid=4215

Sasongko, A. & Sakti, A. (2020). *Sovereign green sukuk: Environmental risk model development*. http://publication-bi.org/repec/idn/wpaper/WP022020.pdfTang, D. Y., & Zhang, Y. (2020). Do shareholders benefit from green bonds? *Journal of Corporate Finance, 61*, 101427.

9   Green Bonds in Modern Portfolios

Risk-Return Dynamics

Bezon Kumar, Afia Mubasshira Tiasha, Atman Shah, and Afrida Jinnurain Urbee

Introduction

In the bond markets, green bonds, which are also known as GBs, have increased in popularity and share. International and local authorities mainly employ them to raise funds for projects that are climate- and environmentally friendly (Tsoukala & Tsiotas, 2021). In 2007, the European Investment Bank (EIB) launched green bonds for the first time. Their features are similar to the traditional fixed-income corporate bonds. Subsequently, their funds can only be allocated to environmentally beneficial initiatives (Naeem et al., 2022).

In addition to gaining importance among investors who care about the environment, green bonds are also becoming a well-known sustainable investment alternative as more and more investors recognize the potentially serious consequences climate change could have for businesses and government rules and regulations (Reboredo, 2018). The key incremental benefit of green bonds is as an "impact investment"—investors in these bonds are aware that they are directly backing programs that address environmental concerns (Hauter, 2018).

There has been an increase in the importance of analyzing green bonds and the structure of investment portfolios in recent times. The funding of green technologies has become a key component of the contemporary global context of sustainable development goals (SDGs), which encourages investors to be socially, politically, and environmentally sustainable (Marín-Rodríguez et al., 2023). This chapter examines the fundamental components of security and bond, which might contribute to the array of knowledge existing in practice. In addition, it aims to portray an overview of the risks and returns of green bond portfolios.

Risk and Return

The risk is the possible economic loss from investing in securities. Risk is the likelihood of losing money made by an investor. On the other hand,

DOI: 10.4324/9781032686844-9

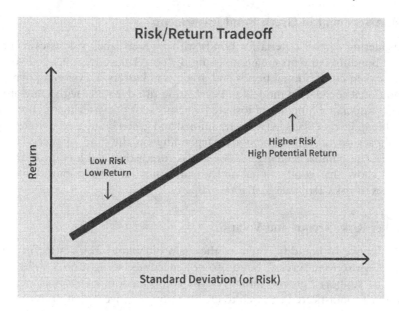

Figure 9.1 Tradeoff between risk and return

Source: Investopedia

return is the possible economic gain from investing in securities. Return is the profit made by an investor. Figure 9.1 displays the tradeoff between risk and return.

Usually, high-risk investments yield better returns, contrarily, and low-risk investments yield lower returns. Risk and return are highly correlated to each other, and it depends on many factors, such as project-competitive risk, industry-specific risk, international risk, specific risk, and market risk. The rule of risk and return is often called "no pain, no gain." This means that an investor chooses to invest in an asset with the lowest risk, the possible return then is often modest. Contrarily, an investment with a high-risk element has a higher probability of making larger profits.

Unique Characteristics of Green Bonds

i It is a special form of fixed-income instrument that is specifically allocated to elevate money for climate and environmental projects.
ii It must adhere to criteria on the use of proceeds, have a process for project evaluation and selection, ensure proper management of any proceeds, and offer detailed reporting.
iii It is typically asset-linked and backed by the issuing entity's balance sheet.
iv It usually carries the same credit rating as their issuers' other debt obligations.
v Fixed coupon payments are made to the bondholders until maturity.

Risk Assessment in Green Bond Investments

Considering several criteria for bonds with a green label, risk assessment in green bond investments entails assessing the correlation dynamics and volatility between conventional bonds and green bond assets. Developing dynamic conditional correlation models and evaluating risk dynamics with value-at-risk and its associated function of loss are two aspects of this assessment. There are notable spillover effects between traditional and green bond assets, which have an impact on offsetting methods. Depending on the kind of green-labeled criteria, these impacts change. Value-at-risk forecasting and loss function estimates show that conventional and green bonds have significantly different degrees of risk (Tsoukala & Tsiotas, 2021).

Market Risk: Trends and Volatility

The absence of liquidity is one of the main difficulties in investing in green bonds. Moreover, "green" bonds do not specify how the money will be utilized to support "green" initiatives. In addition, low yields, mispricing, a dearth of sophisticated research to enable informed investment decisions, and the presence of certain green bond issuers with dubious backgrounds are some additional risks associated with green bonds (Moskowitz, 2022).

Credit Risk: Evaluating Issuer Strength

Green bond issuer strength is critical for investors looking for reputable and effective investment opportunities. The dependability and trustworthiness of issuers in this sector are influenced by a number of critical factors. Adherence to recognized norms and frameworks, such as the International Capital Market Association's (ICMA) Green Bond Principles, demonstrates an issuer's commitment to transparency and environmental responsibility (ICMA, 2020).

Furthermore, issuer credibility is determined by criteria, such as a track record of success in green projects and transparent reporting practices (Climate Bonds Initiative, 2020; Pimbley, 2018). Independent verification and certification of green bond projects by credible authorities strengthens issuer credibility even further, ensuring investors of the legitimacy of the issuer's green obligations (IFC, 2020; Moody's Investors Service, 2021).

Long-term viability and impact assessments of green projects, as emphasized by organizations, such as the World Bank, are critical in establishing issuer strength (The World Bank, 2019). Furthermore, despite global concerns, the market's rise in sustainable debt instruments demonstrates investor trust in issuer commitment and project sustainability (BloombergNEF, 2021).

Liquidity Risk: Accessibility and Trading

Green bond liquidity risk is a specific concern driven by the accessibility and trading dynamics of these products. Green bond accessibility, which is generally decided by market depth and breadth, may have a substantial influence on liquidity. While the green bond market has grown, worries about its smaller size and lack of diversity in comparison to conventional bond markets remain (Climate Bonds Initiative, 2020).

Liquidity risk in green bonds is also influenced by trading dynamics. The presence of specialized market makers, pricing transparency, and trading frequency all play important roles (ICMA, 2020). In the lack of a standardized framework for pricing and valuation, market liquidity might suffer, discouraging potential investors (Pimbley, 2018).

Furthermore, green bond integration into larger financial markets remains a hurdle, hurting their tradability and liquidity. Green bond markets should benefit from more openness, standardization, and governmental backing (Moody's Investors Service, 2021).

Return Metrics for Green Bonds

Return measures for green bonds are critical in assessing their financial success and effect. Yield to maturity, coupon rate, and total return are all important factors (BloombergNEF, 2021). Understanding these indicators in the context of green bonds helps investors to evaluate financial returns as well as environmental effects. Environmental, social, and governance (ESG) aspects are increasingly being considered in return calculations, reflecting the larger aims of sustainable investment (Climate Bonds Initiative, 2020). Evaluating these return criteria provides investors with information about the financial feasibility and environmental benefits of green bond investments.

Yield to Maturity

Yield to maturity (YTM) is the total rate of return that will have been earned by a bond when it makes all interest payments and repays the original principal. YTM is reflected in a long-term bond yield but is stated as an annual rate. YTM is essentially a bond's internal rate of return if held to maturity. Calculating the YTM can be a complicated process, and it assumes all coupon or interest payments can be reinvested at the same rate of return as the bond.

Total Return vs. Yield

Yield is referred to the income return on an investment, which is the interest or dividends received, uttered annually as a percentage based on the investment's cost, its current market value, or its face value. Total return is defined as interest, capital gains, dividends, and distributions grasped over a given period of time. Investors concentrated on yield are generally interested in income and less concerned with growth, such investments may include CDs and bonds. Investors more fretful with the total return will likely elect to emphasize on portfolio growth and associated investments.

Diversification Strategies for Green Bond Portfolios

i **Diversify Thoughtfully**: Diversification is fundamental. To limit the danger of concentration, diversify your holdings among several industries and issuers. Your portfolio can be balanced by diversifying among various green project categories, such as sustainable agriculture, clean transportation, and renewable energy.

ii **Rigorous Due Diligence**: Do your research thoroughly before choosing green bonds. Examine the issuer's track record, their dedication to transparency, and the projects they have funded in terms of their environmental advantages. Check to see if the bonds meet recognized benchmarks and certifications, such as the requirements of the Climate Bonds Initiative.

iii **Align with Sustainability Criteria**: Make sure the investments you make in green bonds support your sustainability goals. Recognize the initiatives you support environmental impact as well as the wider effects of your investments on society and ecosystems.

iv **Balance Risk and Return**: It is crucial to strike a balance between return generation and risk reduction. Consider elements including credit risk, interest rate risk, and sector-specific hazards as you assess the risk profile of your portfolio. Your financial objectives, level of risk tolerance, and investment horizon all play a role in determining the ideal risk-return mix.

v **Monitor and Adapt**: Like all assets, green bonds need constant attention. Keep up to date on the sustainability objectives of the issuer and the environmental performance of the projects you support. Prepare yourself to modify your portfolio as the market and your goals change.

vi **Tax Benefits**: Investigate any potential tax advantages of investing in green bonds. Investors in green bonds may be eligible for tax breaks or credits from some countries.

Asset Allocation and Sector Diversification

The framework of investment is asset allocation and diversification. The process of allocating one's assets is like choosing how many eggs to place in each of the multiple asset classes or baskets. Conversely, diversification entails the distribution of one's investments across several asset categories (Thomas, 2023).

Geographic Diversification

Geographical diversification is a technique of disseminating comparable businesses over diverse countries primarily to increase profits for the business as a whole (Subramaniam & Wasiuzzaman, 2019). Businesses typically reduce their vulnerability to political and economic volatility by deploying specific departments across various parts of the world (Fincash, 2023).

Duration Matching and Interest Rate Risk

Bonds and other fixed-income products are substantially vulnerable to interest rate risks. The fluctuations in interest rates are inversely correlated with bond prices. Hence, a change in interest rates may have an impact on an investor's or a company's investment portfolio. A particular approach to curbing interest rate risk is duration matching. Both individuals and businesses can use this specific method to secure their assets against changes in interest rates (Duration Matching: Interest Rate Risk Management Technique, 2021).

Sustainable Investment Considerations

Being more responsible for the consequences it has on the financial markets has made sustainable investment an intriguing answer to both social and environmental issues. Nowadays, an increasing number of investors desire that their assets address the bigger problems and represent these more expansive ideologies. Sustainable investment and value-based investment are made possible by this. The inclusion of ESG considerations in the process of making investment decisions is known as a sustainable investment (Talan & Sharma, 2019).

ESG Factors in Bond Selection

Investing in bonds can be significantly impacted by ESG factors. Reliability for bond payments may be impacted by enterprises having a bad environmental record since they may be subject to more legal and regulatory issues. Likewise, organizations that exhibit inadequate social practices or governance frameworks may be at greater risk of reputational damage, which could hinder their capacity to secure financing. When it comes to bond investing, investors are increasingly taking ESG factors into account. Bonds issued by companies with high ESG criteria could be more appealing to investors since they are considered to be less risky and more financially secure ("Exploring the Impact of Environmental, Social, and Governance (ESG) Factors on Bond Investing and Their Role in Sustainable Finance," 2023).

Impact Metrics and Reporting

Impact reporting is any form of reporting (by a green bond issuer on the use of proceeds from the bonds) that aims to put a quantifiable figure on the amount of climatic or environmental impact associated with a project or asset. Investors may quantify positive externalities from their investments with the backing of this sort of reporting, which is becoming more and more prevalent in the green bond markets (Climate Bonds Initiative, 2017).

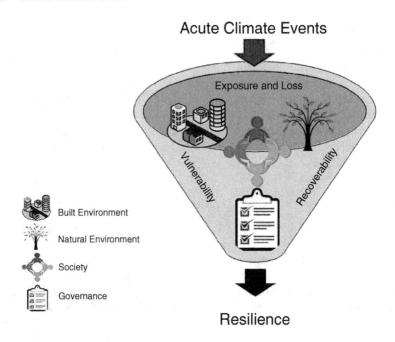

Figure 9.2 Climate risk and resilience assessment

Source: Summers et al. (2017)

Climate Risk and Resilience Assessment

The creation of risk-reduction strategies and related financial investments starts with a thorough assessment of climate risk. Though there are many tools available for doing climate risk assessments, guidelines on how to apply them specifically for participants in the green bond market are still being created. The adaptation advantages of the actions being financed should also be demonstrated for investments that result in the adaptation of other activities, communities, or systems. Given the technical skills required, the majority of issuers will probably need outside assistance to complete the examination. As an alternative, issuers can investigate risk assessments and regional, national, and local climate projections. Figure 9.2 shows climate risk and resilience assessment.

Green Bond Issuer Selection

The issuance of green bonds is open to all entities, including corporations, governments, and financial institutions. The legality of a green bond is typically confirmed by third-party organizations to reassure investors while minimizing false representations. The Climate Bonds Initiative offers a list of independent verifiers for green bonds (Corporate Finance Institute, n.d.).

Issuer Due Diligence

To verify facts or details about an issue under consideration, due diligence is an audit, review, or investigation. When considering a potential deal with another party, due diligence in the financial sector necessitates a review of financial documents (Chen, 2023). In the case of green bonds, the steps involved are, for example, eligibility criteria selection, identifying qualifying green projects and assets, developing a green bond framework, arranging independent verification, setting up tracking and reporting, issuing bonds, and regular reporting (Global Center on Adaptation, 2021).

Credit Ratings and Analysis

Lenders frequently use credit ratings to figure out default risk because every credit is associated with a likelihood of loss. Potential lenders can hire credit-rating entities to help them determine how likely it is that a given company will default, and the lender can determine the extent of the risk based on some classification. Multiple businesses, including banks, insurance providers, and suppliers, employ this service. Moreover, green bonds and corporate social responsibility go closely together since green bonds are intended for the consideration of environmental projects (Czarnitzki & Kraft, 2007).

Monitoring and Surveillance

A monitoring and assessment system with the required technology tools should be guaranteed during the funding process for projects that will reap the advantages of green bonds. The primary objective of the financial sector at the moment is to leverage green bonds as a means of producing greater social and financial returns. The industry can focus its efforts on three sub-objectives to accomplish this (Çavuşoğlu, 2022).

Scenario Analysis and Stress Testing

In a scenario analysis, different risk factors are simulated over several periods to assess prospective future scenarios with an emphasis on a business, sector, or economy. It facilitates determining the essential elements and outcomes of potential occurrences or changes. Nevertheless, stress testing anticipates financial results in highly adverse circumstances by taking along a variety of risk elements and their major, perhaps enduring effects and subsequently examining an economy's or company's resistance to these unlikely but realistic disasters (International Actuarial Association, 2013).

Climate Scenario Analysis

Climate change, environmental deterioration, and natural resource depletion have pushed environmental sustainability to the center of global economic and financial agendas. Governments, businesses, and investors are increasingly searching for new and impactful ways to direct financial resources toward projects that promote sustainability and mitigate environmental hazards. Green bonds are debt instruments of sustainable finance that are commonly associated with low-carbon generating eco-friendly projects (Flammer, 2020). He further pointed out that green bonds add value since green bond issuers outperform non-green bond issuers in the long run. These bonds are also seen as a potential device for addressing climate change (Bloomberg, 2018).

Sensitivity to Environmental Events

Due to the large expenditure required, it is impossible to fund global warming through public investment (Ntsama et al., 2021). Green Bonds have evolved as a financial instrument with the ability to bridge the gap between financial markets and the compelling need to solve critical environmental challenges in this setting. In the endogenous growth model, Nordhus (1990) incorporated global warming. In their pursuit of tackling environmental and sustainable development concerns, SDG 7 and green bonds are inextricably linked. SDG 7 is one of the United Nations' SDGs that aims to provide all people with affordable, reliable, sustainable, and modern energy by 2030. Green Bonds are a type of financial instrument used to fund initiatives that have a clear environmental benefit.

Integration of Green Bonds in a Multi-asset Portfolio

The name "Green Bond" was coined by the EIB in 2007, when it issued bonds to fund renewable energy and energy efficiency projects (EIB, 2007). Since then, global issuance of Green Bonds has grown exponentially, reflecting the growing interest in sustainable investments and environmentally sensitive finance. According to the Climate Bonds Initiative, a leading industry organization, global green bond issuance surpassed USD 200 billion in 2019, representing a significant rise over previous years (Climate Bonds Initiative, 2019). In December 2016, Poland became the first government to issue a green sovereign bond, followed by France in January 2017. Fannie Mae, a government organization in the United States, released the largest green mortgage-backed securities to date, worth $24.9 billion USD. Malaysia issued the world's first green Islamic bond, known as a "green Sukuk," in June 2017 to fund climate-resilient growth (Tang & Zhang, 2018).

Correlation with Other Asset Classes

A "green bond" differs from a standard bond by its label, which indicates a promise to use the funds collected solely to finance or refinance "green" projects, assets, or business activities (ICMA, 2015). The Green Bond Principles, the climate bond standards, and other principles and guidelines recognized and supported by the official sector, including public financial institutions and development banks, have resulted from market and government-led efforts at standardization and definition in the green bond market.

Risk-Adjusted Returns

Bonds can be used to finance or refinance a wide range of projects and activities, including infrastructure, power plants, and the continued operation of businesses . Inderst et al. (2012) define a green bond as a debt security issued by a government entity, a multilateral institution, or a firm to raise funds from investors for a project that contributes to a low-carbon, climate-resilient economy.

Portfolio Optimization Techniques

Green Bonds' broad investor appeal is one of their distinguishing characteristics. They draw a diverse group of participants, ranging from socially conscious individual investors to huge institutional investors and sovereign wealth funds. These bonds are appealing not only for their environmental purpose, but also for providing investors with financial instruments that provide both stability and diversity (Bisson et al., 2019). This broad appeal positions Green Bonds as a way to attract funds from a variety of sources and direct it toward environmental activities.

Regulatory and Policy Considerations

According to the World Bank Group (2023), poor countries are increasingly obtaining funds for climate action through the issuance of green and sustainability bonds. Colombia, Egypt, India, and Indonesia are among 19 emerging-market countries using green bond profits to develop renewable energy and public transit. Egypt's $750 million sovereign green bond was the Middle East and North Africa's first in 2020. In 2021, an Indonesian sustainability bond will fund the Sidrap Wind Farm in South Sulawesi, one of the largest islands in the Indonesian Archipelago. Colombia, known for its environmental initiatives, issued Latin America's first green bond in local currency (Colombian pesos) in 2021.

Regulatory Landscape for Green Bonds

In early 2023, India joined this club, issuing its first green bond to collect approximately $2 billion for initiatives that contribute to climate change mitigation, adaptation, environmental protection, resource and biodiversity conservation, and net zero goals. Green bonds had raised $2.5 trillion globally as of January 2023 to promote green and sustainable projects. Emerging-market governments have raised $74 billion in green, social, and sustainability bonds, accounting for 2% of total green, social, and sustainability bonds issued globally (World Bank 2023).

A green bond portfolio is a collection of green bonds and debt instruments issued by various entities to finance environmentally beneficial projects. These portfolios typically support initiatives addressing climate change, sustainability, and eco-friendly activities, such as renewable energy, energy efficiency, pollution prevention and control, clean transportation, green building, and sustainable agriculture (Bhutta et al., 2022; ICMA, 2021). The careful composition of a green bond portfolio aims to align with an investor's environmental and financial goals, taking into account factors, such as risk tolerance, return expectations, and sustainability impact. These bonds are tied to specific assets and share credit ratings with the issuer's other debt obligations (Deschryver & De Mariz, 2020).

Green bonds, exclusively utilize the funds raised to finance or refinance "green" (or sustainable) projects, assets, or business activities (ICMA, 2021; Kaminker, 2015), sometimes interchangeably referred to as climate bonds, play a significant role in sustainable finance. However, it is crucial to note that while green bond portfolios cover a broad range of environmentally beneficial projects, climate bonds specifically focus on reducing carbon emissions and mitigating climate change effects (Bhutta et al., 2022). The EIB issued the first "Climate Awareness Bond" in 2007 and the World Bank issued the first bond under the term "Green Bond" in 2008 (Azhgaliyeva et al., 2020; The World Bank, 2020; Vivid Economics and Climate Bonds Initiative, 2019). Since then, the global issuance of green bonds has expanded exponentially, from $3.4 billion in 2012 to $556 billion in 2021 (Azhgaliyeva et al., 2020; Caramichael & Rapp, 2022).

Real-World Examples of Green Bond Portfolios

Several entities and regions have embraced green bonds as a means to fund environment-friendly projects. The issuance of green bonds aims at reducing carbon emissions has supported initiatives, such as renewable energy installations and public transportation developments (Marín-Rodríguez et al., 2023; UN ESCAP, 2021). The World Bank (2020), a major green bond issuer, has released substantial funds for global projects primarily in renewable energy, clean transportation, agriculture, and land use. In the corporate sector, companies like Apple and Microsoft issued green bonds to fund renewable energy projects and energy-efficient manufacturing processes, aligning with their sustainability commitments (Hartzmark & Sussman, 2019; Ning et al., 2023).

Understanding historical trends is crucial for effective portfolio management. Lessons from past market movements emphasize the stability of green bond prices during market volatility, highlighting the importance of diversification to mitigate sector-specific risks (Bhutta et al., 2022). Investors increasingly prioritize projects with clear environmental benefits and issuers with a strong track record of accountability, emphasizing the importance of clear environmental objectives and accountability (Hartzmark & Sussman, 2019). Regulatory changes have underscored the need for standardized definitions and reporting requirements, aligning green bond frameworks with internationally recognized standards to enhance market integrity (EU, 2020).

Emerging Trends and Innovations

The green bond market continues to evolve rapidly. In 2021, green bond issuances reached $556 billion, with the United States leading with $50 billion in new issuances (Azhgaliyeva et al., 2020; Caramichael & Rapp, 2022; Climate Bonds Initiative, 2020). Emerging trends include diversification beyond traditional sectors into areas, such as green real estate, sustainable agriculture, water management, circular economy projects, and biodiversity conservation (Khanna, 2020).

Diversification Strategies for Green Bond Portfolios

Diversification is pivotal in managing green bond portfolios and serves as a robust risk mitigation tool. To counter concentration risk, investors diversify across sectors, encompassing sustainable agriculture, clean transportation, and renewable energy. Sectoral diversification minimizes vulnerabilities tied to industry dynamics, ensuring overall portfolio stability. Geographical diversification involves investing across regions and mitigating risks associated with economic variations. Issuer diversification includes bonds from diverse entities to manage credit risk. Duration diversification balances interest rate fluctuations. These strategies cultivate a resilient investment approach (Abuzayed & Al-Fayoumi, 2023).

Relative Value Analysis

Relative value analysis guides green bond investors in assessing risk and return characteristics. Yield spread analysis, endorsed by Hartzmark and Sussman (2019), compares green bonds to traditional bonds, considering sustainability factors in valuation. Performance metrics gauge environmental benefits and carbon impact, aiding informed decisions (Guerry et al., 2015). Comparison with benchmarks, utilizing Climate Transition Benchmarks and Paris-aligned Benchmarks (EU, 2020), helps evaluate portfolio performance. In conclusion, effective diversification and relative value analysis align with sustainable and responsible investment practices, contributing to risk mitigation and informed decision-making in green bond portfolio management.

Innovative Structures

Sustainability-linked bonds incentivize sustainability improvements, while social bonds address social challenges alongside environmental goals, amplifying their social and environmental impact. These trends and innovations reshape risk-return dynamics and affirm the significance of green bonds in the global financial framework (OECD, 2022).

Green Bond Market Evolution

The green bond market's inception was attributed to the EIB in 2007, but a significant acceleration occurred in 2013 with the issuance of officially labeled green bonds. During the 2010s, green bond funds expanded accessibility to individual investors. Notable firms like Allianz S.E., Axa S.A., State Street Corp., TIAA-CREF, BlackRock, AXA World Funds, and HSBC have supported green bond mutual funds and ETFs (Sustainable Research and Analysis, 2020). A major milestone was the publication of the Green Bond Principles in 2014, standardizing guidelines for green bond issuances and enhancing transparency.

New Financial Instruments and Structures

Innovations include sustainability-linked bonds, incentivizing sustainability improvements, and introducing dynamic pricing dynamics. Nature-based bonds finance projects focused on preserving and restoring natural ecosystems, potentially aligning with investor demand for impact-driven investments. These instruments not only expand diversification opportunities but also require specialized knowledge and skills, necessitating a balanced approach that considers returns, risk, and environmental impact.

Technological Advancements in Green Finance

Technology plays a significant role in green finance, including finch platforms streamlining green bond issuance and trading, blockchain technology enhancing transparency, and data analytics assessing environmental impact and sustainability performance. Sustainability-related tools enable investors to quantify environmental benefits and optimize investment strategies with algorithmic trading and AI.

Conclusions and Policies

This chapter navigated the world of green bond portfolios, exploring their evolution, diverse opportunities, innovative instruments, and technological advancements. Key takeaways include the diversification of green bond sectors, the introduction of innovative instruments, and the transformational influence of technology. These insights set the stage for subsequent sections, delving into risk-return dynamics and best practices for effective portfolio management.

Lessons from past market dynamics emphasize asset resilience, investor priorities, and regulatory alignment. Diversification reduces sector-specific risk, and performance against sustainability goals influences returns. Technological advancements enhance transparency, risk assessment, and portfolio management, empowering investors to make informed decisions in a changing landscape of sustainable finance.

Effectively managing green bond portfolios demands a strategic approach that aligns financial objectives with sustainability goals. Here, we outline key best practices to guide investors in navigating the dynamic landscape of green bonds. Green bonds are debt securities designated to fund "green projects" that promote environmental sustainability. Currently, these are the most widely used instruments that specifically encourage the shift to a global economy that is more robust to climate change and sustainable.

References

Abuzayed, B., & Al-Fayoumi, N. (2023). Diversification and Hedging Strategies of Green Bonds in Financial Asset Portfolios during the COVID-19 Pandemic. *Applied Economics*, 55(36), 4228–4238. https://doi.org/10.1016/j.eneco.2022.106111

Azhgaliyeva, D., Kapoor, A., & Liu, Y. (2020). Green Bonds for Financing Renewable Energy and Energy Efficiency in Southeast Asia: A Review of Policies. ADBI Working Paper 1073. Tokyo: Asian Development Bank Institute. https://www.adb.org/publications/greenbonds-financing-renewable-energy-efficiency-southeast-asia

Bhutta, U. S., Tariq, A., Farrukh, M., Raza, A., & Iqbal, M. K. (2022). Green Bonds for Sustainable Development: Review of Literature on Development and Impact of Green Bonds. *Technological Forecasting and Social Change*, 175, 121378. https://doi.org/10.1016/j.techfore.2021.121378

Bisson, S., Lazar, A., & Bellassen, V. (2019). Green Bonds: Selection or Deselection? Evidence from Liquidity and Credit Risk of French Bonds. *Journal of Corporate Finance, 58*, 22–41.

Bloomberg (2018). *Security That Triggered a Recession Reworked to Green the Earth.* Bloomberg. https://www.bloomberg.com/news/articles /2018-10-09/security-that-triggered-a-recession-reworked-to-green-the-earth.

BloombergNEF. (2021). Sustainable Debt Grows in 2020 Despite Pandemic.

Caramichael, J. and Rapp, A. (2022). "The Green Corporate Bond Issuance Premium," International Finance Discussion Papers 1346. Washington: Board of Governors of the Federal Reserve System, https://doi.org/10.17016/IFDP.2022.1346.

Çavuşoğlu, Ş. (2022). Exploring the Ways for Integrating the Green Bond with Decoupling Projects through Monitoring and Evaluation: The Carbon Emission Atlas and Expert System (Kaus) (Master's Thesis, Middle East Technical University).

Chen, J. (2023, April 30). Due Diligence. *Investopedia.* https://www.investopedia.com/terms/d/duediligence.asp

Climate Bonds Initiative. (2017). Impact reporting & Green Bonds: A Closer Look: Analysis from Our Recent Use of Proceeds Report. Climate Bonds Initiative. https://www.climatebonds.net/2017/07/impact-reporting-green-bonds-closer-look-analysis-our-recent-use-proceeds-report

Climate Bonds Initiative. (2020). Green Bonds Market Summary 2020. https://www.climatebonds.net/resources/reports/green-bonds-market-summary-q3-2020

Climate Bonds Initiative. (2020). State of the Market 2020: An Overview of Global Green, Social, and Sustainability (GSS) Bond Market.

Corporate Finance Institute. (n.d.). Green Bond - Overview, How It Works, History, Advantages. https://corporatefinanceinstitute.com/resources/esg/green-bond/

Czarnitzki, D., & Kraft, K. (2007). Are Credit Ratings Valuable Information? *Applied Financial Economics, 17*(13), 1061–1070.

Deschryver, P., & De Mariz, F. (2020). What Future for the Green Bond Market? How Can Policymakers, Companies, and Investors Unlock the Potential of the Green Bond Market? *Journal of Risk and Financial Management, 13*(3), 61. https://doi.org/10.3390/jrfm13030061

Duration Matching – Interest Rate Risk Management Technique. (2021). *Accounting Hub.* https://www.accountinghub-online.com/duration-matching/

EIB. (2007). *Climate Awareness Bonds.* European Investment Bank. Retrieved March 29, 2024, from https://www.eib.org/en/investor-relations/disclaimer.htm

European Union [EU]. (2020). Regulation (EU) 2020/852 of the European Parliament and of the Council of 18 June 2020 on the Establishment of a Framework to Facilitate Sustainable Investment, and Amending Regulation (EU) 2019/2088 (Text with EEA relevance). https://eur-lex.europa.eu/eli/reg/2020/852/oj

Exploring the Impact of Environmental, Social, and Governance (ESG) Factors on Bond Investing and Their Role in Sustainable Finance. (2023). *Sports Changers.* https://www.sportschangers.com/general/exploring-the-impact-of-environmental-social-and-governance-esg-factors-on-bond-investing-and-their-role-in-sustainable-finance/

Fincash. (2023, November 29). *What Is Geographical Diversification?* https://www.fincash.com/l/basics/geographical-diversification

Flammer, C. (2020). Green Bonds: Effectiveness and Implications for Public Policy. *Environmental and Energy Policy and the Economy, 1,* 95–128.

Global Center on Adaptation. (2021). Green Bonds for Climate Resilience: A Guide for Issuers. https://gca.org/wp-content/uploads/2021/11/A-guide-for-issuers-Full-report-online.pdf?_gl=1*1icxjvy*_ga*MTg4MTMwMjIzOS4xNzAxNjMyMjA5*_up*MQ.

Global Center on Adaptation. (2021). Green Bonds for Climate Resilience: State of Play and Roadmap to Scale. Retrieved from Green Bonds for Climate Resilience (gca.org)

Guerry, A. D., Polasky, S., Lubchenco, J., Chaplin-Kramer, R., Daily, G. C., Griffin, R., & Vira, B. (2015). Natural Capital and Ecosystem Services Informing Decisions: From Promise to Practice. *Proceedings of the National academy of Sciences, 112*(24), 7348–7355. https://doi.org/10.1073/pnas.1503751112

Hartzmark, S. M., & Sussman, A. B. (2019). Do Investors Value Sustainability? A Natural Experiment Examining Ranking and Fund Flows. *European Corporate Governance Institute (ECGI) - Finance Working Paper No. 565/2018.* https://doi.org/10.2139/ssrn.3016092

Hauter, A. (2018). *Income and Impact: Adding Green Bonds to Investment Portfolios.* Brown Advisory. https://www.brownadvisory.com/us/insights/income-and-impact-adding-green-bonds-investment-portfolios#:~:text=The%20primary%20incremental%20benefit%20that,projects%20that%20address%20environmental%20challenges

ICMA. (2015). Green Bond principles: Voluntary Process Guidelines for Issuing Green Bond, March.

ICMA. (2020). Green Bond Principles 2020.

IFC. (2020). Green Bond Verification and Certification: Role of Independent Verifiers.

Inderst, G., Kaminker, C., & Stewart, F. (2012). Defining and measuring green investments.

International Actuarial Association. (2013). Stress Testing and Scenario Analysis. https://www.actuaries.org/CTTEES_SOLV/Documents/StressTestingPaper.pdf

International Capital Market Association [ICMA]. (2021). Green Bond Principles Voluntary Process Guidelines for Issuing Green Bonds. *International Capital Market Association.* https://www.icmagroup.org/assets/documents/Sustainable-finance/2022-updates/Green-Bond-Principles-June-2022-060623.pdf

Kaminker, C. (2015). Green Bonds. Mobilising the Debt Capital Markets for a Low-Carbon Transition. *OECD Policy Perspectives.* https://www.oecd.org/environment/cc/Green%20bonds%20PP%20%5Bf3%5D%20%5Blr%5D.pdf

Khanna, M. (2020). Growing Green Business Investments in Asia and the Pacific: Trends and Opportunities. ADB Sustainable Development Working Paper Series. https://doi.org/10.22617/WPS200357-2

Marín-Rodríguez, N. J., González-Ruiz, J. D., & Valencia-Arias, A. (2023). Incorporating Green Bonds into Portfolio Investments: Recent Trends and Further Research. *Sustainability, 15*(20), 14897.

Moody's Investors Service. (2021). Green Bonds Assessment: Moody's Approach to Assessing Green Bond Issuers.

Moskowitz, D. (2022). Opportunities and Risks of Green Bond Investing. *Investopedia.* https://www.investopedia.com/articles/investing/081115/green-bonds-benefits-and-risks.asp

Naeem, M. A., Conlon, T., & Cotter, J. (2022). Green Bonds and Other Assets: Evidence from Extreme Risk Transmission. *Journal of Environmental Management, 305,* 114358.

Ning, Y., Cherian, J., Sial, M. S., Álvarez-Otero, S., Comite, U., & Zia-Ud-Din, M. (2023). Green Bond as a New Determinant of Sustainable Green Financing, Energy Efficiency Investment, and Economic Growth: A Global Perspective. *Environmental Science and Pollution Research, 30*(22), 61324–61339. https://doi.org/10.1007/s11356-021-18454-7

Nordhus, W. D. (1990). A General Equilibrium Model of Policies to Slow Global Warming. In D. Wood (Ed.), *Economic Models of Energy and Environment, Proceedings of a Workshop.*

Ntsama, U. Y. O., Chen, Y., Nasiri, A., & Mboungam, A. H. M. (2021). Green Bonds Issuance: Insights in Low- and Middle-Income Countries. *International Journal of Corporate Social Responsibility, 6*(1), 1–9.

OECD (2022), Green, Social, Sustainability and Sustainability-Linked Bonds in Developing Countries: How Can Donors Support Public Sector Issuances? OECD Publishing, Paris. https://www.oecd.org/dac/green-social-sustainability-and-sustainability-linked-bonds.pdf

Pimbley, C. (2018). Credibility and Green Bonds: The Role of Transparency. Environmental Finance.

Reboredo, J. C. (2018). Green Bond and Financial Markets: Co-movement, Diversification and Price Spillover Effects. *Energy Economics, 74,* 38–50.

Subramaniam, V., & Wasiuzzaman, S. (2019). Geographical Diversification, Firm Size and Profitability in Malaysia: A Quantile Regression Approach. *Heliyon, 5*(10), e02664. https://doi.org/10.1016/j.heliyon.2019.e02664

Summers, J. K., Harwell, L. C. ... (2017). Development of a Climate Resilience Screening Index (CRSI): An Assessment of Resilience to Acute Meteorological Events and Selected Natural Hazards. EPA600/R-17/238.

Sustainable Research and Analysis. (2020). New Green Bond Fund Investing Options Double in Number. https://sustainableinvest.com/new-green-bond-fund-investing-options-double-in-number/

Talan, G., & Sharma, G. D. (2019). Doing Well by Doing Good: A Systematic Review and Research Agenda for Sustainable Investment. *Sustainability, 11*(2), 353.

Tang, D. Y., & Zhang, Y. (2018). Do Shareholders Benefit from Green Bonds? *Social Science Research Network.* https://doi.org/10.2139/ssrn.3259555

The United Nations Economic and Social Commission for Asia and the Pacific (ESCAP) [UN ESCAP]. (2021). Green and Climate Finance Options to Support the Post-Covid-19 Pandemic Recovery and Climate Action. https://www.unescap.org/sites/default/d8files/knowledge-products/Final_Green%20and%20Climate%20%20Finance%20Options%20to%20Support%20the%20Post%20COVID-19%20Pandemic%20Recovery%20and%20%20Climate%20Action.pdf

The World Bank. (2019). Green Bonds: A Key Financial Tool to Fight Climate Change.

The World Bank. (2020). Sustainable Development Bonds and Green Bonds: Impact Report 2020. https://thedocs.worldbank.org/en/doc/e2cd2af46f36e5ecbd3407da177db751-0340022021/original/WB-SDB-Impact-Report-2020-Resources.pdf

Thomas, M. (2023). Asset Allocation and Diversification Are Explained. Which? https://www.which.co.uk/money/investing/learn-how-investing-works/asset-allocation-explained-afeZT2k9iE2S#what-is-asset-allocation

Tsoukala, A. K., & Tsiotas, G. (2021). Assessing Green Bond Risk: An Empirical Investigation. *Green Finance, 3*(2), 222–252.

Vivid Economics and Climate Bonds Initiative. (2019). Green Bonds Development in Bangladesh- A Market Landscape. https://www.bb.org.bd/pub/special/greenbond_dec19.pdf

World Bank. (2023). *IBRD Funding Program.*

10 The Future of Portfolio Management with Green Bonds

Trends and Innovations

Eşref Savaş BAŞCI and Muhammad Saeed Meo

Introduction

The field of portfolio management involving green bonds has experienced significant transformations, primarily influenced by the escalating demand for sustainable investments and the heightened recognition of environmental, social, and governance (ESG) considerations. Green bonds are a unique category of fixed-income financial instruments that are explicitly allocated to finance projects that yield environmental advantages. Therefore, they have attracted considerable interest from portfolio managers and investors for various significant factors (Bhutta et al., 2022, p. 9).

Green bonds offer investors the opportunity to match their investment portfolios with ESG objectives and methods. Portfolio managers can showcase their dedication to promoting sustainability and mitigating climate change by allocating resources towards green bonds, which are specifically designed to finance environmentally friendly initiatives (Sachs et al., 2019, p. 120).

Green bonds present a potential avenue for achieving portfolio diversification, given their tendency to exhibit distinct risk-return characteristics in contrast to conventional fixed-income instruments. Furthermore, with the growing recognition of climate-related hazards, the incorporation of green bonds into investment portfolios can serve as a means to effectively mitigate such risks and perhaps enhance the robustness of investment portfolios.

Governments and regulatory agencies worldwide have implemented various laws and incentives aimed at fostering the growth of sustainable finance and encouraging investments in environmentally friendly initiatives. The establishment of a conducive regulatory framework has facilitated the adoption of green bonds by portfolio managers and investors, prompting their integration into investment strategies.

The demand for sustainable investments is increasing across many categories of investors such as institutional investors, retail investors, and asset managers. Consequently, there has been substantial growth in the green bond market, so offering portfolio managers a wider array of investment prospects and the possibility of favorable financial gains.

DOI: 10.4324/9781032686844-10

The utilization of green bonds is of significant importance in the realm of impact investing, particularly in relation to the financing of initiatives aimed at mitigating climate change and promoting environmental sustainability. Portfolio managers and investors acknowledge the potential influence of these investments in facilitating favorable environmental consequences such as the advancement of renewable energy, enhancements in energy efficiency, and the implementation of sustainable infrastructure initiatives (Buzoianu et al., 2019, p. 64).

Investing in green bonds has the potential to facilitate long-term value development through its support of the transition towards a low-carbon and sustainable economy. There is a growing acknowledgment among portfolio managers regarding the significance of integrating sustainable investment strategies. These strategies aim to not only provide financial returns but also make beneficial contributions to social and environmental aspects in the long run (Sachs et al., 2019, p. 10).

In general, the increasing appeal of green bonds among portfolio managers and investors is indicative of a more extensive trend toward sustainable and ethical investment practices. This trend is motivated by the acknowledgment of the significance of tackling environmental issues and advancing sustainable development. By including green bonds into their investment portfolios, investors have the opportunity to not only pursue financial gains but also make a meaningful contribution toward fostering a more sustainable and resilient global economy.

Green bonds have a significant impact on the development of sustainable finance as they enable the incorporation of environmental factors into investment choices (Bhutta et al., 2022, pp. 7–10). With the increasing worldwide emphasis on sustainability, green bonds have assumed a broader role in sustainable finance, encompassing several facets such as the incorporation of these bonds into investment strategies. This discourse elucidates the transformative impact of green bonds on the realm of sustainable finance, as well as the potential for their seamless integration into investment strategies. There are some strategies listed below to support sustainable finance (Wendt, 2015, p. 7):

1 The promotion of sustainable development is facilitated by green bonds, as they direct financial resources toward endeavors that provide favorable ecological outcomes, including but not limited to renewable energy, energy efficiency, sustainable infrastructure, and climate adaptation activities (Yucel et al., 2023, p. 4). Green bonds play a crucial role in promoting a more sustainable and resilient global economy by providing backing to these projects (Wendt, 2015, p. 64).

2 Green bonds serve as a catalyst for corporate responsibility by providing incentives for corporations to prioritize ecologically sustainable initiatives and publish their environmental performance. Companies that issue

green bonds are frequently obligated to offer openness and responsibility with respect to the utilization of money, so guaranteeing that the allotted resources are directed toward initiatives that yield evident environmental advantages.

3 The inclusion of green bonds has significantly diversified the available investment options in the realm of sustainable finance (Asl et al., 2023, p. 15). The inclusion of ESG criteria in investing strategies enables portfolio managers to achieve portfolio diversification. The expansion in question plays a significant role in fostering the growth of a broader and more varied sustainable investment landscape, which effectively addresses the rising need for financial products that align with ESG criteria (Fleenor, 2004, p. 258).

4 Green bonds are a means to mitigate risk and enhance performance. By integrating environmental issues into investing decisions, portfolio managers have the opportunity to avoid risks related to climate change and uncover opportunities linked to the shift toward a low-carbon economy. The process of integrating several factors can potentially result in enhanced long-term performance and increased resilience of investment portfolios (Sachs et al., 2019, p. 42).

5 Green bonds play a crucial role in driving innovation and market development as they facilitate the expansion of sustainable finance projects. The growing need for green bonds has prompted market participants to create novel financial products and investment solutions that are specifically designed to align with sustainable investment goals (Yucel et al., 2023, p. 7). The aforementioned phenomenon has given rise to novel financial tools and frameworks that facilitate the promotion of sustainable finance on a global scale.

6 The facilitation of policy alignment and impact measurement is achieved through the utilization of green bonds, which adhere to recognized norms and frameworks specific to green bonds. These established criteria serve to guarantee the reliability and openness of green bond offerings, facilitating investors in accurately evaluating the ecological consequences of their investments. Moreover, the incorporation of green bonds into investment strategies enables investors to assess the ecological efficacy of their portfolios and oversee their contributions toward sustainability objectives.

The successful incorporation of green bonds into investing strategies necessitates a thorough comprehension of ESG considerations, and a steadfast dedication to sustainable investment methodologies. By integrating green bonds into their investment portfolios, investors have the potential to make a positive impact on sustainable development while also capitalizing on the financial prospects linked to the increasing demand for environmentally sensitive investments.

Mainstreaming Green Bonds

The integration of green bonds into investment portfolios has gained traction in recent years, with a notable shift toward sustainable investment practices among institutional investors. This mainstreaming of green bonds can be attributed to the increasing emphasis on sustainable development and the growing recognition of environmental risks within investment decision-making processes.

Institutional investors have demonstrated a growing appetite for green bonds, driven by a combination of factors, including regulatory support, investor demand for sustainable investment options, and the potential for achieving attractive risk-adjusted returns. The adoption trends indicate a heightened awareness of the environmental impact of investment decisions and a proactive approach toward integrating sustainability considerations into investment strategies.

The effective incorporation of green bonds into diversified portfolios requires a comprehensive understanding of the unique risk-return profiles associated with these instruments. Strategies such as thematic investing, impact investing, and integration of ESG criteria into investment analysis have proven instrumental in optimizing portfolio diversification while aligning with sustainable investment objectives.

The integration of ESG principles in green bond allocations is crucial for ensuring the alignment of investment portfolios with sustainability goals. By incorporating rigorous ESG assessments and considering environmental performance metrics, investors can identify green bond issuances that adhere to high ESG standards, thereby contributing to the promotion of responsible and impactful investments.

Combining ESG principles with green bond investments entails a holistic approach that encompasses environmental considerations, social impact assessments, and governance practices. This integrated approach enables investors to evaluate the overall sustainability performance of green bond issuers, fostering a more comprehensive understanding of the long-term implications of investment decisions on both financial returns and environmental outcomes.

Optimizing asset allocation for ESG impact involves a strategic allocation of capital toward green bond investments that not only yield financial returns but also generate positive environmental and social impacts. By incorporating ESG criteria into asset allocation frameworks, institutional investors can effectively manage risk, enhance portfolio resilience, and contribute to the advancement of sustainable development goals.

The emergence of new investment vehicles such as sustainability-focused exchange-traded funds, green bond investment funds, and impact investing platforms reflects the growing demand for innovative financial products that promote sustainable finance. Green finance and the related conceptual structure can be seen in Figure 10.1. The investment instruments considered in this context also play a critical role in expanding the accessibility of green bonds to a broader investor base, supporting market liquidity, and promoting further

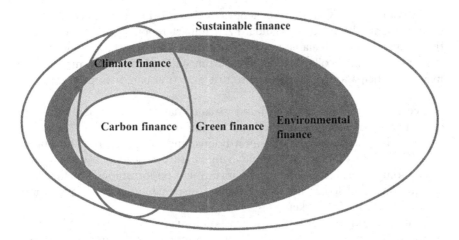

Figure 10.1 Relationship between green finance and environment
Source: Sachs et al. (2019)

growth and development in the sustainable finance sector. Figure 10.1 shows the relationship between green finance and environment.

Green Bond Funds and EFTs

The proliferation of green bond funds and exchange-traded funds has garnered substantial attention within the investment community, reflecting the increasing demand for sustainable investment options. According to OECD (2014) and UNEP-SEFI (2007) reports, the growth and popularity of these investment products can be attributed to their ability to provide diversified exposure to green bonds, facilitate liquidity, and offer investors the opportunity to align their portfolios with environmentally conscious investment objectives.

The selection and management of green bond funds necessitates a rigorous assessment of various factors, including issuer credibility, project transparency, and environmental impact metrics. Strategies such as thorough due diligence, active portfolio monitoring, and adherence to sustainable investment principles are instrumental in selecting and managing green bond funds effectively, ensuring the alignment of investment strategies with sustainability goals.

Impact investing platforms play a critical role in connecting investors with sustainable projects, enabling direct investment in green initiatives that promote environmental sustainability and social impact. These platforms facilitate the democratization of sustainable finance by providing investors with transparent investment opportunities, fostering community engagement, and empowering individuals to contribute to positive environmental and social change.

While impact-driven investment presents significant opportunities for generating both financial returns and positive social and environmental outcomes, it is accompanied by various challenges, including the complexity of impact measurement, the need for standardized impact reporting frameworks, and the requirement for scalable impact investment solutions. Overcoming these challenges requires collaborative efforts from stakeholders, policymakers, and market participants to establish a robust and transparent impact investing ecosystem.

Recent innovations in green bond issuance have transformed the sustainable finance landscape, with the introduction of novel structures, including sustainability-linked bonds, transition bonds, and green securitization products. These innovations reflect the dynamic nature of sustainable finance and the ongoing efforts to diversify green investment opportunities, enhance market liquidity, and foster the integration of sustainability considerations into mainstream financial markets.

In conclusion, the growth of green bond investment products, the emergence of impact investing platforms, and the innovations in green bond issuance signify the increasing momentum of sustainable finance practices in the global investment landscape. By leveraging effective strategies for selecting and managing green bond funds, addressing the challenges associated with impact-driven investment, and embracing innovations in green bond issuance, investors and stakeholders can contribute to the advancement of sustainable development goals while generating positive financial returns and fostering environmental and social impact. Moreover, the continued evolution of sustainable finance practices presents an opportunity for market participants to actively participate in the global transition toward a more sustainable and resilient economy.

Transition Bonds

Transition bonds play a pivotal role in supporting sustainability efforts by facilitating the transition to a low-carbon economy and fostering the alignment of transitional activities with ESG principles. These bonds enable issuers to finance projects that promote sustainable practices, accelerate decarbonization efforts, and address environmental challenges, thereby contributing to the global transition toward a more sustainable and resilient future (Hu & Jin, 2023, pp. 113040–113041).

The inclusion of transition bonds in investment portfolios necessitates the implementation of comprehensive strategies that consider the unique risk-return characteristics of these instruments. Strategies such as thematic investing, impact-oriented allocation, and active engagement with issuers can enable investors to effectively incorporate transition bonds into their portfolios while mitigating transition-related risks and capitalizing on the opportunities associated with the evolving sustainable finance landscape.

The emergence of social and sustainability bonds has expanded the scope of impact beyond environmental considerations, encompassing a broader spectrum of social and governance-related issues. These bonds enable investors to support projects that address social challenges, promote sustainable development goals, and enhance societal well-being, thereby fostering a more holistic approach to sustainable finance and responsible investing practices (Wendt, 2015, p. 404).

The incorporation of social and sustainability bonds into investment portfolios requires a holistic approach that integrates ESG considerations into investment analysis and decision-making processes. By incorporating rigorous impact assessments, fostering stakeholder engagement, and aligning investment strategies with sustainable development objectives, investors can effectively integrate social and sustainability bonds into their portfolios and contribute to the advancement of sustainable and responsible investment practices.

The rapid advancement of technological tools and solutions has revolutionized portfolio management practices, offering investors advanced analytics, real-time risk assessments, and sophisticated portfolio optimization capabilities. These technological advancements enable investors to enhance portfolio diversification, improve risk management strategies, and incorporate ESG considerations more effectively, thereby empowering investors to make informed investment decisions aligned with their sustainability and financial objectives (Mukhtar et al., 2023, p. 11).

The incorporation of transition bonds, social and sustainability bonds, and the integration of technological advancements in portfolio management signify the ongoing evolution of sustainable finance practices and the growing emphasis on holistic and responsible investment approaches. By adopting effective strategies for including transition bonds and social and sustainability bonds in investment portfolios and leveraging technological advancements in portfolio management, investors can contribute to the advancement of sustainable development goals, foster positive environmental and social impact, and achieve long-term financial resilience. Moreover, the continued integration of sustainable finance practices and technological innovations presents an opportunity for investors to actively participate in the global transition toward a more sustainable and equitable future.

Blockchain and Smart Contracts

Blockchain technology and smart contracts have the potential to revolutionize the transparency and accountability of green bond transactions by enabling secure, immutable, and decentralized record-keeping of environmental impact data. These technologies facilitate real-time verification of project eligibility, streamline the issuance process, and enhance trust among investors and stakeholders, thereby fostering greater confidence in the integrity of green bond investments (Bodemer, 2023).

Blockchain technology finds diverse applications in sustainable finance, ranging from the creation of transparent supply chains and carbon credit tracking to the establishment of decentralized autonomous organizations for sustainable project funding. The use of blockchain in these contexts promotes traceability, enhances data security, and empowers stakeholders to make informed decisions based on reliable and verifiable information, ultimately contributing to the advancement of sustainable development goals.

The integration of AI and machine learning techniques in portfolio optimization for green bonds enables investors to leverage data-driven insights, identify market trends, and make informed investment decisions based on predictive analytics and risk management models. By harnessing the power of AI, portfolio managers can optimize asset allocation, mitigate investment risks, and enhance the overall performance and sustainability of green bond portfolios.

AI-driven insights provide portfolio managers with the tools to assess market dynamics, identify investment opportunities, and customize investment strategies tailored to specific ESG criteria. The integration of AI-driven insights in green bond portfolio management enhances portfolio diversification, promotes proactive risk management, and facilitates the integration of sustainable investment practices into decision-making processes, thereby fostering a more resilient and sustainable investment ecosystem.

Case studies highlighting successful AI implementations in the context of green bond portfolio management illustrate the practical application of AI-driven tools and algorithms in optimizing investment strategies, enhancing portfolio performance, and promoting sustainable investment outcomes. These case studies underscore the transformative impact of AI in enabling data-driven decision-making, fostering innovation, and driving positive environmental and financial outcomes in the sustainable finance sector.

The dynamic regulatory and policy landscape in sustainable finance plays a pivotal role in shaping market dynamics, influencing investor behavior, and fostering the adoption of sustainable investment practices. Regulatory developments such as the implementation of standardized ESG reporting frameworks, the introduction of green finance incentives, and the enforcement of disclosure requirements are instrumental in promoting transparency, accountability, and responsible investment practices, thereby creating a conducive environment for sustainable finance initiatives to thrive.

The synergies of blockchain technology, AI, and regulatory dynamics present unprecedented opportunities for the advancement of sustainable finance practices. By leveraging the transformative potential of blockchain technology and smart contracts to enhance transparency and accountability in green bond transactions, harnessing AI-driven insights for effective portfolio management, and embracing regulatory developments that prioritize sustainability and transparency, stakeholders and market participants can collectively contribute to the acceleration of sustainable development goals and the establishment of a more resilient and inclusive global economy.

Evolving Regulatory Frameworks

The continuous evolution of regulatory frameworks surrounding green bond standards and certification processes reflects the growing emphasis on transparency, accountability, and standardization within the sustainable finance landscape. Updates in green bond standards, including the refinement of reporting requirements and the introduction of rigorous certification processes, have profound implications for portfolio management practices, necessitating enhanced due diligence, robust impact measurement methodologies, and comprehensive ESG integration strategies.

The evolving regulatory frameworks in green bond standards and certification processes have significant impacts on portfolio management practices, necessitating the adoption of stringent risk assessment protocols, the implementation of ESG-focused investment strategies, and the integration of sustainability criteria into investment decision-making processes. These impacts underscore the importance of aligning portfolio management practices with established regulatory guidelines and industry best practices to ensure the integrity and credibility of green bond investments and promote the long-term sustainability of investment portfolios.

Government initiatives and incentives aimed at promoting green bond issuance and investment play a pivotal role in stimulating market demand, fostering investor confidence, and incentivizing sustainable investment practices. Policies such as tax incentives, subsidies for green projects, and regulatory support for sustainable finance initiatives create a conducive environment for the growth of green bond markets, encouraging portfolio managers to align their investment strategies with government-led sustainability goals and capitalize on the opportunities presented by the evolving regulatory landscape (Dina et al., 2020, p. 133).

Strategies for aligning investment portfolios with government-led sustainability goals encompass the integration of policy analysis, stakeholder engagement, and ESG-focused investment research into portfolio management frameworks. By proactively identifying investment opportunities aligned with government sustainability targets, adopting proactive risk management strategies, and engaging in dialogue with policymakers and industry stakeholders, portfolio managers can position their portfolios to capture the benefits of government initiatives and contribute to the achievement of national and international sustainability objectives.

The dynamic interplay between evolving regulatory frameworks, government initiatives, and portfolio management practices underscores the integral role of regulatory compliance, policy alignment, and proactive engagement in driving the integration of sustainable finance principles into investment strategies. By proactively adapting to regulatory changes, leveraging government incentives, and aligning investment portfolios with government-led sustainability goals, portfolio managers can navigate the complexities of the evolving sustainable finance landscape, contribute to the advancement of global sustainability objectives, and foster the development of a more resilient and inclusive green bond market (Porath, 2023, pp. 1411–1412).

Global Market Trends and Regional Variances

According to the BIS report (2019), the Asia-Pacific region has emerged as a prominent growth hub for green bonds, driven by the region's increasing focus on sustainable development, supportive regulatory frameworks, and the growing demand for climate-friendly investments. The booming green bond market in Asia-Pacific presents abundant opportunities for portfolio managers to diversify their investment portfolios, engage in sustainable infrastructure financing, and leverage regional partnerships to capitalize on the region's rapidly expanding green finance ecosystem.

Tapping into the opportunities presented by the booming green bond market in the Asia-Pacific region requires the adoption of tailored investment strategies that account for regional market dynamics, regulatory nuances, and cultural intricacies. Strategies such as fostering partnerships with local stakeholders, conducting in-depth market research, and adhering to regional ESG standards can empower portfolio managers to navigate the complexities of the Asia-Pacific market, identify sustainable investment opportunities, and establish a strong foothold in the region's evolving sustainable finance landscape (Sachs et al., 2019, pp. 186–187).

The European Union's (EU) Sustainable Finance Agenda, anchored by the EU Taxonomy and other regulatory developments, reflects the EU's commitment to fostering sustainable investment practices, promoting transparency, and combating greenwashing. The EU Taxonomy, in particular, sets stringent criteria for determining the environmental sustainability of economic activities, thereby influencing the investment decisions and portfolio management practices of financial institutions operating within the EU.

The implications of the EU's Sustainable Finance Agenda for portfolio managers in the EU are multifaceted, encompassing the need for comprehensive ESG integration, robust impact measurement frameworks, and proactive alignment with the EU Taxonomy's sustainability criteria. Portfolio managers must adapt their investment strategies, enhance their risk management frameworks, and prioritize sustainable investment opportunities that comply with the EU's regulatory imperatives, thereby fostering the integration of sustainable finance principles into the fabric of their portfolios and contributing to the advancement of the EU's sustainability objectives.

The effective management of risks in green bond portfolios requires a holistic approach that integrates traditional risk management methodologies with ESG considerations, climate risk assessments, and scenario analysis frameworks. Portfolio managers must proactively identify and mitigate environmental and social risks, monitor the impact of climate-related factors on investment performance, and leverage risk management tools to foster the long-term sustainability and resilience of green bond portfolios in the face of evolving market dynamics and regulatory imperatives.

The global market trends and regional dynamics in green bond portfolio management underscore the importance of proactive market engagement, tailored investment strategies, and robust risk management frameworks in navigating the complexities of the sustainable finance landscape. By leveraging regional opportunities, aligning with regulatory imperatives, and integrating

ESG considerations into risk management practices, portfolio managers can position their portfolios to thrive in diverse regional contexts, contribute to the advancement of global sustainability goals, and foster the development of a more resilient and inclusive green bond market on a global scale.

Environmental and Climate-Related Risk Assessment

The comprehensive assessment of environmental and climate-related risks is crucial in the context of green investments, as it enables investors to identify potential risks associated with climate change, natural disasters, and regulatory shifts. By integrating rigorous risk assessment methodologies, conducting scenario analyses, and prioritizing investments with strong environmental sustainability credentials, investors can proactively mitigate risks and foster the resilience of green investment portfolios in the face of evolving climate dynamics and regulatory landscapes.

The identification and mitigation of risks associated with green investments requires a multifaceted approach that encompasses due diligence, impact assessment, and proactive risk mitigation strategies. By adopting sustainable investment practices, engaging in stakeholder dialogues, and adhering to industry best practices, investors can effectively manage risks, promote responsible investment behaviors, and contribute to the development of a more sustainable and resilient green bond market.

Stress testing portfolios for climate resilience is imperative in evaluating the potential impact of climate-related risks on investment performance and portfolio stability. By simulating various climate scenarios, assessing the vulnerability of portfolio holdings, and incorporating climate risk metrics into investment decision-making processes, investors can enhance their understanding of the resilience of green investment portfolios and implement proactive risk management measures to mitigate potential adverse effects.

Analyzing market dynamics and liquidity considerations in the green bond market is essential for understanding the challenges and opportunities associated with market volatility, supply and demand dynamics, and investor sentiment. By implementing liquidity management strategies, diversifying investment portfolios, and fostering market transparency and efficiency, investors can navigate the complexities of the green bond market, manage market-related risks, and optimize portfolio performance in line with sustainable finance objectives.

The effective management of market-related risks requires the implementation of strategies that prioritize risk diversification, promote liquidity management, and foster the integration of ESG considerations into investment decision-making processes. By leveraging hedging strategies, monitoring market trends, and staying informed about regulatory developments, investors can proactively manage market-related risks, seize investment opportunities, and contribute to the long-term sustainability and resilience of green investment portfolios.

Case studies of innovative green bond portfolios showcase the successful implementation of creative and effective portfolio management approaches, highlighting the integration of ESG criteria, the alignment with sustainability goals, and the pursuit of positive environmental and social impact. These case studies underscore the transformative impact of innovative portfolio management strategies in fostering the development of a more resilient and inclusive green bond market, positioning investors to thrive in the face of evolving market dynamics and regulatory landscapes, and contributing to the advancement of global sustainability objectives.

The effective management of environmental and climate-related risks, proactive stress testing for climate resilience, prudent analysis of market dynamics and liquidity considerations, and the adoption of innovative portfolio management strategies are instrumental in fostering the long-term sustainability and resilience of green investment portfolios. By prioritizing risk management, leveraging market insights, and embracing innovative portfolio management approaches, investors can navigate the complexities of the sustainable finance landscape, contribute to the advancement of global sustainability goals, and foster the development of a more sustainable and resilient green bond market on a global scale.

Real-World Examples of Successful Green Bond Portfolio Management Strategies

Real-world examples of successful green bond portfolio management strategies showcase the practical application of innovative approaches in the context of sustainable finance, highlighting the integration of ESG considerations, the alignment with sustainability goals, and the pursuit of positive environmental and social impact. Several case studies provide valuable insights and lessons learned from implementing innovative approaches, contributing to the advancement of sustainable finance practices and the development of a more resilient and inclusive green bond market (Pertseva, 2023).

BlackRock's Renewable Power Group: BlackRock's Renewable Power Group has successfully implemented a green bond portfolio management strategy that focuses on investing in renewable energy projects worldwide. By leveraging comprehensive ESG integration, rigorous due diligence, and proactive risk management practices, the group has effectively diversified its green bond portfolio, fostered long-term sustainability, and contributed to the global transition toward a low-carbon economy. The key lesson learned from this case study is the importance of adopting a holistic approach that integrates ESG considerations into investment decision-making processes, fosters collaboration with industry stakeholders, and aligns with sustainable development goals (Grove & Clouse, 2021).

California State Treasurer's Green Bond Investments: The California State Treasurer's successful green bond portfolio management strategy emphasizes the alignment of investment portfolios with the state's sustainability goals and climate resilience initiatives. By prioritizing investments in sustainable infra-structure projects such as clean transportation, renewable energy, and water conservation, the California State Treasurer has demonstrated the transforma-tive impact of integrating sustainable finance principles into public investment strategies. The key lesson learned from this case study is the significance of government-led sustainability initiatives, stakeholder engagement, and policy alignment in driving the adoption of sustainable finance practices and fos-tering the development of a more resilient and inclusive green bond market (Chiang, 2017).

Amundi's Green Bond Fund: Amundi's Green Bond Fund serves as a prime example of successful green bond portfolio management, showcasing the inte-gration of innovative investment strategies, robust risk management frame-works, and comprehensive impact measurement methodologies. By leveraging AI-driven insights, proactive engagement with green bond issuers, and adher-ence to industry best practices, Amundi has positioned its Green Bond Fund as a leading sustainable investment vehicle, contributing to the advancement of global sustainability objectives and the promotion of responsible investment practices. The key lesson learned from this case study is the transformative potential of technology-driven solutions, data-driven decision-making, and proactive risk mitigation in fostering the long-term sustainability and resil-ience of green investment portfolios (Pertseva, 2023).

These real-world examples highlight the importance of proactive risk man-agement, the integration of ESG considerations, and the alignment with sus-tainability goals in driving the success of green bond portfolio management strategies. By embracing innovative approaches, prioritizing sustainable invest-ment practices, and fostering collaboration with industry stakeholders and policymakers, investors and portfolio managers can contribute to the advance-ment of sustainable development goals, promote environmental and social impact, and foster the development of a more sustainable and resilient green bond market on a global scale.

Conclusion and Policy Implications

In conclusion, the dynamic landscape of green bond portfolio management is characterized by a multifaceted interplay of technological advancements, regulatory imperatives, market dynamics, and sustainability considerations. The integration of ESG principles, coupled with the adoption of innovative portfolio management strategies, has become instrumental in fostering the long-term sustainability and resilience of green bond investments. From the evolution of regulatory frameworks and government initiatives to the trans-formative potential of blockchain technology, AI-driven insights, and risk management best practices, the global investment community is increasingly recognizing the imperative of aligning investment strategies with sustainable finance principles and contributing to the advancement of global sustainability objectives.

Real-world examples of successful green bond portfolio management strategies underscore the importance of proactive risk management, the integration of ESG considerations, and the alignment with sustainability goals in driving the success of sustainable finance initiatives. By embracing innovative approaches, leveraging technology-driven solutions, and fostering collaboration with industry stakeholders and policymakers, investors and portfolio managers can navigate the complexities of the sustainable finance landscape, contribute to the advancement of global sustainability goals, and foster the development of a more resilient and inclusive green bond market on a global scale.

As the global investment community continues to embrace sustainable finance practices, there is a growing recognition of the transformative potential of green bond investments in driving positive environmental and social impact. By prioritizing the integration of ESG considerations, aligning investment strategies with regulatory imperatives, and fostering the adoption of innovative portfolio management approaches, stakeholders and market participants can contribute to the establishment of a more sustainable and resilient global economy while generating positive financial returns and fostering environmental and social sustainability.

References

Asl, M. G., Rashidi, M. M., Tiwari, A. K., Lee, C. C., & Roubaud, D. (2023). Green bond vs. Islamic bond: Which one is more environmentally friendly? *Journal of Environmental Management, 345*, 118580.

Bhutta, U.S., Tariq, A., Farrukh, M., Raza, A., & Iqbal, M.K. (2022). Green bonds for sustainable development: Review of literature on development and impact of green bonds. *Technological Forecasting and Social Change*, 175. https://doi.org/10.1016/j.techfore.2021.121378.

BIS (2019). *BIS Launches Green Bond Fund for Central Banks*, Press release, 26 September 2019, https://www.bis.org/press/p190926.htm

Bodemer, O. (2023). *Transforming the Insurance Industry with Blockchain and Smart Contracts: Enhancing Efficiency, Transparency, and Trust*. TechRxiv. Preprint. https://doi.org/10.36227/techrxiv.24006237.v1

Buzoianu, O.A.C, Diaconu, A., Mitriță, M., & Dima, C. (2019). Options for sustainable resource strategies in the EU: The case of forest policy, in *BASIQ International Conference: New Trends in Sustainable Business and Consumption -2019*, edited by Rodica Pamfilie, Vasile Dinu, Laurenţiu Tăchiciu, Doru Pleşea, Cristinel Vasiliu, Proceedings of BASIQ Vol. 01.

Chiang, J. (2017). *Growing the US Green Bond Market*. California State Treasurer, California, 1.

Dina A., Anant K. & Yang L. (2020) Green bonds for financing renewable energy and energy efficiency in South-East Asia: A review of policies. *Journal of Sustainable Finance & Investment*, 10(2), 113–140, https://doi.org/10.1080/20430795.2019.1704160

Fleenor, Alice A. (2004). Sustainable development: economy, society, and environment. *Senior Thesis Projects, 2003–2006*. https://trace.tennessee.edu/utk_interstp3/19

Grove, H., & Clouse, M. (2021). Renewable energy commitments versus greenwashing: Board responsibilities. *Corporate Ownership & Control*, 18(3), 423–437.

Hu, Y., & Jin, Y. (2023). Unraveling the influence of green bonds on environmental sustainability and paving the way for sustainable energy projects in green finance. *Environmental Science and Pollution Research*, 1–16.

Mukhtar, B., Shad, M. K., Woon, L. F., & Hamad, S. (2023). Risk management implementation and its efficacy towards green innovation: A conceptual framework for Malaysian solar photovoltaic industry. *Journal of Economic and Administrative Sciences*.

OECD (2014). *Institutional Investors and Long-Term Investment*. Project Report. Available from: http://www.oecd.org/daf/fin/ private-pensions/OECD-LTI-project.pdf

Pertseva, S. Y. (2023). *Current Trends in the Green Bond Market. In Current Problems of the Global Environmental Economy Under the Conditions of Climate Change and the Perspectives of Sustainable Development* (pp. 23–32). Cham: Springer International Publishing.

Porath, U. (2023) Advancing managerial evolution and resource management in contemporary business landscapes. *Modern Economy*, 14, 1404–1420. https://doi.org/10.4236/me.2023.1410072.

Sachs, J. D., Woo, W. T., Yoshino, N., & Taghizadeh-Hesary, F. (Eds.). (2019). *Handbook of Green Finance*. https://doi.org/10.1007/978–981-13-0227-5

UNEP-SEFI (2007). *Global Trends in Sustainable Investment 2007*. Available from: http://www.unep.org/ pdf/72_Glob_Sust_Energy_Inv_Report_(2007).pdf

Wendt, K. (Ed.). (2015). Responsible investment banking. *CSR, Sustainability, Ethics & Governance*. https://doi.org/10.1007/978-3-319-10311-2

Yucel, O., Celik, G., & Yilmaz, Z. (2023). Sustainable investment attitudes based on sustainable finance literacy and perceived environmental impact. *Sustainability*, 15(22).

Index

Note: **Bold** page numbers refer to tables; *italic* page numbers refer to figures and page numbers followed by "n" denote endnotes.

Printed in the United States
by Baker & Taylor Publisher Services